EACL Workshop on Innovative Hybrid Approaches to the Processing of Textual Data 2012

Avignon, France
23-24 April 2012

ISBN: 978-1-62276-474-7

Printed from e-media with permission by:

Curran Associates, Inc.
57 Morehouse Lane
Red Hook, NY 12571

Some format issues inherent in the e-media version may also appear in this print version.

Printed by Curran Associates, Inc. (2013)

For permission requests, please contact the Association for Computational Linguistics at the address below.

Association for Computational Linguistics
209 N. Eighth Street
Stroudsburg, Pennsylvania 18360

Phone: 1-570-476-8006
Fax: 1-570-476-0860

acl@aclweb.org

Additional copies of this publication are available from:

Curran Associates, Inc.
57 Morehouse Lane
Red Hook, NY 12571 USA
Phone: 845-758-0400
Fax: 845-758-2634
Email: curran@proceedings.com
Web: www.proceedings.com

Introduction

The *hybrid approach* term covers a large set of situations in which different approaches are combined in order to better process textual data and to attempt a better achievement of the dedicated task. Hybrid approaches are commonly used in various NLP applications (*i.e.*, automatic creation of linguistic resources, POS tagging, building and structuring of terminologies, information retrieval and filtering, linguistic annotation, semantic labelling).

Among the hybridizations the possible combinations are unlimited. The most frequent combination, as stressed during The Balancing Act in 1994, addressed machine learning and rule-based systems. Beyond this, the hybridization can be augmented with distributional approaches, syntactic and morphological analyses, semantic distances and similarities, graph theory models, co-occurrences of linguistic units (e.g., word and their dependencies, word senses and postag, NEs and semantic roles,...), knowledge-based approaches (terminologies and ontologies), etc.

As a matter of fact, the hybridization implies to define a strategy to efficiently combine several approaches: cooperation between approaches, filtering, voting or ranking of the multiple system outputs, etc. Indeed, the combination of these different methods and approaches appears to provide more complete and efficient results. The reason is that each method is sensitive and efficient with given data and within given contexts. Hence, their combination may improve both precision and recall. The coverage is indeed improved, while the exploitation of different methods may also lead to the improvement of the precision since their use within filtering, voting etc. modes becomes possible.

This workshop has several objectives:

- To bring together researchers working on hybrid approaches independently from the topics and the applications. Indeed, the presented papers and posters address a great variety of applications: machine translation, lexicon and semantic relations acquisition, spell checking, indexing and annotation, syntactic analysis, summarization, named entity recognition, question-answering. We hope the exchange experienced during this workshop will be fruitful for the future research and collaborations.
- To outline future directions for the conception of novel hybrid approaches. For instance, the invited speaker Rada Mihalcea, University of North Texas, USA will give a presentation on the multilingual hybridization methods.

The Hybrid 2012 workshop received 27 submissions. Seven of these have been accepted as full papers and eight as poster presentations.

Acknowledgments

First of all, we are grateful to the authors who chose the Hybrid 2012 workshop to submit and present their innovative work, especially as these authors come from different countries. Without them, this workshop could not have been organized.

We are grateful to the organizers of the EACL conference to have accepted this workshop as one of the joint events of the main conference. This is a really nice place and time to present the research work.

We are very grateful to the members of the Scientific committee who reviewed three submissions in a very short period of time and, for some of them, during the holiday period.

We are particularly grateful to Rada Mihalcea, University of North Texas, USA to have accepted to participate in this workshop and to give the invited speaker talk.

Finally, we are grateful to our labs and institutions for the sponsoring of this workshop.

Organizers:

Natalia Grabar, CNRS UMR 8163 STL, Université Lille 1&3, France
Marie Dupuch, CNRS UMR 8163 STL, Université Lille 1&3, France
Amandine Périnet, LIM&BIO, Université Paris 13, France
Thierry Hamon, LIM&BIO, Université Paris 13, France

Program Committee:

Anders Ardö, EIT, LTH, Lund University, Sweden
Delphine Bernhard, LiLPa, Université de Strasbourg, France
Wray Duntine, NICTA, Australia
Philipp Cimiano, CITEC, University of Bielefeld, Germany
Vincent Claveau, IRISA-CNRS, Rennes, France
Kevin Cohen, University of Colorado Health Sciences Center, USA
Marie-Claude l'Homme, OLST, Université de Montreal, Canada
Béatrice Daille, Université de Nantes, LINA, France
Stefan Th. Gries, University of California, Santa Barbara, USA
Anna Kazantseva, University of Ottawa, Canada
Mikaela Keller, CNRS LIFL UMR8022, Mostrare INRIA, Université Lille 1&3, France
Alistair Kennedy, University of Ottawa, Canada
Ben Leong, University of North Texas, USA
Pierre Nugues, CS, LTH, Lund University, Sweden
Bruno Pouliquen, WIPO, Geneva, Switzerland
Sampo Pyysalo, National Centre for Text Mining, University of Manchester, United Kingdom
Mathieu Roche, LIRMM, Université de Montpellier 2, France
Patrick Ruch, Haute École de Gestion de Genève, Switzerland
Paul Thompson, National Centre for Text Mining, University of Manchester, United Kingdom
Juan-Manuel Torres Moreno, LIA, Université d'Avignon et des Pays de Vaucluse, France
Özlem Uzuner, University at Albany, State University of New York, USA

Invited Speaker:

Rada Mihalcea, University of North Texas, USA

Table of Contents

Conference Program

Monday April 23, 2012

09:00	Introduction
	(09:10) Session 1
09:10	*Experiments on Hybrid Corpus-Based Sentiment Lexicon Acquisition* Goran Glavaš, Jan Šnajder and Bojana Dalbelo Bašić
09:40	*A Study of Hybrid Similarity Measures for Semantic Relation Extraction* Alexander Panchenko and Olga Morozova
10:10	Coffee break
	(10:30) Session 2
10:30	*Hybrid Combination of Constituency and Dependency Trees into an Ensemble Dependency Parser* Nathan Green and Zdeněk Žabokrtský
11:00	*Describing Video Contents in Natural Language* Muhammad Usman Ghani Khan and Yoshihiko Gotoh
11:30	*An Unsupervised and Data-Driven Approach for Spell Checking in Vietnamese OCR-scanned Texts* Cong Duy Vu Hoang and Ai Ti Aw
	(12:00) Short Presentation: Posters
12:30	Lunch break

Monday April 23, 2012 (continued)

(14:00) Invited speaker

14:00 *Multilingual Natural Language Processing*
Rada Mihalcea

(15:30) Coffee break and Poster Session

15:30 *Contrasting Objective and Subjective Portuguese Texts from Heterogeneous Sources*
Michel Généreux and William Martinez

A Joint Named Entity Recognition and Entity Linking System
Rosa Stern, Benoît Sagot and Frédéric Béchet

Collaborative Annotation of Dialogue Acts: Application of a New ISO Standard to the Switchboard Corpus
Alex C. Fang, Harry Bunt, Jing Cao and Xiaoyue Liu

Coupling Knowledge-Based and Data-Driven Systems for Named Entity Recognition
Damien Nouvel, Jean-Yves Antoine, Nathalie Friburger and Arnaud Soulet

A Random Forest System Combination Approach for Error Detection in Digital Dictionaries
Michael Bloodgood, Peng Ye, Paul Rodrigues, David Zajic and David Doermann

Methods Combination and ML-based Re-ranking of Multiple Hypothesis for Question-Answering Systems
Arnaud Grappy, Brigitte Grau and Sophie Rosset

A Generalised Hybrid Architecture for NLP
Alistair Willis, Hui Yang and Anne De Roeck

Monday April 23, 2012 (continued)

(16:30) Session 3

16:30 *Incorporating Linguistic Knowledge in Statistical Machine Translation: Translating Prepositions*
Reshef Shilon, Hanna Fadida and Shuly Wintner

17:00 *Combining Different Summarization Techniques for Legal Text*
Filippo Galgani, Paul Compton and Achim Hoffmann

17:30 Closing

Experiments on Hybrid Corpus-Based Sentiment Lexicon Acquisition

Goran Glavaš, Jan Šnajder and Bojana Dalbelo Bašić
Faculty of Electrical Engineering and Computing
University of Zagreb
Zagreb, Croatia
{goran.glavas, jan.snajder, bojana.dalbelo}@fer.hr

Abstract

Numerous sentiment analysis applications make usage of a sentiment lexicon. In this paper we present experiments on hybrid sentiment lexicon acquisition. The approach is corpus-based and thus suitable for languages lacking general dictionary-based resources. The approach is a hybrid two-step process that combines semi-supervised graph-based algorithms and supervised models. We evaluate the performance on three tasks that capture different aspects of a sentiment lexicon: polarity ranking task, polarity regression task, and sentiment classification task. Extensive evaluation shows that the results are comparable to those of a well-known sentiment lexicon SentiWordNet on the polarity ranking task. On the sentiment classification task, the results are also comparable to SentiWordNet when restricted to *monosentimous* (all senses carry the same sentiment) words. This is satisfactory, given the absence of explicit semantic relations between words in the corpus.

1 Introduction

Knowing someone's attitude towards events, entities, and phenomena can be very important in various areas of human activity. Sentiment analysis is an area of computational linguistics that aims to recognize the subjectivity and attitude expressed in natural language texts. Applications of sentiment analysis are numerous, including sentiment-based document classification (Riloff et al., 2006), opinion-oriented information extraction (Hu and Liu, 2004), and question answering (Somasundaran et al., 2007).

Sentiment analysis combines subjectivity analysis and polarity analysis. Subjectivity analysis answers whether the text unit is subjective or neutral, while polarity analysis determines whether a subjective text unit is positive or negative. The majority of research approaches (Hatzivassiloglou and McKeown, 1997; Turney and Littman, 2003; Wilson et al., 2009) see subjectivity and polarity as categorical terms (i.e., classification problems). Intuitively, not all words express the sentiment with the same intensity. Accordingly, there has been some research effort in assessing subjectivity and polarity as graded values (Baccianella et al., 2010; Andreevskaia and Bergler, 2006). Most of the work on sentence or document level sentiment makes usage of sentiment annotated lexicon providing subjectivity and polarity information for individual words (Wilson et al., 2009; Taboada et al., 2011).

In this paper we present a hybrid approach for automated acquisition of sentiment lexicon. The method is language independent and corpus-based and therefore suitable for languages lacking general lexical resources such as WordNet (Fellbaum, 2010). The two-step hybrid process combines semi-supervised graph-based algorithms and supervised learning models.

We consider three different tasks, each capturing different aspect of a sentiment lexicon:

1. Polarity ranking task – determine the relative rankings of words, i.e., order lexicon items descendingly by positivity and negativity;

2. Polarity regression task – assign each word absolute scores (between 0 and 1) for positivity and negativity;

3. Sentiment classification task – classify each

Proceedings of the Workshop on Innovative Hybrid Approaches to the Processing of Textual Data (Hybrid2012), EACL 2012, pages 1–9,
Avignon, France, April 23 2012. ©2012 Association for Computational Linguistics

word into one of the three sentiment classes (*positive*, *negative*, or *neutral*).

Accordingly, we evaluate our method using three different measures – one to evaluate the quality of the ordering by positivity and negativity, other to evaluate the absolute sentiment scores assigned to each corpus word, and another to evaluate the classification performance.

The rest of the paper is structured as follows. In Section 2 we present the related work on sentiment lexicon acquisition. Section 3 discusses the semi-supervised step of the hybrid approach. In Section 4 we explain the supervised step in more detail. In Section 5 the experimental setup, the evaluation procedure, and the results of the approach are discussed. Section 6 concludes the paper and outlines future work.

2 Related Work

Several approaches have been proposed for determining the prior polarity of words. Most of the approaches can be classified as either dictionary-based (Kamps et al., 2004; Esuli and Sebastiani, 2007; Baccianella et al., 2010) or corpus-based (Hatzivassiloglou and McKeown, 1997; Turney and Littman, 2003). Regardless of the resource used, most of the approaches focus on bootstrapping, starting from a small seed set of manually labeled words (Hatzivassiloglou and McKeown, 1997; Turney and Littman, 2003; Esuli and Sebastiani, 2007). In this paper we also follow this idea of the semi-supervised bootstrapping as the first step of the sentiment lexicon acquisition.

Dictionary-based approaches grow the seed sets according to the explicit paradigmatic semantic relations (synonymy, antonymy, hyponymy, etc.) between words in the dictionary. Kamps et al. (2004) build a graph of adjectives based on synonymy relations gathered from WordNet. They determine the polarity of the adjective based on its shortest path distances from positive and negative seed adjectives *good* and *bad*. Esuli and Sebastiani (2007) first build a graph based on a gloss relation (i.e., *definiens – definiendum* relation) from WordNet. Afterwards they perform a variation of the PageRank algorithm (Page et al., 1999) in two runs. In the first run positive PageRank value is assigned to the vertices of the synsets from the positive seed set and zero value to all other vertices. In the second run the same is done for the synsets from the negative seed set. Word's polarity is then decided based on the difference between its PageRank values of the two runs. We also believe that graph is the appropriate structure for the propagation of sentiment properties of words. Unfortunately, for many languages a precompiled lexical resource like WordNet does not exist. In such a case, semantic relations between words may be extracted from corpus.

In their pioneering work, Hatzivassiloglou and McKeown (1997) attempt to determine the polarity of adjectives based on their co-occurrences in conjunctions. They start with a small manually labeled seed set and build on the observation that adjectives of the same polarity are often conjoined with the conjunction *and*, while adjectives of the opposite polarity are conjoined with the conjunction *but*. Turney and Littman (2003) use pointwise mutual information (PMI) (Church and Hanks, 1990) and latent semantic analysis (LSA) (Dumais, 2004) to determine the similarity of the word of unknown polarity with the words in both positive and negative seed sets. The aforementioned work presumes that there is a correlation between lexical semantics and sentiment. We base our work on the same assumption, but instead of directly comparing the words with the seed sets, we use distributional semantics to build a word similarity graph. In contrast to the approaches above, this allows us to potentially account for similarities between all pairs of words from corpus. To the best of our knowledge, such an approach that combines corpus-based lexical semantics with graph-based propagation has not yet been applied to the task of building sentiment lexicon. However, similar approaches have been proven rather efficient on other tasks such as document level sentiment classification (Goldberg and Zhu, 2006) and word sense disambiguation (Agirre et al., 2006).

3 Semi-supervised Graph-based Methods

The structure of a graph in general provides a good framework for propagation of object properties, which, in our case, are the sentiment values of the words. In a word similarity graph, weights of edges represent the degree of semantic similarity between words.

In the work presented in this paper we build graphs from corpus, using different notions of word similarity. Each vertex in the graph represents a word from corpus. Weights of the edges are calculated in several different ways, using measures of word co-occurrence (co-occurrence frequency and pointwise mutual information) and distributional semantic models (latent semantic analysis and random indexing). We manually compiled positive and negative seed sets, each consisting of 15 words:

> positiveSeeds = {*good, best, excellent, happy, well, new, great, nice, smart, beautiful, smile, win, hope, love, friend*}
>
> negativeSeeds = {*bad, worst, violence, die, poor, terrible, death, war, enemy, accident, murder, lose, wrong, attack, loss*}

In addition to these, we compiled the third seed set consisting of neutral words to serve as sentiment sinks for the employed label propagation algorithm:

> neutralSeeds = {*time, place, company, work, city, house, man, world, woman, country, building, number, system, object, room*}

Once we have built the graph, we label the vertices belonging to the words from the polar seed set with the sentiment score of 1. All other vertices are initially unlabeled (i.e., assigned a sentiment score of 0). We then use the structure of the graph and one of the two random-walk algorithms to propagate the labels from the labeled seed set vertices to the unlabeled ones. The random walk algorithm is executed twice: once with the words from the positive seed set being initially labeled and once with the words from the negative seed set being initially labeled. Once the random walk algorithm converges, all unlabeled vertices will be assigned a sentiment label. However, the final sentiment values obtained after the convergence of the random-walk algorithm are directly dependent on the size of the graph (which, in turn, depends on the size of the corpus), the size of the seed set, and the choice of the seed set words. Thus, they should be interpreted as relative rather than absolute sentiment scores. Nevertheless, the scores obtained from the graph can be used to rank the words by their positivity and negativity.

3.1 Similarity Based on Corpus Co-occurrence

If the two words co-occur in the corpus within a window of a given size, an edge in the graph between their corresponding vertices is added. The weight of the edge should represent the measure of the degree to which the two words co-occur.

There are many word collocation measures that may be used to calculate the weights of edges (Evert, 2008). In this work, we use raw co-occurrence frequency and pointwise mutual information (PMI) (Church and Hanks, 1990). In the former case the edge between two words is assigned a weight indicating a total number of co-occurrences of the corresponding words in the corpus within the window of a given size. In the latter case, we use PMI to account for the individual frequencies of each of the two words along with their co-occurrence frequency. The most frequent corpus words tend to frequently co-occur with most other words in the corpus, including words from both positive and negative seed sets. PMI compensates for this shortcoming of the raw co-occurrence frequency measure.

3.2 Similarity Based on Latent Semantic Analysis

Latent semantic analysis is a well-known technique for identifying semantically related concepts and dimensionality reduction in large vector spaces (Dumais, 2004). The first step is to create a sparse word-document matrix. Matrix elements are frequencies of words occurring in documents, usually transformed using some weighting scheme (e.g., *tf-idf*). The word-document matrix is then decomposed using singular value decomposition (SVD), a well-known linear algebra procedure. Finally, the dimensionality reduction is performed by approximating the original matrix using only the top k largest singular values.

We build two different word-document matrices using different weighting schemes. The elements of the first matrix were calculated using the *tf-idf* weighting scheme, while for the second matrix the *log-entropy* weighting scheme was used. In the *log-entropy* scheme, each matrix element, $m_{w,d}$, is calculated using logarithmic value of word-document frequency and the global word entropy (entropy of word frequency across the documents), as follows:

$$m_{w,d} = \log\left(tf_{w,d} + 1\right) \cdot g_e(w)$$

with

$$g_e(w) = 1 + \frac{1}{\log n} \sum_{d' \in D} \frac{tf_{w,d'}}{gf_w} \log \frac{tf_{w,d'}}{gf_w}$$

where $tf_{w,d}$ represents occurrence frequency of word w in document d, parameter gf_w represents global frequency of word w in corpus D, and n is the number of documents in corpus D. Next, we decompose each of the two matrices using SVD in order to obtain a vector for each word in the vector space of reduced dimensionality k ($k \ll n$). LSA vectors tend to express semantic properties of words. Moreover, the similarity between the LSA vectors may be used as a measure of semantic similarity between the corresponding words. We compute this similarity using the cosine between the LSA vectors and use the obtained values as weights of graph edges. Because running random-walk algorithms on a complete graph would be computationally intractable, we decided to reduce the number of edges by thresholding the similarity values.

3.3 Similarity Based on Random Indexing

Random Indexing (RI) is another word space approach, which presents an efficient and scalable alternative to more commonly used word space methods such as LSA. Random indexing is a dimensionality reduction technique in which a random matrix is used to project the original word-context matrix into the vector space of lower dimensionality. Each context is represented by its *index vector*, a sparse vector with a small number of randomly distributed $+1$ and -1 values, the remaining values being 0 (Sahlgren, 2006). For each corpus word its *context vector* is constructed by summing index vectors of all context elements occurring within contexts of all of its occurrences in the corpus. The semantic similarity of the two words is then expressed as the similarity between its context vectors.

We use two different definitions for the context and context relation. In the first case (referred to as *RI with document context*), each corpus document is considered as a separate context and the word is considered to be in a context relation if it occurs in the document. The context vector of each word is then simply the sum of random index vectors of the documents in which the word occurs. In the second case (referred to as *RI with window context*), each corpus word is considered as a context itself, and the two words are considered to be in a context relation if they co-occur in the corpus within the window of a given size. The context vector of each corpus word is then computed as the sum of random index vectors of all words with which it co-occurs in the corpus inside the window of a given size. Like in the LSA approach, we use the cosine of the angle between the context vectors as a measure of semantic similarity between the word pairs. To reduce the number of edges, we again perform the thresholding of the similarity values.

3.4 Random-Walk Algorithms

Once the graph building phase is done, we start propagating the sentiment scores from the vertices of the seed set words to the unlabeled vertices. To this end, one can use several semi-supervised learning algorithms. The most commonly used algorithm for dictionary-based sentiment lexicon acquisition is PageRank. Along with the PageRank we employ another random-walk algorithm called harmonic function learning.

PageRank

PageRank (Page et al., 1999) was initially designed for ranking web pages by their relevance. The intuition behind PageRank is that a vertex v should have a high score if it has many high-scoring neighbours and these neighbours do not have many other neighbours except the vertex v. Let $\mathbf{W}$ be the weighted row-normalized adjacency matrix of graph G. The algorithm iteratively computes the vector of vertex scores $\mathbf{a}$ in the following way:

$$\mathbf{a}^{(\mathbf{k})} = \alpha \mathbf{a}^{(\mathbf{k-1})} \mathbf{W} + (\mathbf{1} - \alpha)\mathbf{e}$$

where α is the PageRank damping factor. Vector $\mathbf{e}$ models the normalized internal source of score for all vertices and its elements sum up to 1. We assign the value of e_i to be $\frac{1}{|SeedSet|}$ for the vertices whose corresponding words belong to the seed set and $e_i = 0$ for all other vertices.

Harmonic Function

The second graph-based semi-supervised learning algorithm we use is the harmonic function label propagation (also known as absorbing random walk) (Zhu and Goldberg, 2009). Harmonic function tries to propagate labels between sources and sinks of sentiment. We perform two runs of the algorithm: one for positive sentiment, in which we use the words from the positive seed set as sentiment sources, and one for the negative sentiment, in which we use the words from the negative seed set as sentiment sources. In both cases, we use the precompiled seed set of neutral words as sentiment sinks. Note that we could not have used positive seed set words as sources and negative seed set words as sinks (or vice versa) because we aim to predict the positive and negative sentiment scores separately.

The value of the harmonic function for a labeled vertex remains the same as initially labeled, whereas for an unlabeled vertex the value is computed as the weighted average of its neighbours' values (Zhu and Goldberg, 2009):

$$f(v_k) = \frac{\sum_{j \in |V|} w_{kj} \cdot f(v_j)}{\sum_{j \in |V|} w_{kj}}$$

where V is the set of vertices of graph G and w_{kj} is the weight of the edge between the vertices v_k and v_j. If there is no graph edge between vertices v_k and v_j, the value of the weight w_{kj} is 0. This equation also represents the update rule for the iterative computation of the harmonic function. However, it can be shown that there is a closed-form solution of the harmonic function. Let W be the unnormalized weighted adjacency matrix of the graph G, and let D be the diagonal matrix with the element $D_{ii} = \sum_{j \in |V|} w_{ij}$ being the weighted degree of the vertex v_i. Then the unnormalized graph Laplacian is defined with $L = D - W$. Assuming that the labeled seed set vertices are ordered before the unlabeled ones, the graph Laplacian can be partitioned in the following way:

$$L = \begin{pmatrix} L_{ll} & L_{lu} \\ L_{ul} & L_{uu} \end{pmatrix}$$

The closed form solution for the harmonic function of the unlabeled vertices is then given by:

$$\mathbf{f_u} = -\mathbf{L_{uu}^{-1}} \mathbf{L_{ul}} \mathbf{y_l}$$

where $\mathbf{y_l}$ if the vector of labels of the seed set vertices (Zhu and Goldberg, 2009).

4 Supervised Step Hybridization

The sentiment scores obtained by the semi-supervised graph-based approaches described above are relative because they depend on the graph size as well as on the size and content of the seed sets. As such, these values can be used to rank the words by positivity or negativity, but not as absolute positivity and negativity scores. Thus, in the second step of our hybrid approach, we use supervised learning to obtain the absolute sentiment scores (polarity regression task) and the sentiment labels (sentiment classification task).

Each score obtained on each graph represents a single feature for supervised learning. There are altogether 24 different semi-supervised features used as input for the supervised learners. These features are both positive and negative labels generated from six different semi-supervised graphs (co-occurence frequency, co-occurrence PMI, LSA log-entropy, LSA tf-idf, random indexing with document context, and random indexing with window context) using two different random-walk algorithms (harmonic function and PageRank). We used the occurrence frequency of words in corpus as an additional feature.

For polarity regression, learning must be performed twice: once for the negative and once for the positive sentiment score. We performed the regression using SVM with radial-basis kernel. The same set of features used for regression was used for sentiment classification, but the goal was to predict the class of the word (positive, negative, or neutral) instead of separate positivity or negativity scores. SVM with radial-basis kernel was used to perform classification learning as well.

5 Evaluation and Results

All the experiments were performed on the excerpt of the New York Times corpus (years 2002–2007), containing 434,494 articles. The corpus was preprocessed (tokenized, lemmatized, and POS tagged) and only the content lemmas (nouns, verbs, adjectives, and adverbs) occurring at least 80 times in the corpus were considered. Lemmas occurring less than 80 were mainly named entities or their derivatives. The final sentiment lexicon consists of 41,359 lemmas annotated with positivity and negativity scores and sentiment class.[1]

[1]Sentiment lexicon is freely available at `http://takelab.fer.hr/sentilex`

5.1 Sentiment Annotations

To evaluate our methods on the three tasks, we compare the results against the Micro-WN(Op) dataset (Cerini et al., 2007). Micro-WN(Op) contains sentiment annotations for 1105 WordNet 2.0 synsets. Each synset s is manually annotated with the degree of positivity $Pos(s)$ and negativity $Neg(s)$, where $0 \leq Pos(s) \leq 1$, $0 \leq Neg(s) \leq 1$, and $Pos(s) + Neg(s) \leq 1$. Objectivity score is defined as $Obj(s) = 1 - (Pos(s) + Neg(s))$.

This gives us a list of 2800 word-sense pairs with their sentiment annotations. For reasons that we explain below, we retain from this list only those words for which all senses from WordNet have been sentiment-annotated, which leaves us with a list of 1645 word-sense pairs. From this list we then filter out all words that occur less than 80 times in our corpus, leaving us with a list of 1125 word-sense pairs (365 distinct words, of which 152 are monosemous). We refer to this set of 1125 sentiment-annotated word-sense pairs as Micro-WN(Op)-0.

Because our corpus-based methods are unable to discriminate among various senses of a polysemous word, we wish to be able to eliminate the negative effect of polysemy in our evaluation. The motivation for this is twofold: first, it gives us a way of measuring how much polysemy influences our results. Secondly, it provides us with the answer how well our method could perform in an ideal case where all the words from corpus have been pre-disambiguated. Because each of the words in Micro-WN(Op)-0 has all its senses sentiment-annotated, we can determine for each of these words how sentiment depends on its sense. Expectedly, there are words whose sentiment differs radically across its senses or parts-of-speech (e.g., *catch*, *nest*, *shark*, or *hot*), but also words whose sentiment is constant or similar across all its senses. To eliminate the effect of polysemy on sentiment prediction, we further filter the Micro-WN(Op)-0 list by retaining only the words whose sentiment is constant or nearly constant across all their senses. We refer to such words as *monosentimous*. We consider a word to be monosentimous iff (1) pairwise differences between all sentiment scores across senses are less than 0.25 (separately for both positive and negative sentiment) and (2) the sign of the difference between positive and negative sentiment score is constant across all senses. Note that every monosemous word is by definition monosentimous. Out of 365 words in Micro-WN(Op)-0, 225 of them are monosentimous. To obtain the sentiment scores of monosentimous words, we simply average the scores across their senses. We refer to the so-obtained set of 225 sentiment-annotated words as Micro-WN(Op)-1.

5.2 Semi-supervised Step Evaluation

The semi-supervised step was designed to propagate sentiment properties of the labeled words, ordering the words according to their positivity or negativity. Therefore, we decided to use the evaluation metric that measures the quality of the ranking in ordered lists, Kendall τ distance. The performance of the semi-supervised graph-based methods was evaluated both on the Micro-WN(Op)-1 and Micro-WN(Op)-0 sets.

In order to be able to compare our results to SentiWordNet (Baccianella et al., 2010), the *de facto* standard sentiment lexicon for English, we use the p-normalized Kendall τ distance between the rankings generated by our semi-supervised graph-based methods and the gold standard rankings. The p-normalized Kendall τ distance (Fagin et al., 2004) is a version of the standard Kendall τ distance that accounts for ties in the ordering:

$$\tau = \frac{n_d + p \cdot n_t}{Z}$$

where n_d is the number of pairs in disagreement (i.e., pairs of words ordered one way in the gold standard and the opposite way in the ranking under evaluation), n_t is the number of pairs which are ordered in the gold standard and tied in the ranking under evaluation, p is the penalization factor to be assigned to each of the n_t pairs (usually set to $p = \frac{1}{2}$), and Z is the number of pairs of words that are ordered in the gold standard. Table 1 presents the results for each of the methods used to build the sentiment graph and for both random-walk algorithms. The results were obtained by evaluating the relative rankings of words against the Micro-WN(Op)-1 as gold standard. For comparison, the p-normalized Kendall τ scores for SentiWordNet 1.0 and SentiWordNet 3.0 are extracted from (Baccianella et al., 2010).

Rankings for the negative scores are consistently better across all methods and algorithms. We believe that the negative rankings are better

Table 1: The results on the polarity ranking task

	Harmonic function		PageRank	
	Positive	Negative	Positive	Negative
Co-occurrence freq.	0.395	0.298	0.540	0.544
LSA log-entropy	0.425	0.308	0.434	0.370
LSA tf-idf	0.396	0.320	0.417	0.424
Co-occurrence PMI	**0.321**	**0.256**	0.550	0.576
Random indexing document context	0.402	0.433	0.534	0.557
Random indexing window context	0.455	0.398	0.491	0.436
	Positive		Negative	
SentiWordNet 1.0	0.349		0.296	
SentiWordNet 3.0	0.281		0.231	

for two reasons. Firstly, the corpus contains many more articles describing negative events such as wars and accidents than the articles describing positive events such as celebrations and victories. In short, the distribution of articles is significantly skewed towards "negative" events. Secondly, the lemma *new*, which was included in the positive seed set, occurs in the corpus very frequently as a part of named entity collocations such as "New York" and "New Jersey" in which it does not reflect its dominant sense. The harmonic function label propagation generally outperforms the PageRank algorithm. The best performance on the Micro-WN(Op)-0 set was 0.380 for the positive ranking and 0.270 for the negative ranking, showing that the performance deteriorates when polysemy is present. However, the drop in performance, especially for the negative ranking, is not substantial. Our best method (graph built based on PMI of corpus words used in combination with harmonic function label propagation) outperforms SentiWordNet 1.0 and performs slightly worse than SentiWordNet 3.0 for both positive and negative rankings.

5.3 Evaluation of the Supervised Step

Supervised step deals with the polarity regression task and the sentiment classification task. Polarity regression maps the "virtual" sentiment scores obtained on graphs to the absolute sentiment scores (on a scale from 0 to 1). The regression was performed twice: once for the positive scores and once for the negative scores. We evaluate the performance of the polarity regression against the Micro-WN(Op)-0 gold standard in terms of root mean square error (RMSE). We used the average of the labeled polarity scores (positive and negative) of all monosentimous words in Micro-WN(Op)-1 as a baseline for this task.

Sentiment classification uses the scores obtained on graphs as features in order to assign each word with one of the three sentiment labels (*positive*, *negative*, and *neutral*). The classification performance is evaluated in terms of micro-F1 measure. The labels for the classification are assigned according to the positivity and negativity scores (the label *neutral* is assigned if $Obj(s) = 1 - Pos(s) - Neg(s)$ is larger than both $Pos(s)$ and $Neg(s)$). The majority class predictor was used as a baseline for the classification task.

Due to the small size of the labeled sets (e.g., 225 for Micro-WN(Op)-1) we performed the 10 $\times$ 10 CV evaluation (10 cross-validation trials, each on randomly permuted data) (Bouckaert, 2003) both for regression and classification. For comparison, we evaluated the SentiWordNet in the same way – we averaged the SentiWordNet scores for all the senses of monosentimous words from the Micro-WN(Op)-1.

Although the semi-supervised step itself was not designed to deal with polarity regression task and sentiment classification task, we decided to evaluate the results gained from graphs on these tasks as well. This gives us an insight to how much the supervised step adds in terms of performance. The positivity and negativity scores obtained from graphs were directly evaluated on the regression task measuring the RMSE against the gold standard. Classification labels were determined by comparing the positive rank of the word against the negative rank of the word. The word was classified as *neutral* if the absolute difference between its positive and negative rank was below the given treshold t. Empirically determined optimal value of the treshold was $t = 1000$.

Table 2 we present the results of the hybrid method on both the regression (for both positive and negative scores) and classification tasks compared with the performance of the SentiWordNet and the baselines. Additionally, we present the results obtained using only the semi-supervised step. On both the regression and classification task our method outperforms the baseline. The performance is comparable to SentiWordNet on the sentiment classification task. However, the performance of our corpus-based approach is significantly lower than SentiWordNet on the polarity regression task – a more detailed analysis is required to determine the cause of this. The hybrid approach performs significantly better than the semi-supervised method alone, confirming the importance of the supervised step.

Models trained on the Micro-WN(Op)-1 were applied on the set of words from the Micro-WN(Op)-0 not present in the Micro-WN(Op)-1 (i.e., the difference between the two sets) in order to test the performance on non-monosentimous words. The obtained results on this set are, surprisingly, slightly better (positivity regression – 0.337; negativity regression – 0.313; and classification – 57.55%). This is most likely due to the fact that, although not all senses have the same sentiment, most of them have similar sentiment, which is often also the sentiment of the dominant sense in the corpus.

6 Conclusion

We have described a hybrid approach to sentiment lexicon acquisition from corpus. On one hand, the approach combines corpus-based lexical semantics with graph-based label propagation, while on the other hand it combines semi-supervised and supervised learning. We have evaluated the performance on three sentiment prediction tasks: polarity ranking task, polarity regression task, and sentiment classification task. Our experiments suggest that the results on the polarity ranking task are comparable to SentiWordNet. On the sentiment classification task, the results are also comparable to SentiWordNet when restricted to monosentimous words. On the polarity regression task, our results are worse than SentiWordNet, although still above the baseline.

Unlike with the WordNet-based approaches, in which sentiment is predicted based on sentiment-preserving semantic relations between synsets, the corpus-based approach operates at the level of words and thus suffers from two major limitations. Firstly, the semantic relations extracted from corpus are inherently unstructured, vague, and – besides paradigmatic relations – also include syntagmatic and very loose topical relations. Thus, sentiment labels propagate in a less controlled manner and get influenced more easily by the context. For example, words "understandable" and "justifiable" get labeled as predominately negative, because they usually occur in negative contexts. Secondly, in the approach we described, polysemy is not accounted for, which introduces sentiment prediction errors for words that are not monosentimous. It remains to be seen whether this could be remedied by employing WSD prior to sentiment lexicon acquisition.

For future work we intend to investigate how syntax-based information can be used to introduce more semantic structure into the graph. We will experiment with other hybridization approaches that combine semantic links from WordNet with corpus-derived semantic relations.

Acknowledgments

We thank the anonymous reviewers for their useful comments. This work has been supported by the Ministry of Science, Education and Sports, Republic of Croatia under the Grant 036-1300646-1986.

References

E. Agirre, D. Martínez, O.L. de Lacalle, and A. Soroa. 2006. Two graph-based algorithms for state-of-the-art wsd. In *Proc. of the 2006 Conference on Empirical Methods in Natural Language Processing*, pages 585–593. Association for Computational Linguistics.

A. Andreevskaia and S. Bergler. 2006. Mining wordnet for fuzzy sentiment: Sentiment tag extraction from wordnet glosses. In *Proc. of EACL*, volume 6, pages 209–216.

S. Baccianella, A. Esuli, and F. Sebastiani. 2010. Sentiwordnet 3.0: An enhanced lexical resource for sentiment analysis and opinion mining. In

Table 2: The performance on the polarity regression task and sentiment classification task

	Regression (RMSE) Positivity	Regression (RMSE) Negativity	Classification (micro-F1)
Hybrid approach	0.363 ± 0.005	0.387 ± 0.003	0.548 ± 0.126
Baseline	0.383	0.413	0.427
Semi-supervised	0.443	0.466	0.484
SentiWordNet	0.284	0.294	0.582

Proc. of the Seventh International Conference on Language Resources and Evaluation (LREC'10), Valletta, Malta. European Language Resources Association (ELRA).

R.R. Bouckaert. 2003. Choosing between two learning algorithms based on calibrated tests. In *Machine learning-International workshop then conference-*, volume 20, pages 51–58.

S. Cerini, V. Compagnoni, A. Demontis, M. Formentelli, and G. Gandini. 2007. Micro-WNOp: A gold standard for the evaluation of automatically compiled lexical resources for opinion mining. *Language resources and linguistic theory: Typology, second language acquisition, English linguistics*, pages 200–210.

K.W. Church and P. Hanks. 1990. Word association norms, mutual information, and lexicography. *Computational linguistics*, 16(1):22–29.

S.T. Dumais. 2004. Latent semantic analysis. *Annual Review of Information Science and Technology*, 38(1):188–230.

A. Esuli and F. Sebastiani. 2007. Pageranking wordnet synsets: An application to opinion mining. In *Annual meeting-association for computational linguistics*, volume 45, pages 424–431.

S. Evert. 2008. Corpora and collocations. *Corpus Linguistics. An International Handbook*, pages 1212–1248.

R. Fagin, R. Kumar, M. Mahdian, D. Sivakumar, and E. Vee. 2004. Comparing and aggregating rankings with ties. In *Proc. of the twenty-third ACM SIGMOD-SIGACT-SIGART symposium on Principles of database systems*, pages 47–58. ACM.

C. Fellbaum. 2010. Wordnet. *Theory and Applications of Ontology: Computer Applications*, pages 231–243.

A.B. Goldberg and X. Zhu. 2006. Seeing stars when there aren't many stars: graph-based semi-supervised learning for sentiment categorization. In *Proc. of the First Workshop on Graph Based Methods for Natural Language Processing*, pages 45–52. Association for Computational Linguistics.

V. Hatzivassiloglou and K.R. McKeown. 1997. Predicting the semantic orientation of adjectives. In *Proc. of the eighth conference on European chapter of the Association for Computational Linguistics*, pages 174–181. Association for Computational Linguistics.

M. Hu and B. Liu. 2004. Mining opinion features in customer reviews. In *Proc. of the National Conference on Artificial Intelligence*, pages 755–760.

J. Kamps, MJ Marx, R.J. Mokken, and M. De Rijke. 2004. Using WordNet to measure semantic orientations of adjectives.

L. Page, S. Brin, R. Motwani, and T. Winograd. 1999. The PageRank citation ranking: Bringing order to the web.

E. Riloff, S. Patwardhan, and J. Wiebe. 2006. Feature subsumption for opinion analysis. In *Proc. of the 2006 Conference on Empirical Methods in Natural Language Processing*, pages 440–448. Association for Computational Linguistics.

M. Sahlgren. 2006. *The Word-Space Model: Using Distributional Analysis to Represent Syntagmatic and Paradigmatic Relations between Words in High-Dimensional Vector Spaces*. Ph.D. thesis, Stockholm University, Stockholm, Sweden.

S. Somasundaran, T. Wilson, J. Wiebe, and V. Stoyanov. 2007. Qa with attitude: Exploiting opinion type analysis for improving question answering in on-line discussions and the news. In *Proc. of the International Conference on Weblogs and Social Media (ICWSM)*. Citeseer.

M. Taboada, J. Brooke, M. Tofiloski, K. Voll, and M. Stede. 2011. Lexicon-based methods for sentiment analysis. *Computational Linguistics*, (Early Access):1–41.

P. Turney and M.L. Littman. 2003. Measuring praise and criticism: Inference of semantic orientation from association. In *ACM Transactions on Information Systems (TOIS)*.

T. Wilson, J. Wiebe, and P. Hoffmann. 2009. Recognizing contextual polarity: an exploration of features for phrase-level sentiment analysis. *Computational Linguistics*, 35(3):399–433.

X. Zhu and A.B. Goldberg. 2009. Introduction to semi-supervised learning. *Synthesis lectures on artificial intelligence and machine learning*, 3(1):1–130.

A Study of Hybrid Similarity Measures for Semantic Relation Extraction

Alexander Panchenko and Olga Morozova
Center for Natural Language Processing (CENTAL)
Université catholique de Louvain, Belgium
{alexander.panchenko, olga.morozova}@uclouvain.be

Abstract

This paper describes several novel hybrid semantic similarity measures. We study various combinations of 16 baseline measures based on WordNet, Web as a corpus, corpora, dictionaries, and encyclopedia. The hybrid measures rely on 8 combination methods and 3 measure selection techniques and are evaluated on (a) the task of predicting semantic similarity scores and (b) the task of predicting semantic relation between two terms. Our results show that hybrid measures outperform single measures by a wide margin, achieving a correlation up to 0.890 and MAP(20) up to 0.995.

1 Introduction

Semantic similarity measures and relations are proven to be valuable for various NLP and IR applications, such as word sense disambiguation, query expansion, and question answering.

Let R be a set of synonyms, hypernyms, and co-hyponyms of terms C, established by a lexicographer. A *semantic relation extraction* method aims at discovering a set of relations $\hat{R}$ approximating R. The quality of the relations provided by existing extractors is still lower than the quality of the manually constructed relations. This motivates the development of new relation extraction methods.

A well-established approach to relation extraction is based on lexico-syntactic patterns (Auger and Barrière, 2008). In this paper, we study an alternative approach based on *similarity measures*. These methods do not return a type of the relation between words ($\hat{R} \subseteq C \times C$). However, we assume that the methods should retrieve *a mix* of synonyms, hypernyms, and co-hyponyms for practical use in text processing applications and evaluate them accordingly.

A multitude of measures was used in the previous research to extract synonyms, hypernyms, and co-hyponyms. Five key approaches are those based on a distributional analysis (Lin, 1998b), Web as a corpus (Cilibrasi and Vitanyi, 2007), lexico-syntactic patterns (Bollegala et al., 2007), semantic networks (Resnik, 1995), and definitions of dictionaries or encyclopedias (Zesch et al., 2008a). Still, the existing approaches based on these single measures are far from being perfect. For instance, Curran and Moens (2002) compared distributional measures and reported Precision@1 of 76% for the best one. For improving the performance, some attempts were made to combine single measures, such as (Curran, 2002; Cederberg and Widdows, 2003; Mihalcea et al., 2006; Agirre et al., 2009; Yang and Callan, 2009). However, most studies are still not taking into account the whole range of existing measures, combining mostly sporadically different methods.

The main contribution of the paper is a systematic analysis of 16 baseline measures, and their combinations with 8 fusion methods and 3 techniques for the combination set selection. We are first to propose hybrid similarity measures based on all five extraction approaches listed above; our combined techniques are original as they exploit all key types of resources usable for semantic relation extraction – corpus, web corpus, semantic networks, dictionaries, and encyclopedias. Our experiments confirm that the combined measures are more precise than the single ones. The best found hybrid measure combines 15 baseline measures with the supervised learning. It outperforms

Proceedings of the Workshop on Innovative Hybrid Approaches to the Processing of Textual Data (Hybrid2012), EACL 2012, pages 10–18,
Avignon, France, April 23 2012. ©2012 Association for Computational Linguistics

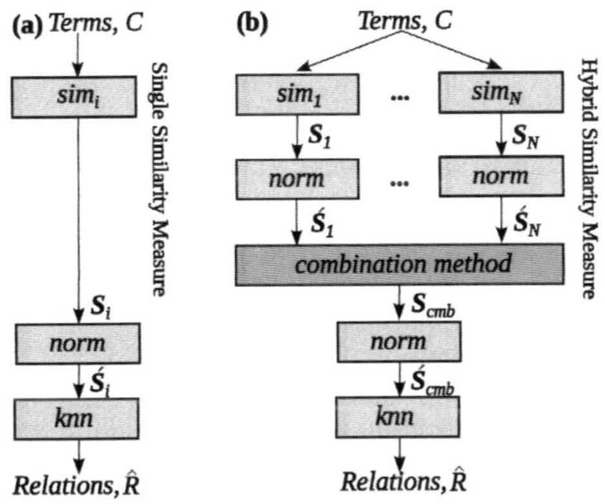

Figure 1: (a) Single and (b) hybrid relation extractors based on similarity measures.

all tested single and combined measures by a large margin, achieving a correlation of 0.870 with human judgements and MAP(20) of 0.995 on the relation recognition task.

2 Similarity-based Relation Extraction

In this paper a similarity-based relation extraction method is used. In contrast to the traditional approaches, relying on a single measure, our method relies on a hybrid measure (see Figure 1). A *hybrid similarity measure* combines several *single similarity measures* with a *combination method* to achieve better extraction results. To extract relations $\hat{R}$ between terms C, the method calculates pairwise similarities between them with the help of a similarity measure. The relations are established between each term $c \in C$ and the terms most similar to c (its nearest neighbors). First, a term-term ($C \times C$) similarity matrix $\mathbf{S}$ is calculated with a similarity measure sim, as depicted in Figure 1 (a). Then, these similarity scores are mapped to the interval $[0;1]$ with a $norm$ function as follows: $\acute{\mathbf{S}} = \frac{\mathbf{S}-min(\mathbf{S})}{max(\mathbf{S})}$. Dissimilarity scores are transformed into similarity scores: $\acute{\mathbf{S}} = \mathbf{1} - norm(\mathbf{S})$. Finally, the knn function calculates semantic relations between terms with a k-NN thresholding: $\hat{R} = \bigcup_{i=1}^{|C|} \{\langle c_i, c_j\rangle : (c_j \in \text{top } k\% \text{ of } c_i) \wedge (s_{ij} > 0)\}$. Here, k is a percent of top similar terms to a term c_i. Thus, the method links each term c_i with $k\%$ of its nearest neighbours.

3 Single Similarity Measures

A similarity measure *extracts* or *recalls* a similarity score $s_{ij} \in \mathbf{S}$ between a pair of terms $c_i, c_j \in C$. In this section we list 16 baseline measures exploited by hybrid measures. The measures were selected as (a) the previous research suggests that they are able to capture synonyms, hypernyms, and co-hyponyms; (b) they rely on all main resources used to derive semantic similarity – semantic networks, Web as a corpus, traditional corpora, dictionaries, and encyclopedia.

3.1 Measures Based on a Semantic Network

We test 5 measures relying on WordNet semantic network (Miller, 1995) to calculate the similarities: Wu and Palmer (1994) (1), Leacock and Chodorow (1998) (2), Resnik (1995) (3), Jiang and Conrath (1997) (4), and Lin (1998a) (5). These measures exploit the lengths of the shortest paths between terms in a network and probability of terms derived from a corpus. We use implementation of the measures available in WordNet::Similarity (Pedersen et al., 2004).

A limitation of these measures is that similarities can only be calculated upon 155.287 English terms from WordNet 3.0. In other words, these measures *recall* rather than *extract* similarities. Therefore, they should be considered as a source of common lexico-semantic knowledge for a hybrid semantic similarity measure.

3.2 Web-based Measures

Web-based metrics use Web search engines for calculation of similarities. They rely on the number of times the terms co-occur in the documents as indexed by an information retrieval system. We use 3 baseline web measures based on index of Yahoo! (6), Bing (7), and Google over the domain `wikipedia.org` (8). These three measures exploit Normalized Google Distance (NGD) formula (Cilibrasi and Vitanyi, 2007) for transforming the number of hits into a similarity score. Our own system implements Bing measure, while Measures of Semantic Relatedness (MSR) web service[1] calculates similarities with Yahoo! and Google.

The coverage of languages and vocabularies by web-based measures is huge. Therefore, it is assumed that they are able to *extract* new lexico-semantic knowledge. Web-based measures are limited by constraints of a search engine API (hundreds of thousands of queries are needed).

[1] `http://cwl-projects.cogsci.rpi.edu/msr/`

3.3 Corpus-based Measures

We tested 5 measures relying on corpora to calculate similarity of terms: two baseline distributional measures, one novel measure based on lexico-syntactic patterns, and two other baseline measures. Each of them uses a different corpus.

Corpus-based measures are able to *extract* similarity between unknown terms. Extraction capabilities of these measures are limited by a corpus. If terms do not occur in a text, then it would be impossible to calculate similarities between them.

Distributional Measures

These measures are based on a distributional analysis of a 800M tokens corpus WaCypedia (Baroni et al., 2009) tagged with TreeTagger and dependency-parsed with MaltParser. We rely on our own implementation of two distributional measures. The distributional measure (9) performs Bag-of-words Distributional Analysis (BDA) (Sahlgren, 2006). We use as features the 5000 most frequent lemmas (nouns, adjectives, and verbs) from a context window of 3 words, excluding stopwords. The distributional measure (10) performs Syntactic Distributional Analysis (SDA) (Lin, 1998b). For this one, we use as features the 100.000 most frequent dependency-lemma pairs. In our implementation of SDA a term c_i is represented with a feature $\langle dt_j, w_k \rangle$, if w_k is not in a stoplist and dt_j has one of the following dependency types: NMOD, P, PMOD, ADV, SBJ, OBJ, VMOD, COORD, CC, VC, DEP, PRD, AMOD, PRN, PRT, LGS, IOBJ, EXP, CLF, GAP . For both BDA and SDA: the feature matrix is normalized with Pointwise Mutual Information; similarities between terms are calculated with a cosine between their respective feature vectors.

Pattern-based Measure

We developed a novel similarity measure PatternWiki (13), which relies on 10 lexico-syntactic patterns. [2] First, we apply the patterns to the WaCypedia corpus and get as a result a list of concordances (see below). Next, we select the concordances which contain at least two terms from the input vocabulary C. The semantic similarity s_{ij} between each two terms $c_i, c_j \in C$ is equal to the number of their co-occurences in the same concordance.

The set of the patterns we used is a compilation of the 6 classical Hearst (1992) patterns, aiming at the extraction of hypernymic relations, as well as 3 patterns retrieving some other hypernyms and co-hyponyms and 1 synonym extraction pattern, which we found in accordance with Hearst's pattern discovery algorithm. The patterns are encoded in a form of finite-state transducers with the help of a corpus processing tool Unitex [3] (Paumier, 2003). The main graph is a cascade of the subgraphs, each of which encodes one of the patterns. For example, Figure 2 presents the graph which extracts, e. g.:

- `such diverse {[occupations]} as {[doctors]}, {[engineers]} and {[scientists]}[PATTERN=1]`

Figure brackets mark the noun phrases, which are in the semantic relation, nouns and compound nouns stand between the square brackets. Unitex enables the exclusion of meaningless adjectives and determiners out of the tagging, while the patterns containing them are still being recognized. So, the notion of a pattern has more general sense with respect to other works such as (Bollegala et al., 2007), where each construction with a different lexical item, a word form or even a punctuation mark is regarded as a unique pattern. The nouns extracted from the square brackets are lemmatized with the help of DELA dictionary[4], which consists of around 300,000 simple and 130,000 compound words. If the noun to extract is a plural form of a noun in the dictionary, then it is re-written into the respective singular form. Semantic similarity score is equal to the number of co-occurences of terms in the square brackets within the same concordance (the number of extractions between the terms).

Other Corpus-based Measures

In addition to the three measures presented above, we use two other corpus-based measures available via the MSR web service. The measure (11) relies on the Latent Semantic Analysis (LSA) (Landauer and Dumais, 1997) trained on the TASA corpus (Veksler et al., 2008). LSA calculates similarity of terms with a cosine between their respective vectors in the "concept space". The measure (12) relies on the NGD formula (see Section 3.2), where counts are derived from the Factiva corpus (Veksler et al., 2008).

[2] Available at http://http://cental.fltr.ucl.ac.be/team/~morozova/pattern-wiki.tar.gz

[3] http://igm.univ-mlv.fr/~unitex/

[4] Available at http://infolingu.univ-mlv.fr/

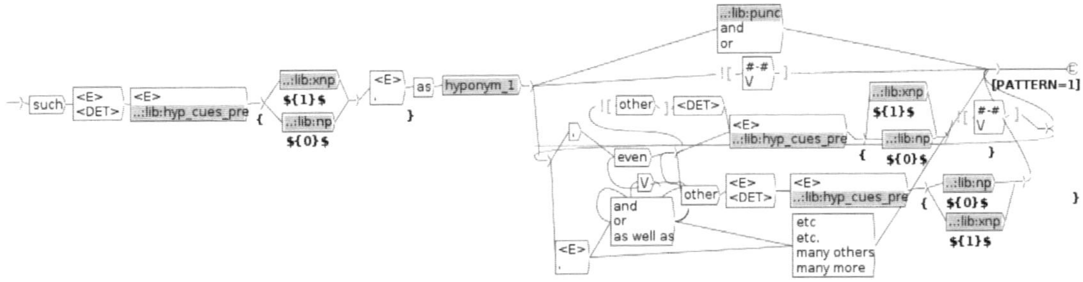

Figure 2: An example of a UNITEX graph for hypernym extraction (subgraphs are marked with gray; <E> defines zero; <DET> defines determiners; bold symbols and letters outside of the boxes are annotation tags)

3.4 Definition-based Measures

We test 3 measures which rely on explicit definitions of terms specified in dictionaries. The first metric WktWiki (14) is a novel similarity measure that stems from the Lesk algorithm (Pedersen et al., 2004) and the work of Zesch et al. (2008a). WktWiki operates on Wiktionary definitions and relations and Wikipedia abstracts. WktWiki calculates similarity as follows. First, definitions for each input term $c \in C$ are built. A "definition" is a union of all available glosses, examples, quotations, related words, and categories from Wiktionary and a short abstract of the corresponding Wikipedia article (a name of the article must exactly match the term c). We use all senses corresponding to a surface form of term c. Then, each term $c \in C$ of the 1000 most frequent lemmas is represented as a bag-of-lemma vector, derived from its "definition". Feature vectors are normalized with Pointwise Mutual Information and similarities between terms are calculated with a cosine between them. Finally, the pairwise similarities between terms $\mathbf{S}$ are corrected. The highest similarity score is assigned to the pairs of terms which are directly related in Wiktionary. [5]

WktWiki is different to the work of Zesch et al. (2008b) in three aspects: (a) terms are represented in a word space, and not in a document space; (b) both texts from Wiktionary and Wikipedia are used; (c) relations of Wiktionary are used to update similarity scores.

In addition to WktWiki, we operate with 2 baseline measures relying on WordNet glosses available in a WORDNET::SIMILARITY package: Gloss Vectors (Patwardhan and Pedersen, 2006) (15) and Extended Lesk (Banerjee and Pedersen, 2003) (16). The key difference between WktWiki and WordNet-based measures is that the latter uses definitions of related terms.

Extraction capabilities of definition-based measures are limited by the number of available definitions. As of October 2011, WordNet contains 117.659 definitions (glosses); Wiktionary contains 536.594 definitions in English and 4.272.902 definitions in all languages; Wikipedia has 3.866.773 English articles and around 20.8 millons of articles in all languages.

4 Hybrid Similarity Measures

A hybrid similarity measure combines several single similarity measures described above with one of the combination methods described below.

4.1 Combination Methods

A goal of a combination method is to produce similarity scores which perform better than the scores of input single measures. A combination method takes as an input a set of similarity matrices $\{\mathbf{S}_1, \ldots, \mathbf{S}_K\}$ produced by K single measures and outputs a combined similarity matrix $\mathbf{S}_{cmb}$. We denote as s_{ij}^k a *pairwise similarity score* of terms c_i and c_j produced by k-th measure. We test the 8 following combination methods:

Mean. A mean of K pairwise similarity scores:

$$\mathbf{S}_{cmb} = \frac{1}{K}\sum_{k=1}^{K}\mathbf{S}_k \Leftrightarrow s_{ij}^{cmb} = \frac{1}{K}\sum_{k=1,K} s_{ij}^k.$$

Mean-Nnz. A mean of those pairwise similarity scores which have a non-zero value:

$$s_{ij}^{cmb} = \frac{1}{|k : s_{ij}^k > 0, k = 1, K|}\sum_{k=1,K} s_{ij}^k.$$

[5] We used JWKTL library (Zesch et al., 2008a), as an API to Wiktionary and `DBpedia.org` as a source of Wikipedia short abstracts (dumps were downloaded in October 2011).

Mean-Zscore. A mean of K similarity scores transformed into Z-scores:

$$s_{ij}^{cmb} = \frac{1}{K}\sum_{k=1}^{K}\frac{s_{ij}^{k} - \mu_k}{\sigma_k},$$

where μ_k is a mean and σ_k is a standard deviation of similarity scores of k-th measure ($\mathbf{S}_k$).

Median. A median of K pairwise similarities:

$$s_{ij}^{cmb} = median(s_{ij}^{1}, \ldots, s_{ij}^{K}).$$

Max. A maximum of K pairwise similarities:

$$s_{ij}^{cmb} = max(s_{ij}^{1}, \ldots, s_{ij}^{K}).$$

Rank Fusion. First, this combination method converts each pairwise similarity score s_{ij}^{k} to a rank r_{ij}^{k}. Here, $r_{ij}^{k} = 5$ means that term c_j is the 5-th nearest neighbor of the term c_i, according to the k-th measure. Then, it calculates a combined similarity score as a mean of these pairwise ranks: $s_{ij}^{cmb} = \frac{1}{K}\sum_{k=1,K} r_{ij}^{k}$.

Relation Fusion. This combination method gathers and unites the best relations provided by each measure. First, the method retrieves relations extracted by single measures with the function knn described in Section 2. We have empirically chosen an "internal" kNN threshold of 20% for this combination method. Then, a set of extracted relations R_k, obtained from the k-th measure, is encoded as an adjacency matrix $\mathbf{R}_k$. An element of this matrix indicates whether terms c_i and c_j are related:

$$r_{ij}^{k} = \begin{cases} 1 & \text{if semantic relation } \langle c_i, c_j\rangle \in R_k \\ 0 & \text{else} \end{cases}$$

The final similarity score is a mean of adjacency matrices: $\mathbf{S}_{cmb} = \frac{1}{K}\sum_{i=1}^{K}\mathbf{R}_i$. Thus, if two measures are combined and the first extracted the relation between c_i and c_j, while the second did not, then the similarity s_{ij} will be equal to 0.5.

Logit. This combination method is based on logistic regression (Agresti, 2002). We train a binary classifier on a set of manually constructed semantic relations R (we use BLESS and SN datasets described in Section 5). Positive training examples are "meaningful" relations (synonyms, hyponyms, etc.), while negative training examples are pairs of semantically unrelated words (generated randomly and verified manually). A semantic relation $\langle c_i, c_j\rangle \in R$ is represented with a vector of pairwise similarities between terms c_i, c_j calculated with K measures $(s_{ij}^{1}, \ldots, s_{ij}^{K})$ and a binary variable r_{ij} (category):

$$r_{ij} = \begin{cases} 0 & \text{if } \langle c_i, c_j\rangle \text{ is a random relation} \\ 1 & \text{otherwise} \end{cases}$$

For evaluation purposes, we use a special 10-fold cross validation ensuring that all relations of one term c are always in the same training/test fold. The results of the training are $K + 1$ coefficients of regression $(w_0, w_1, \ldots, w_K)$. We apply the model to combine similarity measures as follows:

$$s_{ij}^{cmb} = \frac{1}{1+e^{-z}}, z = w_0 + \sum_{k=1}^{K} w_k s_{ij}^{k}.$$

4.2 Combination Sets

Any of the 8 combination methods presented above may combine from 2 to 16 single measures. Thus, there are $\sum_{m=2}^{16} C_{16}^{m} = \sum_{m=2}^{16} \frac{16!}{m!(16-m)!} = 65535$ ways to choose which single measures to use in *a* combination method. We apply three methods to find an efficient combination of measures in this search space: expert choice of measures, forward stepwise procedure, and analysis of a logistic regression model.

Expert choice of measures is based on the analytical and empirical properties of the measures. We chose 5 or 9 measures which perform well and rely on complimentary resources: corpus, Web, WordNet, etc. Additionally, we selected a group of all measures except for one which has shown the worst results on all datasets. Thus, according to this selection method we have chosen three groups of measures (see Section 3 and Table 1 for notation):

- $E5 = \{3, 9, 10, 13, 14\}$
- $E9 = \{1, 3, 9 - 11, 13 - 16\}$
- $E15 = \{1, 2, 3, 4, 5, 6, 8 - 16\}$

Forward stepwise procedure is a greedy algorithm which works as follows. It takes as an input all measures, a method of their combination such as *Mean*, and a criterion such as Precision at $k = 50$. It starts with a void set of measures. Then, at each iteration it adds to the combination one measure which brings the biggest improvement to the criterion. The algorithm stops when no measure can improve the criteria. According to this method, we have chosen four groups of the measures [6]:

- $S7 = \{9-11, 13-16\}$
- $S8a = \{9-16\}$
- $S8b = \{1, 9-11, 13-16\}$
- $S10 = \{1, 6, 9-16\}$

The last measure selection technique is based on analysis of *logistic regression* trained on all 16 measures as features. Only measures with positive coefficients are selected. According to this method, 12 measures were chosen:

- $R12 = \{3, 5, 6, 8-16\}$

We test combination methods on the 8 sets of measures specified above. Remarkably, all three selection techniques constantly choose six following measures – $9, 10, 11, 14, 15, 16$, i. e., C-BowDA, C-SynDA, C-LSA-Tasa, D-WktWiki, N-GlossVectors, and N-ExtendedLesk.

5 Evaluation

Evaluation relies on human judgements about semantic similarity and on manually constructed semantic relations. [7]

Human Judgements Datasets. This kind of ground truth enables *direct* assessment of measure performance and *indirect* assessment of extraction quality with this measure. Each of these datasets consists of N tuples $\langle c_i, c_j, s_{ij}\rangle$, where c_i, c_j are terms, and s_{ij} is their similarity obtained by human judgement. We use three standard human judgements datasets – MC (Miller and Charles, 1991), RG (Rubenstein and Goodenough, 1965) and WordSim353 (Finkelstein et al., 2001), composed of 30, 65, and 353 pairs of terms respectively. Let $\mathrm{s} = (s_{i1}, s_{i2}, \ldots, s_{iN})$ be a vector of ground truth scores, and $\hat{\mathrm{s}} = (\hat{s}_{i1}, \hat{s}_{i2}, \ldots, \hat{s}_{iN})$ be a vector of similarity scores calculated with a similarity measure. Then, the quality of this measure is assessed with Spearman's correlation between s and ŝ.

Semantic Relations Datasets. This kind of ground truth enables *indirect* assessment of measure performance and *direct* assessment of extraction quality with the measure. Each of these datasets consists of a set of semantic relations R, such as ⟨agitator, syn, activist⟩, ⟨hawk , hyper, predator⟩, ⟨gun, syn,weapon⟩, and ⟨dishwasher, cohypo, reezer⟩. Each "target" term has roughly the same number of meaningful and random relations. We use two semantic relation datasets: BLESS (Baroni and Lenci, 2011) and SN. The first is used to assess *hypernyms* and *cohyponyms* extraction. BLESS relates 200 target terms (100 animate and 100 inanimate nouns) to 8625 relatum terms with 26554 semantic relations (14440 are meaningful and 12154 are random). Every relation has one of the following types: hypernym, co-hyponym, meronym, attribute, event, or random. We use the second dataset to evaluate synonymy extraction. SN relates 462 target terms (nouns) to 5910 relatum terms with 14682 semantic relations (7341 are meaningful and 7341 are random). We built SN from WordNet, Roget's thesaurus, and a synonyms database [8].

This kind of evaluation is based on the number of correctly extracted relations with the method described in Section 2. Let $\hat{R}_k$ be a set of extracted semantic relations at a certain level of the kNN threshold k. Then, precision, recall, and mean average precision (MAP) at k are calculated correspondingly as follows: $P(k) = \frac{|R \cap \hat{R}_k|}{|\hat{R}_k|}$, $R(k) = \frac{|R \cap \hat{R}_k|}{|R|}$, $M(k) = \frac{1}{k}\sum_{i=1}^{k} P(i)$. The quality of a similarity measure is assessed with the six following statistics: $P(10)$, $P(20)$, $P(50)$, $R(50)$, $M(20)$, and $M(50)$.

6 Results

Table 1 and Figure 3 present performance of the single and hybrid measures on the five ground truth datasets listed above. The first three columns of the table contain correlations with human judgements, while the other columns present performance on the relation extraction task.

The first part of the table reports on scores of 16 single measures. Our results show that the measures are indeed complimentary – there is no measure which performs best on all datasets. For instance, the measure based on a syntactic distributional analysis C-SynDA performed best on the MC dataset achieving a correlation of 0.790; the WordNet measure WN-LeacockChodorow achieved the top score of 0.789 on the RG dataset;

[6] We used Mean as a hybrid measure and the following criteria: MAP(20), MAP(50), P(10), P(20) and P(50). We kept measures which were selected by most of the criteria.

[7] An evaluation script is available at `http://cental.fltr.ucl.ac.be/team/~panchenko/sre-eval/`

[8] `http://synonyms-database.downloadaces.com`

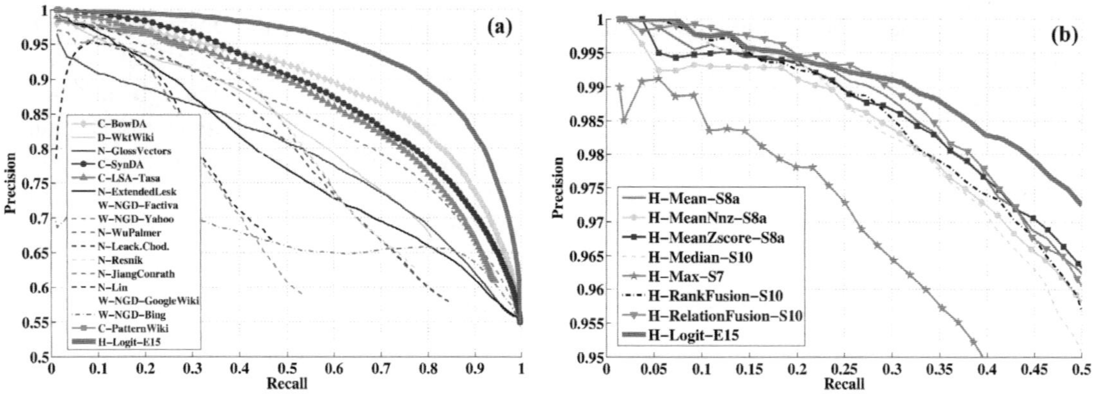

Figure 3: Precision-Recall graphs calculated on the BLESS dataset of (a) 16 single measures and the best hybrid measure H-Logit-E15; (b) 8 hybrid measures.

the corpus based measure C-NGD-Factiva was best on the WordSim353 dataset, achieving a correlation of 0.600. On the BLESS dataset, syntactic distributional analysis C-SynDA performed best for high precision among single measures achieving MAP(20) of 0.984, while the bag-of-words distributional measure C-BowDA was the best for high recall with R(50) of 0.772. On the SN dataset, the WordNet-based measure N-WuPalmer was best both for precision and recall.

The second part of Table 1 presents performance of the hybrid measures. Our results show that if signals from complimentary resources are used, then the retrieval of semantically similar words is significantly improved. Most of the hybrid measures outperform the single measures on all the datasets. We tested each of the 8 combination methods presented in Section 4.1 with each of the 8 sets of measures specified in Section 4.2. We report on the best metrics among all 64 hybrid measures. A notion H-Mean-S8a means that the *Mean* combination method provides the best results with the set of measures *S8a*.

Measures based on the mean of non-zero similarities H-MeanNnz-S8a and H-MeanNnz-E5 performed best on MC and WordSim353 datasets respectively. They achieved correlations of 0.878 and 0.740, which is higher than scores of any other measure. At the same time, measure H-MeanZscore-S8b provided the best scores on the RG dataset among all single and hybrid measures, achieving correlation of 0.890. Supervised measure H-Logit-E15 based on Logistic Regression provided the very best results on both semantic relations datasets BLESS and SN. Furthermore, it outperformed all single and hybrid measures on that task, in terms of both precision and recall, achieving MAP(20) of 0.995 and R(50) of 0.818 on BLESS and MAP(20) of 0.993 and R(50) of 0.819 on SN. H-Logit-E15 makes use of 15 similarity measures and disregards only the worst single measure W-NGD-Bing.

As we can see in Figure 3 (b), combining similarity scores with a *Max* function appears to be the worst solution. Combination methods based on an average and a median, including Rank and Relation Fusion, perform much better. These methods provide quite similar results: in the high precision range, they perform nearly as well as a supervised combination. Relation Fusion even manages to slightly outperform Logit on the first 10-15 k-NN (see Figure 3). However, all unsupervised combination methods are significantly worse if higher recall is needed.

We conclude that the H-Logit-E15 is the best hybrid similarity measure for semantic relation extraction and in terms of plausibility with human judgements among all single and hybrid measures examined in this paper.

7 Discussion

Hybrid measures achieve higher precision and recall than single measures. First, it is due to the reuse of common lexico-semantic information (such as that a "car" is a synonym of a "vehicle") via knowledge- and definition-based measures. Measures based on WordNet and dictionary definitions achieve high precision as they rely on fine-grained manually constructed resources. However, due to limited coverage of these resources,

Similarity Measure	MC	RG	WS	BLESS						SN					
	ρ	ρ	ρ	*P(10)*	*P (20)*	*M(20)*	*P(50)*	*M(50)*	*R(50)*	*P(10)*	*P(20)*	*M(20)*	*P(50)*	*M(50)*	*R(50)*
Random	*0.056*	*-0.047*	*-0.122*	0.546	0.542	0.549	0.544	0.546	0.522	0.504	0.502	0.507	0.499	0.502	0.498
1. N-WuPalmer	0.742	0.775	0.331	0.974	0.929	0.972	0.702	0.879	0.674	0.982	0.959	**0.981**	0.766	0.917	**0.763**
2. N-Leack.Chod.	0.724	**0.789**	0.295	0.953	0.901	0.954	0.702	0.863	0.648	0.984	0.953	**0.981**	0.757	0.913	0.755
3. N-Resnik	0.784	0.757	0.331	0.970	0.933	0.970	0.700	0.879	0.647	0.948	0.908	0.948	0.724	0.874	0.722
4. N-JiangConrath	0.719	0.588	0.175	0.956	0.872	0.920	0.645	0.817	0.458	0.931	0.857	0.911	0.625	0.808	0.570
5. N-Lin	0.754	0.619	0.204	0.949	0.884	0.918	0.682	0.822	0.451	0.939	0.877	0.920	0.611	0.827	0.566
6. W-NGD-Yahoo	*0.330*	0.445	0.254	0.940	0.907	0.941	0.783	0.885	0.648	—	—	—	—	—	—
7. W-NGD-Bing	*0.063*	*0.181*	*0.060*	0.724	0.706	0.713	0.650	0.690	0.600	0.659	0.619	0.671	0.633	0.648	0.633
8. W-NGD-GoogleWiki	*0.334*	0.502	0.251	0.874	0.837	0.872	0.703	0.814	0.649	—	—	—	—	—	—
9. C-BowDA	0.693	0.782	0.466	0.971	0.947	0.969	0.836	0.928	**0.772**	0.974	0.932	0.968	0.742	0.896	0.740
10. C-SynDA	**0.790**	0.786	0.491	0.985	0.953	**0.984**	0.811	0.925	0.749	0.978	0.945	0.972	0.751	0.907	0.743
11. C-LSA-Tasa	0.694	0.605	0.566	0.968	0.937	0.967	0.802	0.912	0.740	0.903	0.846	0.895	0.641	0.803	0.609
12. C-NGD-Factiva	0.603	0.599	**0.600**	0.959	0.916	0.959	0.786	0.894	0.681	0.906	0.857	0.904	0.731	0.835	0.543
13. C-PatternWiki	0.461	0.542	0.357	0.972	0.951	0.976	0.944	0.957	0.287	0.920	0.904	0.907	0.891	0.900	0.295
14. D-WktWiki	0.759	0.754	0.521	0.943	0.905	0.946	0.750	0.876	0.679	0.922	0.887	0.918	0.725	0.854	0.656
15. D-GlossVectors	0.653	0.738	0.322	0.894	0.860	0.901	0.742	0.843	0.686	0.932	0.899	0.933	0.722	0.864	0.709
16. D-ExtenedLesk	0.792	0.718	0.409	0.937	0.866	0.939	0.711	0.843	0.657	0.952	0.873	0.943	0.655	0.832	0.654
H-Mean-S8a	0.834	0.864	0.734	0.994	0.980	0.994	0.870	0.960	0.804	0.985	0.965	0.985	0.788	0.928	0.787
H-MeanZscore-S8a	0.830	0.864	0.728	0.994	0.981	0.993	0.874	0.961	0.808	0.986	0.967	0.986	0.793	0.932	0.792
H-MeanNnz-S8a	**0.843**	0.847	**0.740**	0.993	0.977	0.991	0.865	0.956	0.799	0.986	0.967	0.985	0.803	0.933	0.802
H-Median-S10	0.821	0.842	0.647	0.995	0.976	0.992	0.843	0.950	0.779	0.975	0.934	0.970	0.724	0.892	0.721
H-Max-S7	0.802	0.816	0.654	0.979	0.957	0.979	0.839	0.936	0.775	0.980	0.957	0.979	0.786	0.922	0.785
H-RankFusion-S10	—	—	—	0.994	0.978	0.993	0.864	0.956	0.798	0.976	0.929	0.971	0.745	0.896	0.744
H-RelationFusion-S10	—	—	—	0.996	0.982	0.995	0.840	0.952	0.758	0.986	0.963	0.981	0.781	0.920	0.749
H-Logit-E15	0.793	**0.870**	0.690	0.995	0.987	**0.995**	0.885	0.968	**0.818**	0.995	0.984	**0.993**	0.821	0.951	**0.819**
H-MeanNnz-E5	**0.878**	0.878	0.482	0.986	0.956	0.984	0.784	0.922	0.725	0.975	0.938	0.969	0.768	0.906	0.766
H-MeanZscore-S8b	0.844	**0.890**	0.616	0.992	0.977	0.991	0.844	0.953	0.780	0.995	0.985	0.995	0.815	0.950	0.814

Table 1: Performance of 16 single and 8 hybrid similarity measures on human judgements datasets (MC, RG, WordSim353) and semantic relation datasets (BLESS and SN). The best scores in a group (single/hybrid) are in bold; the very best scores are in grey. Correlations *in italics* mean $p > 0.05$, otherwise $p \leq 0.05$.

they only can determine relations between a limited number of terms. On the other hand, measures based on web and corpora are nearly unlimited in their coverage, but provide less precise results. Combination of the measures enables keeping high precision for frequent terms (e. g., "disease") present in WordNet and dictionaries, and empowers calculation of relations between rare terms unlisted in the handcrafted resources (e. g., "bronchocele") with web and corpus measures.

Second, combinations work well because, as it was found in previous research (Sahlgren, 2006; Heylen et al., 2008), different measures provide complementary types of semantic relations. For instance, WordNet-based measures score higher hypernyms than associative relations; distributional analysis score high co-hyponyms and synonyms, etc. In that respect, a combination helps to recall more different relations. For example, a WordNet-based measure may return a hypernym $\langle$salmon, seafood$\rangle$, while a corpus-based measure would extract a co-hyponym $\langle$salmon, mackerel$\rangle$.

Finally, the supervised combination method works better than unsupervised ones because of two reasons. First, the measures generate scores which have quite different distributions on the range $[0; 1]$. The averaging of such scores may be suboptimal. Logistic Regression overcomes this issue by assigning appropriate weights $(w_1, \ldots, w_k)$ to the measures in the linear combination z. Second, training procedure enables the model to assign higher weights to the measures which provide better results, while for the methods based on averaging all weight are equal.

8 Conclusion

In this work, we designed and studied several hybrid similarity measures in the context of semantic relation extraction. We have undertaken a systematic analysis of 16 baseline measures, 8 combination methods, and 3 measure selection techniques. The combined measures were thoroughly evaluated on five ground truth datasets: MC, RG, WordSim353, BLESS, and SN. Our results have shown that the hybrid measures outperform the single measures on all datasets. In particular, a combination of 15 baseline corpus-, web-, network-, and dictionary-based measures with Logistic Regression provided the best results. This method achieved a correlation of 0.870 with human judgements and MAP(20) of 0.995 and Recall(50) of 0.818 at predicting semantic relation between terms.

This paper also sketched two novel single similarity measures performing comparably with the baselines – WktWiki, based on definitions of Wikipedia and Wiktionary; and PatternWiki, based on patterns applied on Wikipedia abstracts. In the future research, we are going to apply the developed methods to query expansion.

References

Eneko Agirre, Enrique Alfonseca, Keith Hall, Jana Kravalova, Marius Paşca, and Aitor Soroa. 2009. A study on similarity and relatedness using distributional and wordnet-based approaches. In *Proceedings of NAACL-HLT 2009*, pages 19–27.

Alan Agresti. 2002. *Categorical Data Analysis (Wiley Series in Probability and Statistics)*. 2 edition.

Alain Auger and Caroline Barrière. 2008. Pattern-based approaches to semantic relation extraction: A state-of-the-art. *Terminology Journal*, 14(1):1–19.

Satanjeev Banerjee and Ted Pedersen. 2003. Extended gloss overlaps as a measure of semantic relatedness. In *IJCAI*, volume 18, pages 805–810.

Marco Baroni and Alexandro Lenci. 2011. How we blessed distributional semantic evaluation. *GEMS (EMNLP), 2011*, pages 1–11.

Marco Baroni, Silvia Bernardini, Adriano Ferraresi, and Eros Zanchetta. 2009. The wacky wide web: A collection of very large linguistically processed web-crawled corpora. *LREC*, 43(3):209–226.

D. Bollegala, Y. Matsuo, and M. Ishizuka. 2007. Measuring semantic similarity between words using web search engines. In *WWW*, volume 766.

S. Cederberg and D. Widdows. 2003. Using LSA and noun coordination information to improve the precision and recall of automatic hyponymy extraction. In *Proceedings HLT-NAACL*, page 111118.

Rudi L. Cilibrasi and Paul M. B. Vitanyi. 2007. The Google Similarity Distance. *IEEE Trans. on Knowl. and Data Eng.*, 19(3):370–383.

James R. Curran and Marc Moens. 2002. Improvements in automatic thesaurus extraction. In *Proceedings of the ACL-02 workshop on Unsupervised Lexical Acquisition*, pages 59–66.

James R. Curran. 2002. Ensemble methods for automatic thesaurus extraction. In *Proceedings of the EMNLP-02*, pages 222–229. ACL.

Lev Finkelstein, Evgeniy Gabrilovich, Yossi Matias, Ehud Rivlin, Zach Solan, Gadi Wolfman, and Eytan Ruppin. 2001. Placing search in context: The concept revisited. In *WWW 2001*, pages 406–414.

Marti A. Hearst. 1992. Automatic acquisition of hyponyms from large text corpora. In *ACL*, pages 539–545.

Kris Heylen, Yves Peirsman, Dirk Geeraerts, and Dirk Speelman. 2008. Modelling word similarity: an evaluation of automatic synonymy extraction algorithms. *LREC'08*, pages 3243–3249.

Jay J. Jiang and David W. Conrath. 1997. Semantic Similarity Based on Corpus Statistics and Lexical Taxonomy. In *ROCLING X*, pages 19–33.

Thomas K. Landauer and Susan T. Dumais. 1997. A solution to plato's problem: The latent semantic analysis theory of acquisition, induction, and representation of knowledge. *Psych. review*, 104(2):211.

Claudia Leacock and Martin Chodorow. 1998. Combining Local Context and WordNet Similarity for Word Sense Identification. *An Electronic Lexical Database*, pages 265–283.

Dekang Lin. 1998a. An Information-Theoretic Definition of Similarity. In *ICML*, pages 296–304.

Dekang Lin. 1998b. Automatic retrieval and clustering of similar words. In *ACL*, pages 768–774.

Rada Mihalcea, Courtney Corley, and Carlo Strapparava. 2006. Corpus-based and knowledge-based measures of text semantic similarity. In *AAAI'06*, pages 775–780.

George A. Miller and Walter G. Charles. 1991. Contextual correlates of semantic similarity. *Language and Cognitive Processes*, 6(1):1–28.

G. A. Miller. 1995. Wordnet: a lexical database for english. *Communications of ACM*, 38(11):39–41.

Siddharth Patwardhan and Ted Pedersen. 2006. Using WordNet-based context vectors to estimate the semantic relatedness of concepts. *Making Sense of Sense: Bringing Psycholinguistics and Computational Linguistics Together*, page 1.

Sébastien Paumier. 2003. *De la reconnaissance de formes linguistiques à l'analyse syntaxique*. Ph.D. thesis, Université de Marne-la-Vallée.

Ted Pedersen, Siddaharth Patwardhan, and Jason Michelizzi. 2004. Wordnet:: Similarity: measuring the relatedness of concepts. In *Demonstration Papers at HLT-NAACL 2004*, pages 38–41. ACL.

Philip Resnik. 1995. Using Information Content to Evaluate Semantic Similarity in a Taxonomy. In *IJCAI*, volume 1, pages 448–453.

Herbert Rubenstein and John B. Goodenough. 1965. Contextual correlates of synonymy. *Communications of the ACM*, 8(10):627–633.

Magnus Sahlgren. 2006. *The Word-Space Model: Using distributional analysis to represent syntagmatic and paradigmatic relations between words in high-dimensional vector spaces*. Ph.D. thesis.

Vladislav D. Veksler, Ryan Z. Govostes, and Wayne D. Gray. 2008. Defining the dimensions of the human semantic space. In *30th Annual Meeting of the Cognitive Science Society*, pages 1282–1287.

Zhibiao Wu and Martha Palmer. 1994. Verbs semantics and lexical selection. In *Proceedings of ACL'1994*, pages 133–138.

Hui Yang and Jamie Callan. 2009. A metric-based framework for automatic taxonomy induction. In *ACL-IJCNLP*, page 271279.

Torsen Zesch, Christof Müller, and Irina Gurevych. 2008a. Extracting lexical semantic knowledge from wikipedia and wiktionary. In *Proceedings of LREC'08*, pages 1646–1652.

Torsen Zesch, Christof Müller, and Irina Gurevych. 2008b. Using wiktionary for computing semantic relatedness. In *Proceedings of AAAI*, page 45.

Hybrid Combination of Constituency and Dependency Trees into an Ensemble Dependency Parser

Nathan David Green and Zdeněk Žabokrtský
Charles University in Prague
Institute of Formal and Applied Linguistics
Faculty of Mathematics and Physics
Prague, Czech Republic
{green,zabokrtsky}@ufal.mff.cuni.cz

Abstract

Dependency parsing has made many advancements in recent years, in particular for English. There are a few dependency parsers that achieve comparable accuracy scores with each other but with very different types of errors. This paper examines creating a new dependency structure through ensemble learning using a hybrid of the outputs of various parsers. We combine all tree outputs into a weighted edge graph, using 4 weighting mechanisms. The weighted edge graph is the input into our ensemble system and is a hybrid of very different parsing techniques (constituent parsers, transition-based dependency parsers, and a graph-based parser). From this graph we take a maximum spanning tree. We examine the new dependency structure in terms of accuracy and errors on individual part-of-speech values.

The results indicate that using a greater number of more varied parsers will improve accuracy results. The combined ensemble system, using 5 parsers based on 3 different parsing techniques, achieves an accuracy score of 92.58%, beating all single parsers on the Wall Street Journal section 23 test set. Additionally, the ensemble system reduces the average relative error on selected POS tags by 9.82%.

1 Introduction

Dependency parsing has made many advancements in recent years. A prime reason for the quick advancement has been the CoNLL shared task competitions. These competitions gave the community a common training/testing framework along with many open source systems. These systems have, for certain languages, achieved fairly high accuracy. Many of the top systems have comparable accuracy but vary on the types of errors they make. The approaches used in the shared task vary from graph-based techniques to transition-based techniques to the conversion of constituent trees produced by state-of-the-art constituent parsers. This varied error distribution makes dependency parsing a prime area for the application of new hybrid and ensemble algorithms.

Increasing accuracy of dependency parsing often is in the realm of feature tweaking and optimization. The idea behind ensemble learning is to take the best of each parser as it currently is and allow the ensemble system to combine the outputs to form a better overall parse using prior knowledge of each individual parser. This is often done by different weighting or voting schemes.

2 Related Work

Ensemble learning (Dietterich, 2000) has been used for a variety of machine learning tasks and recently has been applied to dependency parsing in various ways and with different levels of success. (Surdeanu and Manning, 2010; Haffari et al., 2011) showed a successful combination of parse trees through a linear combination of trees with various weighting formulations. To keep their tree constraint, they applied Eisner's algorithm for reparsing (Eisner, 1996).

Parser combination with dependency trees has been examined in terms of accuracy (Sagae and Lavie, 2006; Sagae and Tsujii, 2007; Zeman and Žabokrtský, 2005). However, the various techniques have generally examined similar parsers

Proceedings of the Workshop on Innovative Hybrid Approaches to the Processing of Textual Data (Hybrid2012), EACL 2012, pages 19–26,
Avignon, France, April 23 2012.

or parsers which have generated various different models. To the best of our knowledge, our experiments are the first to look at the accuracy and part of speech error distribution when combining together constituent and dependency parsers that use many different techniques. However, POS tags were used in parser combination in (Hall et al., 2007) for combining a set of Malt Parser models with success.

Other methods of parser combinations have shown to be successful such as using one parser to generate features for another parser. This was shown in (Nivre and McDonald, 2008), in which Malt Parser was used as a feature to MST Parser. The result was a successful combination of a transition-based and graph-based parser, but did not address adding other types of parsers into the framework.

3 Methodology

The following sections describe the process flow, choice of parsers, and datasets needed for others to recreate the results listed in this paper. Although we describe the specific parsers and datasets used in this paper, this process flow should work for any number of hybrid combinations of parsers and datasets.

3.1 Process Flow

To generate a single ensemble parse tree, our system takes N parse trees as input. The inputs are from a variety of parsers as described in 3.2. All edges in these parse trees are combined into a graph structure. This graph structure accepts weighted edges. So if more than one parse tree contains the same tree edge, the graph is weighted appropriately according to a chosen weighting algorithm. The weighting algorithms used in our experiments are described in 3.5.

Once the system has a weighted graph, it then uses an algorithm to find a corresponding tree structure so there are no cycles. In this set of experiments, we constructed a tree by finding the maximum spanning tree using ChuLiu/Edmonds' algorithm, which is a standard choice for MST tasks. Figure 1 graphically shows the decisions one needs to make in this framework to create an ensemble parse.

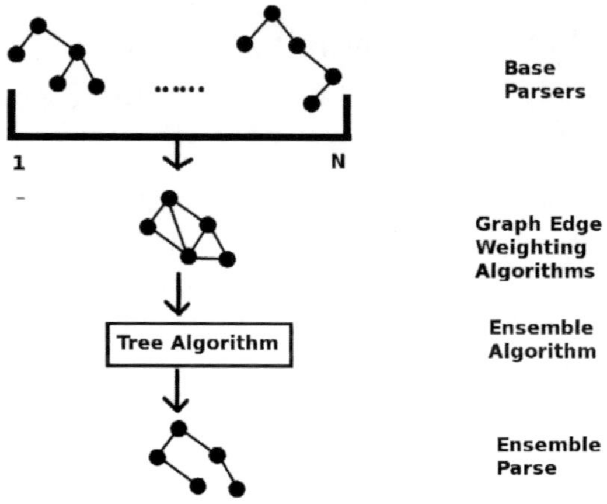

Figure 1: General flow to create an ensemble parse tree.

3.2 Parsers

To get a complete representation of parsers in our ensemble learning framework we use 5 of the most commonly used parsers. They range from graph-based approaches to transition-based approaches to constituent parsers. Constituency output is converted to dependency structures using a converter (Johansson and Nugues, 2007). All parsers are integrated into the Treex framework (Žabokrtský et al., 2008; Popel et al., 2011) using the publicly released parsers from the respective authors but with Perl wrappers to allow them to work on a common tree structure.

- **Graph-Based:** A dependency tree is a special case of a weighted edge graph that spawns from an artificial root and is acyclic. Because of this we can look at a large history of work in graph theory to address finding the best spanning tree for each dependency graph. In this paper we use MST Parser (McDonald et al., 2005) as an input to our ensemble parser.

- **Transition-Based:** Transition-based parsing creates a dependency structure that is parameterized over the transitions used to create a dependency tree. This is closely related to shift-reduce constituency parsing algorithms. The benefit of transition-based parsing is the use of greedy algorithms which have a linear time complexity. However, due to the greedy algorithms, longer arc parses can cause error propagation across each transition (Kübler et al., 2009). We make use of Malt Parser (Nivre et al., 2007b), which in the shared tasks was often tied with the best performing systems. Additionally we use Zpar (Zhang and Clark, 2011) which is based on Malt Parser but with a different set of non-local features.

- **Constituent Transformation** While not a true dependency parser, one technique often applied is to take a state-of-the-art constituent parser and transform its phrase based output into dependency relations. This has been shown to also be state-of-the-art in accuracy for dependency parsing in English. In this paper we transformed the constituency structure into dependencies using the Penn Converter conversion tool (Johansson and Nugues, 2007). A version of this converter was used in the CoNLL shared task to create dependency treebanks as well. For the following ensemble experiments we make use of both (Charniak and Johnson, 2005) and Stanford's (Klein and Manning, 2003) constituent parsers.

In addition to these 5 parsers, we also report the accuracy of an Oracle Parser. This parser is simply the best possible parse of all the edges of the combined dependency trees. If the reference, gold standard, tree has an edge that any of the 5 parsers contain, we include that edge in the Oracle parse. Initially all nodes of the tree are attached to an artificial root in order to maintain connectedness. Since only edges that exist in a reference tree are added, the Oracle Parser maintains the acyclic constraint. This can be viewed as the maximum accuracy that a hybrid approach could achieve with this set of parsers and with the given data sets.

3.3 Datasets

Much of the current progress in dependency parsing has been a result of the availability of common data sets in a variety of languages, made available through the CoNLL shared task (Nivre et al., 2007a). This data is in 13 languages and 7 language families. Later shared tasks also released data in other genres to allow for domain adaptation. The availability of standard competition, gold level, data has been an important factor in dependency based research.

For this study we use the English CoNLL data. This data comes from the Wall Street Journal (WSJ) section of the Penn treebank (Marcus et al., 1993). All parsers are trained on sections 02-21 of the WSJ except for the Stanford parser which uses sections 01-21. Charniak, Stanford and Zpar use pre-trained models *ec50spfinal*, *wsjPCFG.ser.gz*, *english.tar.gz* respectively. For testing we use section 23 of the WSJ for comparability reasons with other papers. This test data contains 56,684 tokens. For tuning we use section 22. This data is used for determining some of the weighting features.

3.4 Evaluation

As an artifact of the CoNLL shared tasks competition, two standard metrics for comparing dependency parsing systems emerged. *L*abeled *a*ttachment *s*core (LAS) and *u*nlabeled *a*ttachment *s*core (UAS). UAS studies the structure of a dependency tree and assesses whether the output has the correct head and dependency arcs. In addition to the structure score in UAS, LAS also measures the accuracy of the dependency labels on each arc. A third, but less common metric, is used to judge the percentage of sentences that are completely correct in regards to their LAS score. For this paper since we are primarily concerned with the merging of tree structures we only evaluate UAS (Buchholz and Marsi, 2006).

3.5 Weighting

Currently we are applying four weighting algorithms to the graph structure. First we give each parser the same uniform weight. Second we examine weighting each parser output by the UAS score of the individual parser taken from our tuning data. Third we use plural voting weights (De Pauw et al., 2006) based on parser ranks from our tuning data. Due to the success of Plural voting, we try to exaggerate the differences in the parsers by using UAS^{10} weighting. All four of these are simple weighting techniques but even in their simplicity we can see the benefit of this type of combination in an ensemble parser.

- **Uniform Weights**: an edge in the graph gets incremented +1 weight for each matching edge in each parser. If an edge occurs in 4 parsers, the weight is 4.

- **UAS Weighted**: Each edge in the graph gets

incremented by the value of it's parsers individual accuracy. So in the UAS results in Table 1 an edge in Charniak's tree gets .92 added while MST gets .86 added to every edge they share with the resulting graph. This weighting should allow us to add poor parsers with very little harm to the overall score.

- **Plural Voting Weights**: In Plural Voting the parsers are rated according to their rank in our tuning data and each gets a "vote" based on their quality. With N parsers the best parser gets N votes while the last place parser gets 1 vote. In this paper, Charniak received 5 votes, Stanford received 4 votes, MST Parser received 3 votes, Malt Parser received 2 votes, and Zpar received 1 vote. Votes in this case are added to each edge as a weight.

- **UAS^{10}**: For this weighting scheme we took each UAS value to the 10th power. This gave us the desired affect of making the differences in accuracy more apparent and giving more distance from the best to worse parser. This exponent was empirically selected from results with our tuning data set.

4 Results

Table 1 contains the results of different parser combinations of the 5 parsers and Table 2 shows the baseline scores of the respective individual parsers. The results indicate that using two parsers will result in an "average" score, and no combination of 2 parsers gave an improvement over the individual parsers, these were left out of the table. Ensemble learning seems to start to have a benefit when using 3 or more parsers with a few combinations having a better UAS score than any of the baseline parsers, these cases are in bold throughout the table. When we add a 4th parser to the mix almost all configurations lead to an improved score when the edges are not weighted uniformly. The only case in which this does not occur is when Stanford's Parser is not used.

Uniform voting gives us an improved score in a few of the model combinations but in most cases does not produce an output that beats the best individual system. UAS weighting is not the best overall but it does give improved performance in the majority of model combinations. Problematically UAS weighted trees do not give an improved accuracy when all 5 parsers are used. Given the slight differences in UAS scores of the baseline models in Table 2 this is not surprising as the best graph edge can be outvoted as the number of N parsers increases. The slight differences in weight do not seem to change the MST parse dramatically when all 5 parsers are used over Uniform weighting. Based on the UAS scores learned in our tuning data set, we next looked to amplify the weight differences using Plural Voting. For the majority of model combinations in Plural voting we achieve improved results over the individual systems. When all 5 parsers are used together with Plural Voting, the ensemble parser improves over the highest individual parser's UAS score. With the success of Plural voting we looked to amplify the UAS score differences in a more systematic way. We looked at using UAS^x where x was found experimentally in our tuning data. UAS^{10} matched Plural voting in the amount of system combinations that improved over their individual components. The top overall score is when we use UAS^{10} weighting with all parsers. For parser combinations that do not feature Charniak's parser, we also find an increase in overall accuracy score compared to each individual parser, although never beating Charniak's individual score.

To see the maximum accuracy a hybrid combination can achieve we include an Oracle Ensemble Parser in Table 1. The Oracle Parser takes the edges from all dependency trees and only adds each edge to the Oracle Tree if the corresponding edge is in the reference tree. This gives us a ceiling on what ensemble learning can achieve. As we can see in Table 1, the ceiling of ensemble learning is 97.41% accuracy. Because of this high value with only 5 parsers, ensemble learning and other hybrid approaches should be a very prosperous area for dependency parsing research.

In (Kübler et al., 2009) the authors confirm that two parsers, MST Parser and Malt Parser, give similar accuracy results but with very different errors. MST parser, a maximum spanning tree graph-based algorithm, has evenly distributed errors while Malt Parser, a transition based parser, has errors on mainly longer sentences. This re-

System	Uniform Weighting	UAS Weighted	Plural Voting	UAS^{10} Weighted	Oracle UAS
Charniak-Stanford-Mst	91.86	**92.27**	**92.28**	**92.25**	96.48
Charniak-Stanford-Malt	91.77	**92.28**	**92.3**	92.08	96.49
Charniak-Stanford-Zpar	91.22	91.99	92.02	92.08	95.94
Charniak-Mst-Malt	88.80	89.55	90.77	92.08	96.3
Charniak-Mst-Zpar	90.44	91.59	92.08	92.08	96.16
Charniak-Malt-Zpar	88.61	91.3	92.08	92.08	96.21
Stanford-Mst-Malt	87.84	**88.28**	**88.26**	**88.28**	95.62
Stanford-Mst-Zpar	**89.12**	**89.88**	**88.84**	**89.91**	95.57
Stanford-Malt-Zpar	**88.61**	**89.57**	87.88	87.88	95.47
Mst-Malt-Zpar	**86.99**	**87.34**	**86.82**	86.49	93.79
Charniak-Stanford-Mst-Malt	90.45	**92.09**	**92.34**	**92.56**	97.09
Charniak-Stanford-Mst-Zpar	91.57	**92.24**	**92.27**	**92.26**	96.97
Charniak-Stanford-Malt-Zpar	91.31	**92.14**	**92.4**	**92.42**	97.03
Charniak-Mst-Malt-Zpar	89.60	89.48	91.71	92.08	96.79
Stanford-Mst-Malt-Zpar	**88.76**	**88.45**	**88.95**	**88.44**	96.36
All	91.43	91.77	**92.44**	**92.58**	97.41

Table 1: Results of the maximum spanning tree algorithm on a combined edge graph. Scores are in **bold** when the ensemble system increased the UAS score over all individual systems.

Parser	UAS
Charniak	92.08
Stanford	87.88
MST	86.49
Malt	84.51
Zpar	76.06

Table 2: Our baseline parsers and corresponding UAS used in our ensemble experiments

sult comes from the approaches themselves. MST parser is globally trained so the best mean solution should be found. This is why errors on the longer sentences are about the same as the shorter sentences. Malt Parser on the other hand uses a greedy algorithm with a classifier that chooses a particular transition at each vertex. This leads to the possibility of the propagation of errors further in a sentence. Along with this line of research, we look at the error distribution for all 5 parsers along with our best ensemble parser configuration. Much like the previous work, we expect different types of errors, given that our parsers are from 3 different parsing techniques. To examine if the ensemble parser is substantially changing the parse tree or is just taking the best parse tree and substituting a few edges, we examine the part of speech accuracies and relative error reduction in Table 3.

As we can see the range of POS errors varies dramatically depending on which parser we examine. For instance for *CC*, Charniak has 83.54% accuracy while MST has only 71.16% accuracy. The performance for certain POS tags is almost universally low such as the left parenthesis *(*. Given the large difference in POS errors, weighting an ensemble system by POS would seem like a logical choice in future work. As we can see in Figure 2, the varying POS accuracies indicate that the parsing techniques we have incorporated into our ensemble parser, are significantly different. In almost every case in Table 3, our ensemble parser achieves the best accuracy for each POS, while reducing the average relative error rate by 9.82%.

The current weighting systems do not simply default to the best parser or to an average of all errors. In the majority of cases our ensemble parser obtains the top accuracy. The ability of the ensemble system to use maximum spanning tree on a graph allows the ensemble parser to connect nodes which might have been unconnected in a subset of the parsers for an overall gain, which is preferable to techniques which only select the best model for a particular tree. In all cases, our ensemble parser is never the worst parser. In

POS	Charniak	Stanford	MST	Malt	Zpar	Best Ensemble	Relative Error Reduction
CC	83.54	74.73	71.16	65.84	20.39	**84.63**	6.62
NNP	94.59	92.16	88.04	87.17	73.67	**95.02**	7.95
VBN	91.72	89.81	90.35	89.17	88.26	**93.81**	25.24
CD	94.91	92.67	85.19	84.46	82.64	**94.96**	0.98
RP	96.15	95.05	97.25	95.60	94.51	**97.80**	42.86
JJ	95.41	92.99	94.47	93.90	89.45	**95.85**	9.59
PRP	97.82	96.21	96.68	95.64	95.45	**98.39**	26.15
TO	94.52	89.44	91.29	90.73	88.63	94.35	-3.10
WRB	63.91	60.90	68.42	73.68	4.51	63.91	0.00
RB	86.26	79.88	81.49	81.44	80.61	**87.19**	6.77
WDT	97.14	95.36	96.43	95.00	9.29	**97.50**	12.59
VBZ	91.97	87.35	83.86	80.78	57.91	**92.46**	6.10
(	73.61	75.00	54.17	58.33	15.28	73.61	0.00
POS	98.18	96.54	98.54	98.72	0.18	**98.36**	9.89
VB	93.04	88.48	91.33	90.95	84.37	**94.24**	17.24
MD	89.55	82.02	83.05	78.77	51.54	**89.90**	3.35
NNS	93.10	89.51	90.68	88.65	78.93	**93.67**	8.26
NN	93.62	90.29	88.45	86.98	83.84	**94.00**	5.96
VBD	93.25	87.20	86.27	82.73	64.32	**93.52**	4.00
DT	97.61	96.47	97.30	97.01	92.19	**97.97**	15.06
RBS	90.00	76.67	93.33	93.33	86.67	90.00	0.00
IN	87.80	78.66	83.45	80.78	73.08	87.48	-2.66
)	70.83	77.78	96.46	55.56	12.50	**72.22**	4.77
VBG	85.19	82.13	82.74	82.25	81.27	**89.35**	28.09
Average							**9.82**

Table 3: POS accuracies for each of our systems that are used in the ensemble system. We use these accuracies to obtain the POS error distribution for our best ensemble system, which is the combination of all parsers using UAS^{10} weighting. Relative error reduction is calculated between our best ensemble system against the Charniak Parser which had the best individual scores.

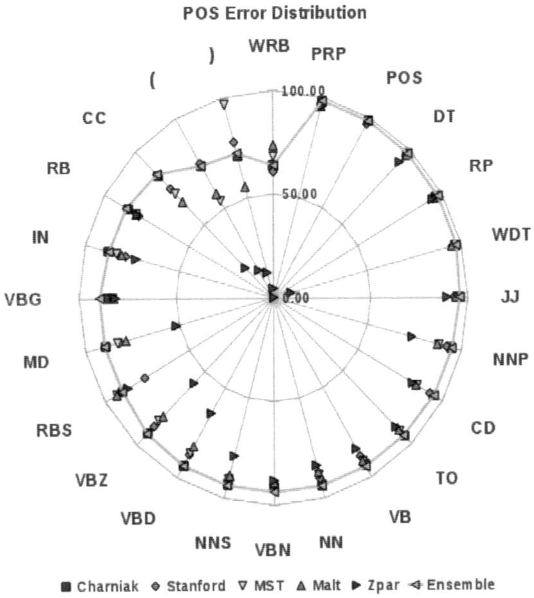

Figure 2: POS errors of all 5 parsers and the best ensemble system

cases where the POS is less frequent, our ensemble parser appears to average out the error distribution.

5 Conclusion

We have shown the benefits of using a maximum spanning tree algorithm in ensemble learning for dependency parsing, especially for the hybrid combination of constituent parsers with other dependency parsing techniques. This ensemble method shows improvements over the current state of the art for each individual parser. We also show a theoretical maximum oracle parser which indicates that much more work in this field can take place to improve dependency parsing accuracy toward the oracle score of 97.41%.

We demonstrated that using parsers of different techniques, especially including transformed constituent parsers, can lead to the best accuracy within this ensemble framework. The improvements in accuracy are not simply due to a few edge changes but can be seen to improve the accuracy of the majority of POS tags over all individual systems.

While we have only shown this for English, we expect the results to be similar for other languages since our methodology is language independent. Future work will contain different weighting mechanisms as well as application to other languages which are included in CoNLL data sets.

6 Acknowledgments

This research has received funding from the European Commission's 7th Framework Program (FP7) under grant agreement n° 238405 (CLARA)

References

Sabine Buchholz and Erwin Marsi. 2006. CoNLL-X shared task on multilingual dependency parsing. In *Proceedings of the Tenth Conference on Computational Natural Language Learning*, CoNLL-X '06, pages 149–164, Stroudsburg, PA, USA. Association for Computational Linguistics.

Eugene Charniak and Mark Johnson. 2005. Coarse-to-fine n-best parsing and maxent discriminative reranking. In *Proceedings of the 43rd Annual Meeting on Association for Computational Linguistics*, ACL '05, pages 173–180, Stroudsburg, PA, USA. Association for Computational Linguistics.

Guy De Pauw, Gilles-Maurice de Schryver, and Peter Wagacha. 2006. Data-driven part-of-speech tagging of kiswahili. In Petr Sojka, Ivan Kopecek, and Karel Pala, editors, *Text, Speech and Dialogue*, volume 4188 of *Lecture Notes in Computer Science*, pages 197–204. Springer Berlin / Heidelberg.

Thomas G. Dietterich. 2000. Ensemble methods in machine learning. In *Proceedings of the First International Workshop on Multiple Classifier Systems*, MCS '00, pages 1–15, London, UK. Springer-Verlag.

Jason Eisner. 1996. Three new probabilistic models for dependency parsing: An exploration. In *Proceedings of the 16th International Conference on Computational Linguistics (COLING-96)*, pages 340–345, Copenhagen, August.

Gholamreza Haffari, Marzieh Razavi, and Anoop Sarkar. 2011. An ensemble model that combines syntactic and semantic clustering for discriminative dependency parsing. In *Proceedings of the 49th Annual Meeting of the Association for Computational Linguistics: Human Language Technologies*, pages 710–714, Portland, Oregon, USA, June. Association for Computational Linguistics.

Johan Hall, Jens Nilsson, Joakim Nivre, Gülsen Eryigit, Beáta Megyesi, Mattias Nilsson, and Markus Saers. 2007. Single malt or blended? a study in multilingual parser optimization. In *Proceedings of the CoNLL Shared Task Session of EMNLP-CoNLL 2007*, pages 933–939.

Richard Johansson and Pierre Nugues. 2007. Extended constituent-to-dependency conversion for

English. In *Proceedings of NODALIDA 2007*, pages 105–112, Tartu, Estonia, May 25-26.

Dan Klein and Christopher D. Manning. 2003. Accurate unlexicalized parsing. In *Proceedings of the 41st Annual Meeting on Association for Computational Linguistics - Volume 1*, ACL '03, pages 423–430, Stroudsburg, PA, USA. Association for Computational Linguistics.

S. Kübler, R. McDonald, and J. Nivre. 2009. *Dependency parsing*. Synthesis lectures on human language technologies. Morgan & Claypool, US.

Mitchell P. Marcus, Mary Ann Marcinkiewicz, and Beatrice Santorini. 1993. Building a large annotated corpus of english: the Penn Treebank. *Comput. Linguist.*, 19:313–330, June.

Ryan McDonald, Fernando Pereira, Kiril Ribarov, and Jan Hajic. 2005. Non-projective dependency parsing using spanning tree algorithms. In *Proceedings of Human Language Technology Conference and Conference on Empirical Methods in Natural Language Processing*, pages 523–530, Vancouver, British Columbia, Canada, October. Association for Computational Linguistics.

Joakim Nivre and Ryan McDonald. 2008. Integrating graph-based and transition-based dependency parsers. In *Proceedings of ACL-08: HLT*, pages 950–958, Columbus, Ohio, June. Association for Computational Linguistics.

Joakim Nivre, Johan Hall, Sandra Kübler, Ryan McDonald, Jens Nilsson, Sebastian Riedel, and Deniz Yuret. 2007a. The CoNLL 2007 shared task on dependency parsing. In *Proceedings of the CoNLL Shared Task Session of EMNLP-CoNLL 2007*, pages 915–932, Prague, Czech Republic, June. Association for Computational Linguistics.

Joakim Nivre, Johan Hall, Jens Nilsson, Atanas Chanev, Gulsen Eryigit, Sandra Kübler, Svetoslav Marinov, and Erwin Marsi. 2007b. MaltParser: A language-independent system for data-driven dependency parsing. *Natural Language Engineering*, 13(2):95–135.

Martin Popel, David Mareček, Nathan Green, and Zdeněk Žabokrtský. 2011. Influence of parser choice on dependency-based mt. In *Proceedings of the Sixth Workshop on Statistical Machine Translation*, pages 433–439, Edinburgh, Scotland, July. Association for Computational Linguistics.

Kenji Sagae and Alon Lavie. 2006. Parser combination by reparsing. In *Proceedings of the Human Language Technology Conference of the NAACL, Companion Volume: Short Papers*, pages 129–132, New York City, USA, June. Association for Computational Linguistics.

Kenji Sagae and Jun'ichi Tsujii. 2007. Dependency parsing and domain adaptation with LR models and parser ensembles. In *Proceedings of the CoNLL Shared Task Session of EMNLP-CoNLL 2007*, pages 1044–1050, Prague, Czech Republic, June. Association for Computational Linguistics.

Mihai Surdeanu and Christopher D. Manning. 2010. Ensemble models for dependency parsing: cheap and good? In *Human Language Technologies: The 2010 Annual Conference of the North American Chapter of the Association for Computational Linguistics*, HLT '10, pages 649–652, Stroudsburg, PA, USA. Association for Computational Linguistics.

Zdeněk Žabokrtský, Jan Ptáček, and Petr Pajas. 2008. TectoMT: Highly Modular MT System with Tectogrammatics Used as Transfer Layer. In *Proceedings of the 3rd Workshop on Statistical Machine Translation, ACL*, pages 167–170.

Daniel Zeman and Zdeněk Žabokrtský. 2005. Improving parsing accuracy by combining diverse dependency parsers. In *In: Proceedings of the 9th International Workshop on Parsing Technologies.*

Yue Zhang and Stephen Clark. 2011. Syntactic processing using the generalized perceptron and beam search. *Computational Linguistics*, 37(1):105–151.

Describing Video Contents in Natural Language

Muhammad Usman Ghani Khan
University of Sheffield
United Kingdom
ughani@dcs.shef.ac.uk

Yoshihiko Gotoh
University of Sheffield
United Kingdom
y.gotoh@dcs.shef.ac.uk

Abstract

This contribution addresses generation of natural language descriptions for human actions, behaviour and their relations with other objects observed in video streams. The work starts with implementation of conventional image processing techniques to extract high level features from video. These features are converted into natural language descriptions using context free grammar. Although feature extraction processes are erroneous at various levels, we explore approaches to putting them together to produce a coherent description. Evaluation is made by calculating ROUGE scores between human annotated and machine generated descriptions. Further we introduce a task based evaluation by human subjects which provides qualitative evaluation of generated descriptions.

1 Introduction

In recent years video has established its dominance in communication and has become an integrated part of our everyday life ranging from hand-held videos to broadcast news video (from unstructured to highly structured). There is a need for formalising video semantics to help users gain useful and refined information relevant to their demands and requirements. Human language is a natural way of communication. Useful entities extracted from videos and their inter-relations can be presented by natural language in a syntactically and semantically correct formulation.

While literature relating to object recognition (Galleguillos and Belongie, 2010), human action recognition (Torralba et al., 2008), and emotion detection (Zheng et al., 2010) are moving towards maturity, automatic description of visual scenes is still in its infancy. Most studies in video retrieval have been based on keywords (Bolle et al., 1998). An interesting extension to a keyword based scheme is natural language textual description of video streams. They are more human friendly. They can clarify context between keywords by capturing their relations. Descriptions can guide generation of video summaries by converting a video to natural language. They can provide basis for creating a multimedia repository for video analysis, retrieval and summarisation tasks.

Kojima et al. (2002) presented a method for describing human activities in videos based on a concept hierarchy of actions. They described head, hands and body movements using natural language. For a traffic control application, Nagel (2004) investigated automatic visual surveillance systems where human behaviour was presented by scenarios, consisting of predefined sequences of events. The scenario was evaluated and automatically translated into a text by analysing the visual contents over time, and deciding on the most suitable event. Lee et al. (2008) introduced a framework for semantic annotation of visual events in three steps; image parsing, event inference and language generation. Instead of humans and their specific activities, they focused on object detection, their inter-relations and events that were present in videos. Baiget et al. (2007) performed human identification and scene modelling manually and focused on human behaviour description for crosswalk scenes. Yao et al. (2010) introduced their work on video to text description which is dependent on the significant amount of annotated data, a requirement that is avoided in this paper. Yang et al. (2011) presented a

Proceedings of the Workshop on Innovative Hybrid Approaches to the Processing of Textual Data (Hybrid2012), EACL 2012, pages 27–35,
Avignon, France, April 23 2012.

framework for static images to textual descriptions where they contained to image with up to two objects. In contrast, this paper presents a work on video streams, handling not only objects but also other features such as actions, age, gender and emotions.

The study presented in this paper is concerned with production of natural language description for visual scenes in a time series using a bottom-up approach. Initially high level features (HLFs) are identified in video frames. They may be 'keywords', such as a particular object and its position/moves, used for a semantic indexing task in video retrieval. Spatial relations between HLFs are important when explaining the semantics of visual scene. Extracted HLFs are then presented by syntactically and semantically correct expressions using a template based approach. Image processing techniques are far from perfect; there can be many missing, misidentified and erroneously extracted HLFs. We present scenarios to overcome these shortcomings and to generate coherent natural descriptions. The approach is evaluated using video segments drafted manually from the TREC video dataset. ROUGE scores is calculated between human annotated and machine generated descriptions. A task based evaluation is performed by human subjects, providing qualitative evaluation of generated descriptions.

2 Dataset Creation

The dataset was manually created from a subset of rushes and HLF extraction task videos in 2007/2008 TREC video evaluations (Over et al., 2007). It consists of 140 segments, with each segment containing one camera shot, spanning 10 to 30 seconds in length. There are 20 video segments for each of the seven categories:

Action: Human can be seen performing some action (*e.g.*, sit, walk)

Closeup: Facial expressions/emotions can be seen (*e.g.*, happy, sad)

News: Anchor/reporter may be seen; particular scene settings (*e.g.*, weather board in the background)

Meeting: Multiple humans are seen interacting; presence of objects such as chairs and a table

Grouping: Multiple humans are seen but not in meeting scenarios; chairs and table may not be present

Traffic: Vehicles (*e.g.*, car, bus, truck) / traffic signals are seen

Indoor/Outdoor: Scene settings are more obvious than human activities (*e.g.*, park scene, office)

13 human subjects individually annotated these videos in one to seven short sentences. They are referred to as **hand annotations** in the rest of this paper.

3 Processing High Level Features

Identification of human face or body can prove the presence of human in a video. The method by Kuchi et al. (2002) is adopted for face detection using colour and motion information. The method works against variations in lightning conditions, skin colours, backgrounds, face sizes and orientations. When the background is close to the skin colour, movement across successive frames is tested to confirm the presence of a human face. Facial features play an important role in identifying age, gender and emotion information (Maglogiannis et al., 2009). Human emotion can be estimated using eyes, lips and their measures (gradient, distance of eyelids or lips). The same set of facial features and measures can be used to identify a human gender[1].

To recognise human actions the approach based on a star skeleton and a hidden Markov model (HMM) is implemented (Chen et al., 2006). Commonly observed actions, such as 'walking', 'running', 'standing', and 'sitting', can be identified. Human body is presented in the form of sticks to generate features such as torso, arm length and angle, leg angle and stride (Sundaresan et al., 2003). Further Haar features are extracted and classifiers are trained to identify non-human objects (Viola and Jones, 2001). They include car, bus, motorbike, bicycle, building, tree, table, chair, cup, bottle and TV-monitor. Scene settings — indoor or outdoor — can be identified based on the edge oriented histogram (EOH) and the colour oriented histogram (COH) (Kim et al., 2010).

3.1 Performance of HLF Extraction

In the experiments, video frames were extracted using *ffmpeg*[2], sampled at 1 fps (frame per second), resulting in 2520 frames in total. Most of

[1] www.virtualffs.co.uk/In_a_Nutshell.html

[2] Ffmpeg is a command line tool composed of a collection of free software and open source libraries. It can record, convert and stream digital audio and video in numerous formats. The default conversion rate is 25 fps. See http://www.ffmpeg.org/

	(ground truth)	
	exist	not exist
exist	1795	29
not exist	95	601

(a) human detection

	(ground truth)	
	male	female
male	911	216
female	226	537

(b) gender identification

Table 1: Confusion tables for (a) human detection and (b) gender identification. Columns show the ground truth, and rows indicate the automatic recognition results. The human detection task is biased towards existence of human, while in the gender identification presence of male and female are roughly balanced.

	(ground truth)					
	stand	sit	walk	run	wave	clap
stand	98	12	19	3	0	0
sit	0	68	0	0	0	0
walk	22	9	105	8	0	0
run	4	0	18	27	0	0
wave	2	5	0	0	19	2
clap	0	0	0	0	4	9

Table 2: Confusion table for human action recognition. Columns show the ground truth, and rows indicate the automatic recognition results. Some actions (*e.g.*, 'standing') were more commonly seen than others (*e.g.*, 'waving').

	(ground truth)				
	angry	serious	happy	sad	surprised
angry	59	0	0	15	16
serious	0	661	0	164	40
happy	0	35	427	27	8
sad	61	13	0	281	2
surprised	9	19	0	0	53

Table 3: Confusion table for human emotion recognition. Columns show the ground truth, and rows indicate the automatic recognition results.

HLFs required one frame to evaluate. Human activities were shown in 45 videos and they were sampled at 4 fps, yielding 3600 frames. Upon several trials, we decided to use eight frames (roughly two seconds) for human action recognition. Consequently tags were assigned for each set of eight frames, totalling 450 sets of actions.

Table 1(a) presents a confusion matrix for human detection. It was a heavily biased dataset where human(s) were present in 1890 out of 2520 frames. Of these 1890, misclassification occurred on 95 occasions. On the other hand gender identification is not always an easy task even for humans. Table 1(b) shows a confusion matrix for gender identification. Out of 1890 frames in which human(s) were present, frontal faces were shown in 1349 images. The total of 3555 humans were present in 1890 frames (1168 frames contained multiple humans), however the table shows the results when at least one gender is correctly identified. Female identification was often more difficult due to make ups, variety of hair styles and wearing hats, veils and scarfs.

Table 2 shows the human action recognition performance tested with a set of 450 actions. It was difficult to recognise 'sitting' actions, probably because HMMs were trained on postures of a complete human body, while a complete posture was often not available when a person was sitting. 'Hand waving' and 'clapping' were related to movements in upper body parts, and 'walking' and 'running' were based on lower body movements. In particular 'waving' appeared an easy action to identify because of its significant moves of upper body parts. Table 3 shows the confusion for human emotion recognition. 'Serious', 'happy' and 'sad' were most common emotions in this dataset, in particular 'happy' emotion was most correctly identified.

There were 15 videos where human or any other moving HLF (*e.g.*, car, bus) were absent. Out of these 15 videos, 12 were related to outdoor environments where trees, greenery, or buildings were present. Three videos showed indoor settings with objects such as chairs, tables and cups. All frames from outdoor scenes were correctly identified; for indoor scenes 80% of frames were correct. Presence of multiple objects seems to have caused negative impact on EOH and COH features, hence resulted in some erroneous classifications. The recognition performances for non-human objects were also evaluated with the dataset. We found their average precision[3] scores ranging between 44.8 (table) and 77.8 (car).

3.2 Formalising Spatial Relations

To develop a grammar robust for describing human related scenes, there is a need for formalising spatial relations among multiple HLFs. Their effective use leads to smooth description of visual scenes. Spatial relations can be categorised into

static: relations between not moving objects;

dynamic: direction and path of moving objects;

inter-static and dynamic: relations between moving and not moving objects.

[3]defined by Everingham et al. (2010).

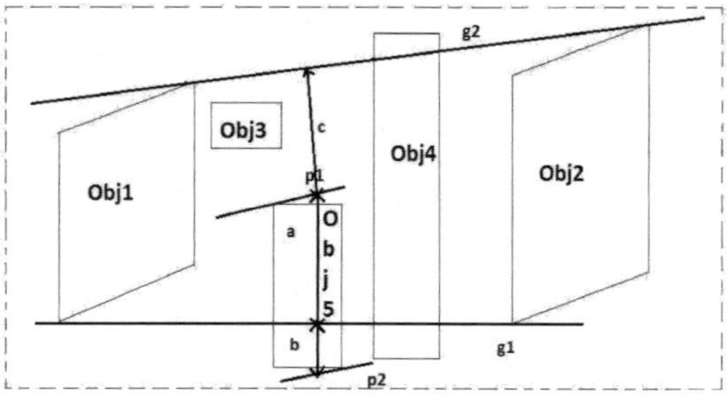

Figure 1: Procedure for calculating the 'between' relation. Obj 1 and 2 are the two reference objects, while Obj 3, 4 and 5 are the target objects.

Static relations can establish the scene settings (*e.g.*, '*chairs around a table*' may imply an indoor scene). Dynamic relations are used for finding activities present in the video (*e.g.*, '*a man is running with a dog*'). Inter-static and dynamic relations are a mixture of stationary and non stationary objects; they explain semantics of the complete scene (*e.g.*, '*persons are sitting on the chairs around the table*' indicates a meeting scene).

Spatial relations are estimated using positions of humans and other objects (or their bounding boxes, to be more precise). Following relationships can be recognised between two or three objects: 'in front of', 'behind', 'to the left', 'to the right', 'beside', 'at', 'on', 'in', and 'between'. Figure 1 illustrates steps for calculating the three-place relationship 'between'. Schirra et al. (1987) explained the algorithm:

- Calculate the two tangents g_1 and g_2 between the reference objects using their closed-rectangle representation;
- If (1) both tangents cross the target or its rectangle representation (see Obj 4 in the figure), or (2) the target is totally enclosed by the tangents and the references (Obj 3), the relationship 'between' is true.
- If only one tangent intersects the subject (Obj 5), the applicability depends on its penetration depth in the area between the tangents, thus calculate: max(a/(a+b), a/(a+c))
- Otherwise 'between' relation does not hold.

3.3 Predicates for Sentence Generation

Figure 2 presents a list of predicates to be used for natural language generation. Some predicates are derived by combining multiple HLFs extracted, *e.g.*, 'boy' may be inferred when a human is a 'male' and a 'child'. Apart from objects, only one value can be selected from candidates at one time, *e.g.*, gender can be male or female, action can be only one of those listed. Note that predicates listed in Figure 2 are for describing single human scenes; combination of these predicates may be used if multiple humans are present.

Human structure related
human (yes, no)
gender (male, female)
age (baby, child, young, old)
body parts (hand, head, body)
grouping (one, two, many)

Human actions and emotions
action (stand, sit, walk, run, wave, clap)
emotion (happy, sad, serious, surprise, angry)

Objects and scene settings
scene setting (indoor, outdoor)
objects (car, cup, table, chair, bicycle, TV-monitor)

Spatial relations among objects
in front of, behind, to the left, to the right, beside, at, on, in, between

Figure 2: Predicates for single human scenes.

4 Natural Language Generation

HLFs acquired by image processing require abstraction and fine tuning for generating syntactically and semantically sound natural language expressions. Firstly, a part of speech (POS) tag is assigned to each HLF using NLTK[4] POS tagger. Further humans and objects need to be assigned proper semantic roles. In this study, a human is treated as a subject, performing a certain action. Other HLFs are treated as objects, affected by human's activities. These objects are usually helpful for description of background and scene settings.

A template filling approach based on context free grammar (CFG) is implemented for sentence generation. A template is a pre-defined structure with slots for user specified parameters. Each template requires three parts for proper functioning: lexicons, template rules and grammar. Lexicon is a vocabulary containing HLFs extracted from a video stream (Figure 3). Grammar assures syntactical correctness of the sentence. Template rules are defined for selection of proper lexicons

[4] www.nltk.org/

Noun	→	man | woman | car | cup | table| chair | cycle | head | hand | body
Verb	→	stand | walk | sit | run | wave
Adjective	→	happy | sad | serious | surprise | angry | one | two | many | young old | middle-aged | child | baby
Pronoun	→	me | i | you | it | she | he
Determiner	→	the | a | an | this | these | that
Preposition	→	from | on | to | near | while
Conjunction	→	and | or | but

Figure 3: Lexicons and their POS tags.

with well defined grammar.

4.1 Template Rules

Template rules are employed for the selection of appropriate lexicons for sentence generation. Followings are some template rules used in this work:

Base returns a pre-defined string (*e.g.*, when no HLF is detected)

If same as an if-then statement of programming languages, returning a result when the antecedent of the rule is true

Select 1 same as a condition statement of programming languages, returning a result when one of antecedent conditions is true

Select n is used for returning a result while more than one antecedent conditions is true

Concatenation appends the the result of one template rule with the results of a second rule

Alternative is used for selecting the most specific template when multiple templates can be used

Elaboration evaluates the value of a template slot

Figure 4 illustrates template rules selection procedure. This example assumes human presence in the video. **If-else** statements are used for fitting proper gender in the template. Human can be performing only one action at a time referred by **Select 1**. There can be multiple objects which are either part of background or interacting with humans. Objects are selected by **Select n** rule. These values can be directly attained from HLFs extraction step. **Elaboration** rule is used for generating new words by joining multiple HLFs. '*Driving*' is achieved by combing '*person is inside car*' and '*car is moving*'.

If (gender == male) then *man* **else** *woman*
Select 1 (Action == *walk, run, wave, clap, sit, stand*)
Select n (Object == *car, chair, table, bike*)
Elaboration (**If** '*the car is moving*' and '*person is inside the car*') then '*person is driving the car*'

Figure 4: Template rules applied for creating a sentence '*man is driving the car*'.

4.2 Grammar

Grammar is the body of rules that describe the structure of expressions in any language. We make use of context free grammar (CFG) for the sentence generation task. CFG based formulation enables us to define a hierarchical presentation for sentence generation; *e.g.*, a description for multiple humans is comprised of single human actions. CFG is formalised by 4-tuple:

$$G = (T, N, S, R)$$

where T is set of terminals (lexicon) shown in Figure 3, N is a set of non-terminals (usually POS tags), S is a start symbol (one of non-terminals). Finally R is rules / productions of the form $X \rightarrow \gamma$, where X is a non-terminal and γ is a sequence of terminals and non-terminals which may be empty.

For implementing the templates, *simpleNLG* is used (Gatt and Reiter, 2009). It also performs some extra processing automatically: (1) the first letter of each sentence is capitalised, (2) '*-ing*' is added to the end of a verb as the progressive aspect of the verb is desired, (3) all words are put together in a grammatical form, (4) appropriate white spaces are inserted between words, and (5) a full stop is placed at the end of the sentence.

4.3 Hierarchical Sentence Generation

In this work we define a CFG based presentation for expressing activities by multiple humans. Ryoo and Aggarwal (2009) used CFG for hierarchical presentation of human actions where complex actions were composed of simpler actions. In contrast we allow a scenario where there is no interaction between humans, *i.e.*, they perform individual actions without a particular relation — imagine a situation whereby three people are sitting around a desk while one person is passing behind them.

Figure 5 shows an example for sentence generation related to a single human. This mechanism is built with three blocks when only one subject[5] is present. The first block expresses a

[5]Non human subject is also allowed in the mechanism.

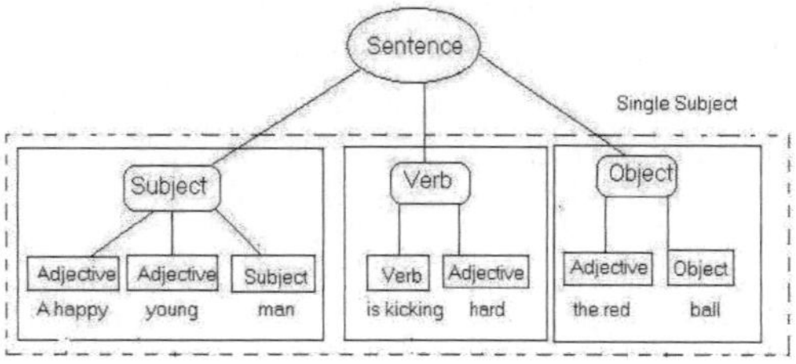

Figure 5: A scenario with a single human.

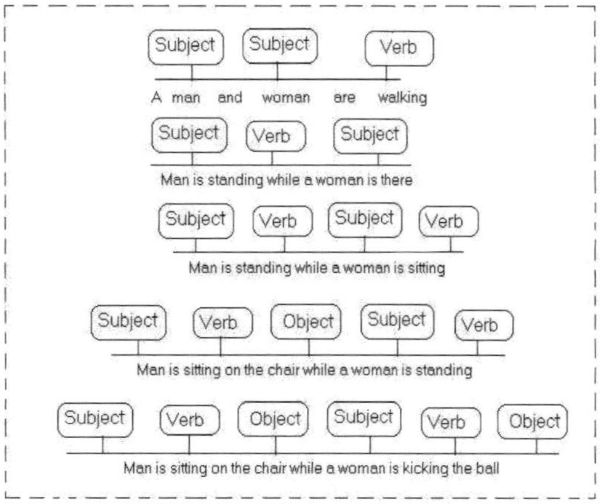

Figure 6: A scenario with two humans.

human subject with age, gender and emotion information. The second block contains a verb describing a human action, to explain the relation between the first and the third blocks. Spatial relation between the subject and other objects can also be presented. The third block captures other objects which may be either a part of background or a target for subject's action.

The approach is hierarchical in the sense that we start with creating a single human grammar, then build up to express interactions between two or more than two humans as a combination of single human activities. Figure 6 presents examples involving two subjects. There can be three scenarios; firstly two persons interact with each other to generate some common single activity (*e.g.*, 'hand shake' scene). The second scenario involves two related humans performing individual actions but they do not create a single action (*e.g.*, both persons are walking together, sitting or standing). Finally two persons happen to be in the same scene at the same time, but there is no particular relation between them (*e.g.*, one person walks, passing behind the other person sitting on a chair). Figure 7 shows an example that involves an extension of a

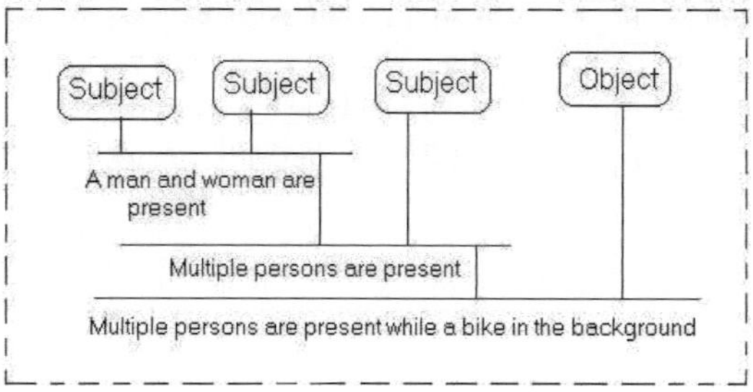

Figure 7: A scenario with multiple humans.

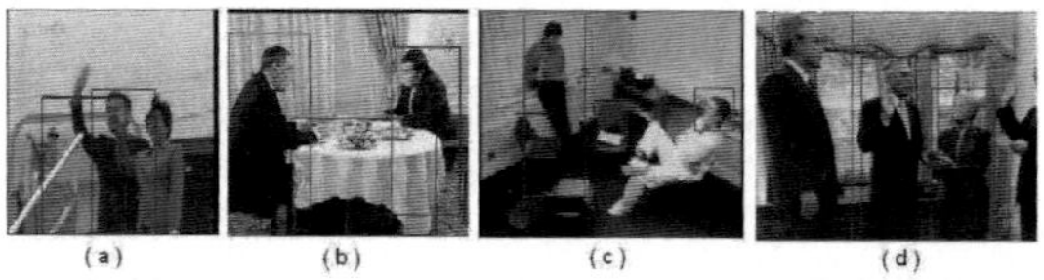

Figure 8: Template selection: (a) subject + subject + verb: '*man and woman are waving hands*'; (b) subject + subject + object: '*two persons around the table*'; (c) subject + verb, noun phrase / subject, noun phrase / subject: '*a man is standing; a person is present; there are two chairs*'; (d) subject + subject + subject + verb: '*multiple persons are present*'.

single human scenario to more than two subjects. Similarly to two-human scenarios, multiple subjects can create a single action, separate actions, or different actions altogether.

4.4 Application Scenarios

This section overviews different scenarios for application of the sentence generation framework. Figure 8 presents examples for template selection procedure. Although syntactically and semantically correct sentences can be generated in all scenes, immaturity of image processing would cause some errors and missing information.

Missing HLFs. For example, action ('*sitting*') was not identified in Figure 8(b). Further, detec-

Figure 9: Image processing can be erroneous: (a) only three cars are identified although there are many vehicles prominent, (b) five persons (in red rectangles) are detected although four are present; (c) one male is identified correctly, other male is identified as 'female'; (d) detected emotion is 'smiling' though he shows a serious face.

Figure 10: Closeup of a man talking to someone in the outdoor scene — seen in '*MS206410*' from the 2007 rushes summarisation task. **Machine annotation:** A serious man is speaking; There are humans in the background. **Hand annotation 1:** A man is talking to someone; He is wearing a formal suit; A police man is standing behind him; Some people in the background are wearing hats. **Hand annotation 2:** A man with brown hair is talking to someone; He is standing at some outdoor place; He is wearing formal clothes; He looks serious; It is windy.

tion of food on the table might have led to more semantic description of the scene (*e.g.*, '*dinning scene*'). In 8(d), fourth human and actions by two humans ('*raising hands*') were not extracted. Recognition of the road and many more vehicles in Figure 9(a) could have produced more semantic expression (*e.g.*, '*heavy traffic scene*').

Non human subjects. Suppose a human is absent, or failed to be extracted, the scene is explained on the basis of objects. They are treated as subjects for which sentences are generated. Figure 9(a) presents such a scenario; description generated was '*multiple cars are moving*'.

Errors in HLF extraction. In Figure 9(c), one person was found correctly but the other was erroneously identified as female. Description generated was '*a smiling adult man is present with a woman*'. Detected emotion was 'smile' in 9(d) though real emotion was 'serious'. Description generated was '*a man is smiling*'.

5 Experiments

5.1 Machine Generated Annotation Samples

Figures 10 to 12 present machine generated annotation and two hand annotations for randomly selected videos related to three categories from dataset.

Face closeup (Figure 10). Main interest was to find human gender and emotion information. Machine generated description was able to capture human emotion and background information. Hand annotations explained the sequence more, *e.g.*, dressing, identity of a person as policeman, hair colour and windy outdoor scene settings.

Traffic scene (Figure 11). Humans were absent in most of traffic video. Object detector was able to identify most prominent objects (*e.g.*, car, bus) for description. Hand annotations produced further details such as colours of car and other objects (*e.g.*, flyover, bridge). This sequence was also described as a highway.

Figure 11: A traffic scene with many vehicles — seen in '*20041101_110000_CCTV4_NEWS3_CHN*' from the HLF extraction task. **Machine annotation:** Many cars are present; Cars are moving; A bus is present. **Hand annotation 1:** There is a red bus, one yellow and many other cars on the highway; This is a scene of daytime traffic; There is a blue road sign on the big tower; There is also a bridge on the road. **Hand annotation 2:** There are many cars; There is a fly-over; Some buses are running on the fly-over; There is vehicle parapet; This is a traffic scene on a highway.

Figure 12: An action scene of two humans — seen in '*20041101_160000_CCTV4_DAILY_NEWS_CHN*' from the HLF extraction task. **Machine annotation:** A woman is sitting while a man is standing; There is a bus in the background; There is a car in the background. **Hand annotation 1:** Two persons are talking; One is a man and other is woman; The man is wearing formal clothes; The man is standing and woman is sitting; A bus is travellings behind. **Hand annotation 2:** Young woman is sitting on a chair in a park and talking to man who is standing next to her.

Action scene (Figure 12). Main interest was to find humans and their activities. Successful recognition of man, woman and their actions (*e.g.*, 'sitting', 'standing') led to well phrased description. The bus and the car at the background were also identified. In hand annotations dressing was noted and location was reported as a park.

5.2 Evaluation with ROUGE

Difficulty in evaluating natural language descriptions stems from the fact that it is not a simple task to define the criteria. We adopted ROUGE, widely used for evaluating automatic summarisation (Lin, 2004), to calculate the overlap between machine generated and hand annotations. Table 4 shows the results where higher ROUGE score indicates closer match between them.

In overall scores were not very high, demonstrating the fact that humans have different observations and interests while watching the same video. Descriptions were often subjective, de-

	Action	Closeup	In/Outdoor	Grouping	Meeting	News	Traffic
ROUGE-1	0.4369	0.5385	0.2544	0.3067	0.3330	0.4321	0.3121
ROUGE-2	0.3087	0.3109	0.1877	0.2619	0.2462	0.3218	0.1268
ROUGE-3	0.2994	0.2106	0.1302	0.1229	0.2400	0.2219	0.1250
ROUGE-L	0.4369	0.4110	0.2544	0.3067	0.3330	0.3321	0.3121
ROUGE-W	0.4147	0.4385	0.2877	0.3619	0.3265	0.3318	0.3147
ROUGE-S	0.3563	0.4193	0.2302	0.2229	0.2648	0.3233	0.3236
ROUGE-SU	0.3686	0.4413	0.2544	0.3067	0.2754	0.3419	0.3407

Table 4: ROUGE scores between machine generated descriptions (reference) and 13 hand annotations (model). ROUGE 1-3 shows n-gram overlap similarity between reference and model descriptions. ROUGE-L is based on longest common subsequence (LCS). ROUGE-W is for weighted LCS. ROUGE-S skips bigram co-occurrence without gap length. ROUGE-SU shows results for skip bigram co-occurrence with unigrams.

pendent on one's perception and understanding, that might have been affected by their educational and professional background, personal interests and experiences. Nevertheless ROUGE scores were not hopelessly low for machine generated descriptions; Closeup, Action and News videos had higher scores because of presence of humans with well defined actions and emotions. Indoor/Outdoor videos show the poorest results due to the limited capability of image processing techniques.

5.3 Task Based Evaluation by Human

Similar to human in the loop evaluation (Nwogu et al., 2011), a task based evaluation was performed to make qualitative evaluation of the generated descriptions. Given a machine generated description, human subjects were instructed to find a corresponding video stream out of 10 candidate videos having the same theme (*e.g.*, a description of a Closeup against 10 Closeup videos). Once a choice was made, each subject was provided with the correct video stream and a questionnaire. The first question was how well the description explained the actual video, rating from 'explained completely', 'satisfactorily', 'fairly', 'poorly', or 'does not explain'. The second question was concerned with the ranking of usefulness for including various visual contents (*e.g.*, human, objects, their moves, their relations, background) in the description.

Seven human subjects conducted this evaluation searching a corresponding video for each of ten machine generated descriptions. They did not involve creation of the dataset, hence they saw these videos for the first time. On average, they were able to identify correct videos for 53%[6] of descriptions. They rated 68%, 48%, and 40% of descriptions explained the actual video 'fairly', 'satisfactorily', and 'completely'. Because multiple videos might have very similar text descriptions, it was worth testing meaningfulness of descriptions for choosing the corresponding video. Finally, usefulness of visual contents had mix results. For about 84% of descriptions, subjects were able to identify videos based on information related to humans, their actions, emotions and interactions with other objects.

6 Conclusion

This paper explored the bottom up approach to describing video contents in natural language. The conversion from quantitative information to qualitative predicates was suitable for conceptual data manipulation and natural language generation. The outcome of the experiments indicates that the natural language formalism makes it possible to generate fluent, rich descriptions, allowing for detailed and refined expressions. Future works include detection of groups, extension of behavioural models, more complex interactions among humans and other objects.

Acknowledgements

Muhammad Usman Ghani Khan thanks University of Engineering & Technology, Lahore, Pakistan for funding his work under the Faculty Development Program.

[6] It is interesting to note the correct identification rate went up to 70% for three subjects who also conducted creation of the dataset.

References

P. Baiget, C. Fernández, X. Roca, and J. Gonzàlez. 2007. Automatic learning of conceptual knowledge in image sequences for human behavior interpretation. *Pattern Recognition and Image Analysis*, pages 507–514.

R.M. Bolle, B.L. Yeo, and M.M. Yeung. 1998. Video query: Research directions. *IBM Journal of Research and Development*, 42(2):233–252.

H.S. Chen, H.T. Chen, Y.W. Chen, and S.Y. Lee. 2006. Human action recognition using star skeleton. In *Proceedings of the 4th ACM international workshop on Video surveillance and sensor networks*, pages 171–178. ACM.

M. Everingham, L. Van Gool, C.K.I. Williams, J. Winn, and A. Zisserman. 2010. The pascal visual object classes (voc) challenge. *International Journal of Computer Vision*, 88(2):303–338.

C. Galleguillos and S. Belongie. 2010. Context based object categorization: A critical survey. *Computer Vision and Image Understanding*, 114(6):712–722.

A. Gatt and E. Reiter. 2009. SimpleNLG: A realisation engine for practical applications. In *Proceedings of the 12th European Workshop on Natural Language Generation*, pages 90–93. Association for Computational Linguistics.

W. Kim, J. Park, and C. Kim. 2010. A novel method for efficient indoor–outdoor image classification. *Journal of Signal Processing Systems*, pages 1–8.

A. Kojima, T. Tamura, and K. Fukunaga. 2002. Natural language description of human activities from video images based on concept hierarchy of actions. *International Journal of Computer Vision*, 50(2):171–184.

P. Kuchi, P. Gabbur, P. SUBBANNA BHAT, et al. 2002. Human face detection and tracking using skin color modeling and connected component operators. *IETE journal of research*, 48(3-4):289–293.

M.W. Lee, A. Hakeem, N. Haering, and S.C. Zhu. 2008. Save: A framework for semantic annotation of visual events. In *Computer Vision and Pattern Recognition Workshops. CVPRW'08*, pages 1–8. IEEE.

C.Y. Lin. 2004. Rouge: A package for automatic evaluation of summaries. In *WAS*.

I. Maglogiannis, D. Vouyioukas, and C. Aggelopoulos. 2009. Face detection and recognition of natural human emotion using markov random fields. *Personal and Ubiquitous Computing*, 13(1):95–101.

H.H. Nagel. 2004. Steps toward a cognitive vision system. *AI Magazine*, 25(2):31.

I. Nwogu, Y. Zhou, and C. Brown. 2011. Disco: Describing images using scene contexts and objects. In *Twenty-Fifth AAAI Conference on Artificial Intelligence*.

P. Over, W. Kraaij, and A.F. Smeaton. 2007. Trecvid 2007: an introduction. In *TREC Video retrieval evaluation online proceedings*.

M.S. Ryoo and J.K. Aggarwal. 2009. Semantic representation and recognition of continued and recursive human activities. *International journal of computer vision*, 82(1):1–24.

J.R.J. Schirra, G. Bosch, CK Sung, and G. Zimmermann. 1987. From image sequences to natural language: a first step toward automatic perception and description of motions. *Applied Artificial Intelligence an International Journal*, 1(4):287–305.

A. Sundaresan, A. RoyChowdhury, and R. Chellappa. 2003. A hidden markov model based framework for recognition of humans from gait sequences. In *International Conference on Image Processing, ICIP 2003*, volume 2. IEEE.

A. Torralba, K.P. Murphy, W.T. Freeman, and M.A. Rubin. 2008. Context-based vision system for place and object recognition. In *Ninth IEEE International Conference on Computer Vision*, pages 273–280. IEEE.

P. Viola and M. Jones. 2001. Rapid object detection using a boosted cascade of simple features. In *IEEE Computer Society Conference on Computer Vision and Pattern Recognition*, volume 1.

Y. Yang, C.L. Teo, H. Daumé III, C. Fermüller, and Y. Aloimonos. 2011. Corpus-guided sentence gereration of natural images. In *EMNLP*.

B.Z. Yao, X. Yang, L. Lin, M.W. Lee, and S.C. Zhu. 2010. I2t: Image parsing to text description. *Proceedings of the IEEE*, 98(8):1485–1508.

W. Zheng, H. Tang, Z. Lin, and T. Huang. 2010. Emotion recognition from arbitrary view facial images. *Computer Vision–ECCV 2010*, pages 490–503.

An Unsupervised and Data-Driven Approach for Spell Checking in Vietnamese OCR-scanned Texts

Cong Duy Vu HOANG & Ai Ti AW
Department of Human Language Technology (HLT)
Institute for Infocomm Research (I2R)
A*STAR, Singapore
{cdvhoang,aaiti}@i2r.a-star.edu.sg

Abstract

OCR (Optical Character Recognition) scanners do not always produce 100% accuracy in recognizing text documents, leading to spelling errors that make the texts hard to process further. This paper presents an investigation for the task of spell checking for OCR-scanned text documents. First, we conduct a detailed analysis on characteristics of spelling errors given by an OCR scanner. Then, we propose a fully automatic approach combining both error detection and correction phases within a unique scheme. The scheme is designed in an unsupervised & data-driven manner, suitable for resource-poor languages. Based on the evaluation on real dataset in Vietnamese language, our approach gives an acceptable performance (detection accuracy 86%, correction accuracy 71%). In addition, we also give a result analysis to show how accurate our approach can achieve.

1 Introduction and Related Work

Documents that are only available in print require scanning from OCR devices for retrieval or e-archiving purposes (Tseng, 2002; Magdy and Darwish, 2008). However, OCR scanners do not always produce 100% accuracy in recognizing text documents, leading to spelling errors that make the texts texts hard to process further. Some factors may cause those errors. For instance, shape or visual similarity forces OCR scanners to misunderstand some characters; or input text documents do not have good quality, causing noises in resulting scanned texts. The task of spell checking for OCR-scanned text documents proposed aims to solve the above situation.

Researchers in the literature used to approach this task for various languages such as: **English** (Tong and Evans, 1996; Taghva and Stofsky, 2001; Kolak and Resnik, 2002), **Chinese** (Zhuang et al., 2004), **Japanese** (Nagata, 1996; Nagata, 1998), **Arabic** (Magdy and Darwish, 2006), and **Thai** (Meknavin et al., 1998).

The most common approach is to involve users for their intervention with computer support. Taghva and Stofsky (2001) designed an **interactive** system (called OCRSpell) that assists users as many interactive features as possible during their correction, such as: choose word boundary, memorize user-corrected words for future correction, provide specific prior knowledge about typical errors. For certain applications requiring automation, the interactive scheme may not work.

Unlike (Taghva and Stofsky, 2001), **non-interactive** (or fully automatic) approaches have been investigated. Such approaches need pre-specified lexicons & confusion resources (Tong and Evans, 1996), language-specific knowledge (Meknavin et al., 1998) or manually-created phonetic transformation rules (Hodge and Austin, 2003) to assist correction process.

Other approaches used **supervised** mechanisms for OCR error correction, such as: statistical language models (Nagata, 1996; Zhuang et al., 2004; Magdy and Darwish, 2006), noisy channel model (Kolak and Resnik, 2002). These approaches performed well but are limited due to requiring large annotated training data specific to OCR spell checking in languages that are very hard to obtain.

Further, research in spell checking for Vietnamese language has been understudied.

Proceedings of the Workshop on Innovative Hybrid Approaches to the Processing of Textual Data (Hybrid2012), EACL 2012, pages 36–44,
Avignon, France, April 23 2012. ©2012 Association for Computational Linguistics

Hunspell−spellcheck−vn[1] & Aspell[2] are **interactive** spell checking tools that work based on pre-defined dictionaries.

According to our best knowledge, there is no work in the literature reported the task of spell checking for Vietnamese OCR-scanned text documents. In this paper, we approach this task in terms of 1) fully automatic scheme; 2) without using any annotated corpora; 3) capable of solving both non-word & real-word spelling errors simultaneously. Such an approach will be beneficial for a poor-resource language like Vietnamese.

2 Error Characteristics

First of all, we would like to observe and analyse the characteristics of OCR-induced errors in compared with typographical errors in a real dataset.

2.1 Data Overview

We used a total of 24 samples of Vietnamese OCR-scanned text documents for our analysis. Each sample contains real & OCR texts, referring to texts without & with spelling errors, respectively. Our manual sentence segmentation gives a result of totally 283 sentences for the above 24 samples, with 103 (good, no errors) and 180 (bad, errors existed) sentences. Also, the number of syllables[3] in real & OCR sentences (over all samples) are 2392 & 2551, respectively.

2.2 Error Classification

We carried out an in-depth analysis on spelling errors, identified existing errors, and then manually classified them into three pre-defined error classes. For each class, we also figured out how an error is formed.

As a result, we classified OCR-induced spelling errors into three classes:

Typographic or Non-syllable Errors (Class 1): refer to incorrect syllables (not included in a standard dictionary). Normally, at least one character of a syllable is expected misspelled.

Real-syllable or Context-based Errors (Class 2): refer to syllables that are **correct** in terms of their existence in a standard dictionary but **incorrect** in terms of their meaning in the context of given sentence.

Unexpected Errors (Class 3): are accidentally formed by unknown operators, such as: insert non-alphabet characters, do incorrect upper-/lower- case, split/merge/remove syllable(s), change syllable orders, ...

Note that errors in **Class 1 & 2** can be formed by applying one of 4 operators[4] (Insertion, Deletion, Substitution, Transposition). **Class 3** is exclusive, formed by unexpected operators. Table 1 gives some examples of 3 error classes.

An important note is that an erroneous syllable can contain errors across different classes. **Class 3** can appear with **Class 1** or **Class 2** but **Class 1** never appears with **Class 2**. For example:

− **h**o**à**n (correct) || **Hò**an (incorrect) (Class 3 & 1)
− b**ắ**t (correct) || bặt’ (incorrect) (Class 3 & 2)

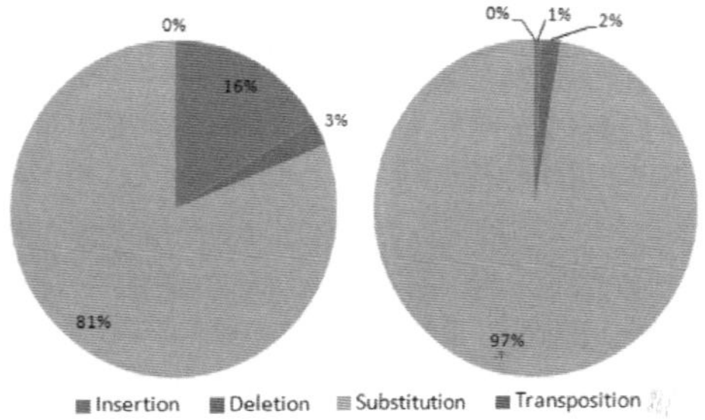

Figure 1: Distribution of operators used in **Class 1** (left) & **Class 2** (right).

2.3 Error Distribution

Our analysis reveals that there are totally 551 recognized errors over all 283 sentences. Each error is classified into three wide classes (Class 1, Class 2, Class 3). Specifically, we also tried to identify operators used in **Class 1** & **Class 2**. As a result, we have totally 9 more fine-grained error classes (1A..1D, 2A..2D, 3)[5].

We explored the distribution of 3 error classes in our analysis. **Class 1** distributed the most, following by **Class 3** (slightly less) and **Class 2**.

[1] `http://code.google.com/p/hunspell-spellcheck-vi/`

[2] `http://en.wikipedia.org/wiki/GNU_Aspell/`

[3] In Vietnamese language, we will use the word "syllable" instead of "token" to mention a unit that is separated by spaces.

[4] Their definitions can be found in (Damerau, 1964).

[5] A, B, C, and D represent for Insertion, Deletion, Substitution, and Transposition, respectively. For instance, **1A** means **Insertion** in **Class 1**.

Class	**Insertion**	**Deletion**	**Substitution**	**Transposition**[a]
Class 1	áp (correct) ‖ á**i**p (incorrect) ("i" inserted)	không (correct) ‖ kh_ (incorrect). ("ô", "n", and "g" deleted)	**y**ếu (correct) ‖ **y**ếu (incorrect). ("y" substituted by "y")	N.A.
Class 2	lên (correct) ‖ l**i**ên (contextually incorrect). ("i" inserted)	t**r**ình (correct) ‖ tình (contextually incorrect). ("r" deleted)	ng**a**y (correct) ‖ ng**â**y (contextually incorrect). ("a" substituted by "â")	N.A.
Class 3	xác nhận là (correct) ‖ x‖nha0a (incorrect). 3 syllables were misspelled & accidentally merged.			

[a]Our analysis reveals no examples for this operator.

Table 1: Examples of error classes.

Generally, each class contributed a certain quantity of errors (38%, 37%, & 25%), making the correction process of errors more challenging. In addition, there are totally 613 counts for 9 fine-grained classes (over 551 errors of 283 sentences), yielding an average & standard deviation 3.41 & 2.78, respectively. Also, one erroneous syllable is able to contain the number of (fine-grained) error classes as follows: 1(492), 2(56), 3(3), 4(0) ((N) is count of cases).

We can also observe more about the distribution of operators that were used within each error class in Figure 1. The **Substitution** operator was used the most in both **Class 1** & **Class 2**, holding 81% & 97%, respectively. Only a few other operators (**Insertion**, **Deletion**) were used. Specially, the **Transposition** operator were not used in both **Class 1** & **Class 2**. This justifies the fact that OCR scanners normally have ambiguity in recognizing similar characters.

3 Proposed Approach

The architecture of our proposed approach (namely (VOSE)) is outlined in Figure 2. Our purpose is to develop VOSE as an unsupervised data-driven approach. It means VOSE will only use textual data (un-annotated) to induce the detection & correction strategies. This makes VOSE unique and generic to adapt to other languages easily.

In VOSE, potential errors will be detected locally within each error class and will then be corrected globally under a ranking scheme. Specifically, VOSE implements two different detectors (**Non-syllable Detector** & **Real-syllable Detector**) for two error groups of **Class 1/3** & **Class 2**, respectively. Then, a corrector combines the outputs from two above detectors based on ranking scheme to produce the final output. Currently, VOSE implements two different correctors, a **Contextual Corrector** and a **Weighting-based Corrector**. **Contextual Corrector** employs language modelling to rank a list of potential candidates in the scope of whole sentence whereas **Weighting-based Corrector** chooses the best candidate for each syllable that has the highest weights. The following will give detailed descriptions for all components developed in VOSE.

3.1 Pre-processor

Pre-processor will take in the input text, do tokenization & normalization steps. Tokenization in Vietnamese is similar to one in English. Normalization step includes: normalize Vietnamese tone & vowel (e.g. h**ò**a –> ho**à**), standardize upper-/lower- cases, find numbers/punctuations/abbreviations, remove noise characters, ...

This step also extracts unigrams. Each of them will then be checked whether they exist in a pre-built list of unigrams (from large raw text data). Unigrams that do not exist in the list will be regarded as **Potential Class 1 & 3 errors** and then turned into **Non-syllable Detector**. Other unigrams will be regarded as **Potential Class 2 errors** passed into **Real-syllable Detector**.

3.2 Non-syllable Detector

Non-syllable Detector is to detect errors that do not exist in a pre-built combined dictionary (Class 1 & 3) and then generate a top-k list of potential candidates for replacement. A pre-built combined dictionary includes all syllables (unigrams) extracted from large raw text data.

In VOSE, we propose a novel approach that uses **pattern retrieval** technique for **Non-syllable**

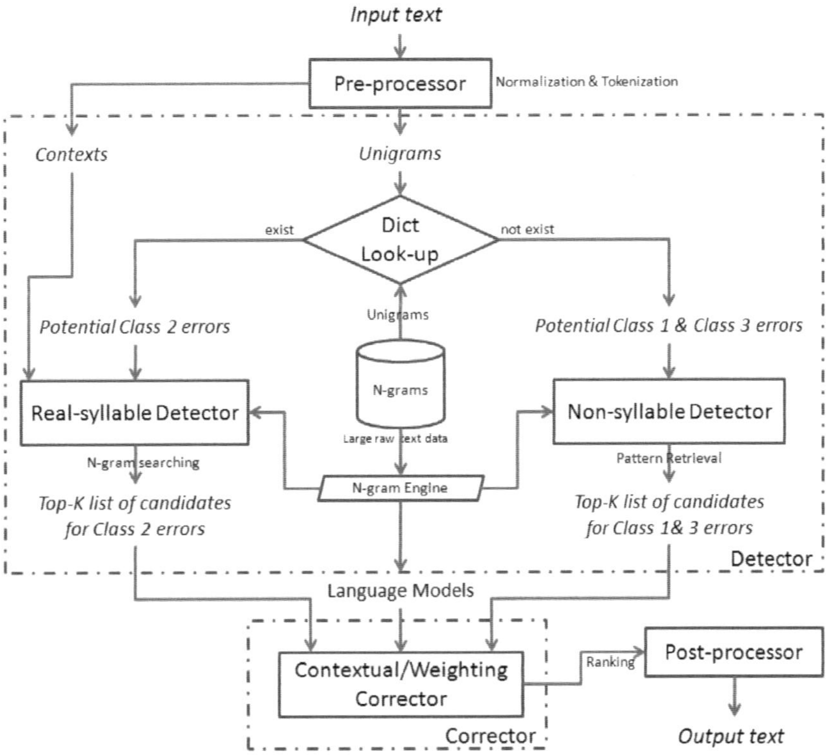

Figure 2: Proposed architecture of our approach

Detector. This approach aims to retrieve all n-gram patterns (n can be 2,3) from textual data, check approximate similarity with original erroneous syllables, and then produce a top list of potential candidates for replacement.

We believe that this approach will be able to not only handle errors with arbitrary changes on syllables but also utilize contexts (within 2/3 window size), making possible replacement candidates more reliable, and more semantically to some extent.

This idea will be implemented in the **N-gram Engine** component.

3.3 Real-syllable Detector

Real-syllable Detector is to detect all possible real-syllable errors (Class 2) and then produce the top-K list of potential candidates for replacement. The core idea of **Real-syllable Detector** is to measure the cohesion of contexts surrounding a target syllable to check whether it is possibly erroneous or not. The cohesion is measured by counts & probabilities estimated from textual data.

Assume that a K-size contextual window with a target syllable at central position is chosen.

$s_1\ s_2\ \cdots\ [\mathbf{s_c}]\ \cdots\ s_{K-1}\ s_K$ (K syllables, s_c to be checked, K is an experimental odd value (can be 3, 5, 7, 9).)

The cohesion of a sequence of syllables s_1^K biased to central syllable s_c can be measured by one of three following formulas:

Formula 1:

$$cohesion_1(s_1^K) = \log(P(s_1^K)) = \log(P(s_c) * \prod_{i \neq c, i=1}^{K} P(s_i|s_c)) \quad (1)$$

Formula 2:

$$cohesion_2(s_1^K) = count_{exist?}(s_{c-2}s_{c-1}s_c, s_{c-1}s_cs_{c+1}, s_cs_{c+1}s_{c+2}, s_{c-1}s_c, s_cs_{c+1}) \quad (2)$$

Formula 3:

$$cohesion_3(s_1^K) = count_{exist?}(s_{c-2} * s_c, s_{c-1}s_c, s_c * s_{c+2}, s_cs_{c+1}) \quad (3)$$

where:
– $cohesion(s_1^K)$ is cohesion measure of sequence s_1^K.

– $P(s_c)$ is estimated from large raw text data computed by $\frac{c(s_c)}{C}$, whereas $c(s_c)$ is unigram count and C is total count of all unigrams from data.
– $P(s_i|s_c)$ is computed by:

$$P(s_i|s_c) = \frac{P(s_i, s_c)}{P(s_c)} = \frac{c(s_i, s_c, |i-c|)}{c(s_c)} \quad (4)$$

where:
– $c(s_i, s_c, |i-c|)$ is a distance-sensitive count of two unigrams s_i and s_c co-occurred and the gap between them is $|i-c|$ unigrams.

For **Formula 1**, if $cohesion(s_1^K) < T_c$ with T_c is a pre-defined threshold, the target syllable is possibly erroneous.

For **Formula 2**, instead of probabilities as in **Formula 1**, we use counting on existence of n-grams within a context. It's maximum value is 5. **Formula 3** is a generalized version of Formula 2 (the wild-card "*" means any syllable). It's maximum value is 4.

N-gram Engine. The N-gram Engine component is very important in VOSE. All detectors & correctors use it.

Data Structure. It is worthy noting that in order to compute probabilities like $c(s_i, s_c, |i-c|)$ or query the patterns from data, an efficient data structure needs to be designed carefully. It MUST satisfy two criteria: 1) **space** to suit memory requirements 2) **speed** to suit real-time speed requirement. In this work, **N-gram Engine** employs inverted index (Zobel and Moffat, 2006), a well-known data structure used in text search engines.

Pattern Retrieval. After detecting potential errors, both **Non-syllable Detector** and **Real-syllable Detector** use **N-gram Engine** to find a set of possible replacement syllables by querying the textual data using 3-gram patterns ($s_{c-2}s_{c-1}[\mathbf{s_c^*}]$, $s_{c-1}[\mathbf{s_c^*}]s_{c+1}$, and $[\mathbf{s_c^*}]s_{c+1}s_{c+2}$) or 2-gram patterns ($s_{c-1}[\mathbf{s_c^*}]$, $[\mathbf{s_c^*}]s_{c+1}$), where $[\mathbf{s_c^*}]$ is a potential candidate. To rank a list of top candidates, we compute the weight for each candidate using the following formula:

$$weight(s_i) = \alpha \times Sim(s_i, s_c^*) + (1-\alpha) \times Freq(s_i) \quad (5)$$

where:
– $Sim(s_i, s_c^*)$ is the string similarity between candidate syllable s_i and erroneous syllable s_c^*.
– $Freq(s_i)$ is normalized frequency of s_i over a retrieved list of possible candidates.
– α is a value to control the weight biased to string similarity or frequency.

In order to compute the string similarity, we followed a combined weighted string similarity (CWSS) computation in (Islam and Inkpen, 2009) as follows:

$$\begin{aligned} Sim(s_i, s_c^*) &= \beta_1 \times NLCS(s_i, s_c^*) \\ &+\beta_2 \times NCLCS_1(s_i, s_c^*) + \beta_3 \times NCLCS_n(s_i, s_c^*) \\ &+\beta_4 \times NCLCS_z(s_i, s_c^*) \end{aligned} \quad (6)$$

where:
– β_1, β_2, β_3, and β_4 are pre-defined weights for each similarity computation. Initially, all β are set equal to $1/4$.
– $NLCS(s_i, s_c^*)$ is normalized length of longest common subsequence between s_i and s_c^*.
– $NCLCS_1(s_i, s_c^*)$, $NCLCS_n(s_i, s_c^*)$, and $NCLCS_z(s_i, s_c^*)$ is normalized length of maximal consecutive longest common subsequence between s_i and s_c^* starting from the first character, from any character, and from the last character, respectively.
– $Sim(s_i, s_c^*)$ has its value in range of $[0, 1]$.

We believe that the CWSS method will obtain better performance than standard methods (e.g. Levenshtein-based String Matching (Navarro, 2001) or n-gram based similarity (Lin, 1998)) because it can exactly capture more information (beginning, body, ending) of incomplete syllables caused by OCR errors. As a result, this step will produce a ranked top-k list of potential candidates for possibly erroneous syllables. In addition, **N-gram Engine** also stores computation utilities relating the language models which are then provided to **Contextual Corrector**.

3.4 Corrector

In **VOSE**, we propose two possible correctors:

Weighting-based Corrector

Given a ranked top-K list of potential candidates from **Non-syllable Detector** and **Real-syllable Detector**, **Weighting-based Corrector** simply chooses the best candidates based on their weights (Equation 5) to produce the final output.

Contextual Corrector

Given a ranked top-K list of potential candidates from **Non-syllable Detector** and **Real-syllable Detector**, **Contextual Corrector** globally ranks the best candidate combination using language modelling scheme.

Specifically, **Contextual Corrector** employs the language modelling based scheme which chooses the combination of candidates $(s_1^n)^*$ that makes $PP((s_1^n)^*)$ maximized over all combinations as follows:

$$(s_1^n)^*_{best} = \arg\max_{(s_1^n)^*} PP((s_1^n)^*) \quad (7)$$

where: $PP(.)$ is a language modelling score or perplexity (Jurafsky and Martin, 2008; Koehn, 2010).

In our current implementation, we used Depth-First Traversal (DFS) strategy to examine over all combinations. The weakness of DFS strategy is the explosion of combinations if the number of nodes (syllables in our case) grows more than 10. In this case, the speed of DFS-based **Contextual Corrector** is getting slow. Future work can consider **beam search** decoding idea in Statistical Machine Translation (Koehn, 2010) to adapt for **Contextual Corrector**.

3.5 Prior Language-specific Knowledge

Since **VOSE** is an unsupervised & data-driven approach, its performance depends on the quality and quantity of raw textual data. VOSE's current design allows us to integrate prior language-specific knowledge easily.

Some possible sources of prior knowledge could be utilized as follows:

– **Vietnamese Character Fuzzy Matching** - In Vietnamese language, some characters look very similar, forcing OCR scanners mis-recognition. Thus, we created a manual list of highly similar characters (as shown in Table 2) and then integrate this into VOSE. Note that this integration takes place in the process of string similarity computation.

– **English Words & Vietnamese Abbreviations Filtering** - In some cases, there exist English words or Vietnamese abbreviations. VOSE may suggest wrong replacements for those cases. Thus, a syllable in either English words or Vietnamese abbreviations will be ignored in VOSE.

4 Experiments

4.1 Baseline Systems

According to our best knowledge, previous systems that are able to simultaneously handle both non-syllable and real-syllable errors do not exist, especially apply for Vietnamese language. We believe that VOSE is the first one to do that.

No.	**Character**	**Similar Characters**
1	a	{á ạ à ả â ấ ậ ầ}
2	e	{ẽ ê ế ề} + **{c}**
3	i	{ỉ ĩ} + **{l}**
4	o	{ò ơ ờ ở ỡ}
5	u	{ũ ư ự ừ ữ}
6	y	{ý ỵ}
7	d	{đ}

Table 2: Vietnamese similar characters.

4.2 N-gram Extraction Data

In VOSE, we extracted ngrams from the raw textual data. Table 3 shows data statistics used in our experiments.

4.3 Evaluation Measure

We used the following measure to evaluate the performance of VOSE:

- For **Detection**:

$$DF = \frac{2 \times DR \times DP}{DR + DP} \quad (8)$$

Where:

– DR (Detection Recall) = the fraction of errors correctly detected.

– DP (Detection Precision) = the fraction of detected errors that are correct.

– DF (Detection F-Measure) = the combination of detection recall and precision.

- For **Correction**:

$$CF = \frac{2 \times CR \times CP}{CR + CP} \quad (9)$$

Where:

– CR (Correction Recall) = the fraction of errors correctly amended.

– CP (Correction Precision) = the fraction of amended errors that are correct.

– CF (Correction F-Measure) = the combination of correction recall and precision.

4.4 Results

We carried out our evaluation based on the real dataset as described in Section 2. In our evaluation, we intend:

– To evaluate whether VOSE can benefit from addition of more data, meaning that VOSE is actually a data-driven system.

– To evaluate the effectiveness of language modelling based corrector in compared to weighing

No	Dataset	NumOfSents	Vocabulary	N-grams			
				2-gram	3-gram	4-gram	5-gram
1	DS1	1,328,506	102,945	1,567,045	8,515,894	17,767,103	24,700,815
2	DS2[a]	2,012,066	169,488	2,175,454	12,610,281	27,961,302	40,295,888
3	DS3[b]	283	1,546	6,956	9,030	9,671	9,946
4	DS4[c]	344	1,755	6,583	7,877	8,232	8,383

[a]includes DS1 and more
[b]annotated test data (not included in DS1 & DS2) as described in Section 2
[c]web contexts data (not included in others) crawled from the Internet

Table 3: Ngram extraction data statistics.

based corrector.
– To evaluate whether prior knowledge specific to Vietnamese language can help VOSE.

The overall evaluation result (in terms of detection & correction accuracy) is shown in Table 4. In our experiments, all VOSE(s) except of VOSE 6 used contextual corrector (Section 3.4). Also, **Real-syllable Detector** (Section 3.3) used Equation 3 which revealed the best result in our pre-evaluation (we do not show the results because spaces do not permit).

We noticed the tone & vowel normalization step in **Pre-processor** module. This step is important specific to Vietnamese language. VOSE 2a in Table 4 shows that VOSE using that step gives a significant improvement (vs. VOSE 1) in both detection & correction.

We also tried to assess the impact of language modelling order factor in VOSE. VOSE using 3-gram language modelling gives the best result (VOSE 2a vs. VOSE 2b & 2c). Because of this, we chose 3-gram for next VOSE set-ups.

We experiment how data addition affects VOSE. First, we used bigger data (DS2) for ngram extraction and found the significant improvement (VOSE 3a vs. VOSE 2a). Second, we tried an interesting set-up in which VOSE utilized ngram extraction data with annotated test data (Dataset DS3) only in order to observe the recall ability of VOSE. Resulting VOSE (VOSE 3b) performed extremely well.

As discussed in Section 3.5, VOSE allows integrated prior language-specific knowledge that helps improve the performance (VOSE 4). This justifies that statistical method in combined with such prior knowledge is very effective.

Specifically, for each error in test data, we crawled the web sentences containing contexts in which that error occurs (called web contexts). We added such web contexts into ngram extraction data. With this strategy, we can improve the performance of VOSE significantly (VOSE 5), obtaining the best result. Again, we've proved that more data VOSE has, more accurate it performs.

The result of VOSE 6 is to show the superiority of VOSE using contextual corrector in compared with using weighting-based corrector (VOSE 6 vs. VOSE 4). However, weighting-based corrector has much faster speed in correction than contextual corrector which is limited due to DFS traversal & language modelling ranking.

Based on the above observations, we have two following important claims:
– First, the addition of more data in ngram extraction process is really useful for VOSE.
– Second, prior knowledge specific to Vietnamese language helps to improve the performance of VOSE.
– Third, contextual corrector with language modelling is superior than weighting-based corrector in terms of the accuracy.

4.5 Result Analysis

Based on the best results produced by our approach (VOSE), we recognize & categorize cases that VOSE is currently unlikely to detect & correct properly.

Consecutive Cases (Category 1)

When there are 2 or 3 consecutive errors, their contexts are limited or lost. This issue will affect the algorithm implemented in VOSE utilizing the contexts to predict the potential replacements. VOSE can handle such errors to limited extent.

Merging Cases (Category 2)

In this case, two or more erroneous syllables are accidentally merged. Currently, VOSE cannot

Set-up	Detection Accuracy			Correction Accuracy			Remark
	Recall	Precision	F1	Recall	Precision	F1	
VOSE 1	0.8782	0.5954	0.7097	0.6849	0.4644	0.5535	w/o TVN + 3-LM + DS1
VOSE 2a	0.8782	**0.6552**	**0.7504**	**0.6807**	**0.5078**	**0.5817**	w/ TVN + 3-LM + DS1
VOSE 2b	0.8782	0.6552	0.7504	0.6744	0.5031	0.5763	w/ TVN + 4-LM + DS1
VOSE 2c	0.8782	0.6552	0.7504	0.6765	0.5047	0.5781	w/ TVN + 5-LM + DS1
VOSE 3a	**0.8584**	**0.7342**	**0.7914**	**0.6829**	**0.5841**	**0.6296**	w/ TVN + 3-LM + DS2
VOSE 3b	0.9727	0.9830	0.9778	0.9223	0.9321	0.9271	w/ TVN + 3-LM + DS3
VOSE 4	0.8695	0.7988	0.8327	0.7095	0.6518	0.6794	VOSE 3a + PK
VOSE 5	**0.8674**	**0.8460**	**0.8565**	**0.7200**	**0.7023**	**0.7110**	VOSE 4 + DS4
VOSE 6	0.8695	0.7988	0.8327	0.6337	0.5822	0.6069	VOSE 4 but uses WC

Table 4: **Evaluation results**. Abbreviations: **TVN** (Tone & Vowel Normalization); **N-LM** (N-order Language Modelling); **DS** (Dataset); **PK** (Prior Knowledge); **WC** (Weighting-based Corrector).

handle such cases. We aim to investigate this in our future work.

Proper Noun/Abbreviation/Number Cases (both in English, Vietnamese) (Category 3)

Abbreviations or proper nouns or numbers are unknown (for VOSE) because they do not appear in ngram extraction data. If VOSE marks them as errors, it could not correct them properly.

Ambiguous Cases (Category 4)

Ambiguity can happen in:
– cases in which punctuation marks (e.g. comma, dot, dash, ...) are accidentally added between two different syllable or within one syllable.
– cases never seen in ngram extraction data.
– cases relating to semantics in Vietnamese.
– cases where one Vietnamese syllable that is changed incorrectly becomes an English word.

Lost Cases (Category 5)

This case happens when a syllable which is accidentally lost most of its characters or too short becomes extremely hard to correct.

Additionally, we conducted to observe the distribution of the above categories (Figure 3). As can be seen, Category 4 dominates more than 70% cases that VOSE has troubles for detection & correction.

5 Conclusion & Future Work

In this paper, we've proposed & developed a new approach for spell checking task (both detection and correction) for Vietnamese OCR-scanned text documents. The approach is designed in an unsupervised & data-driven manner. Also, it allows

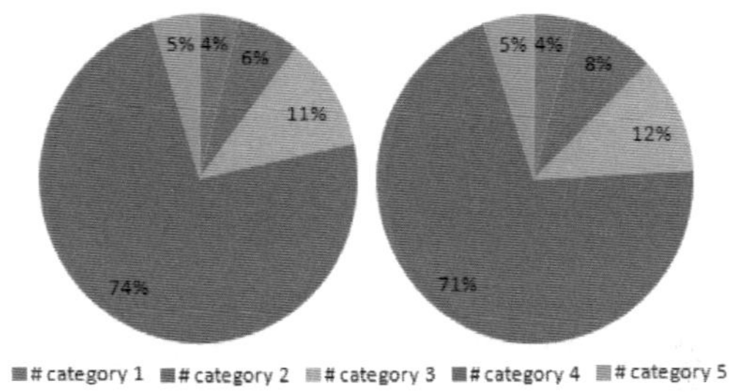

Figure 3: Distribution of categories in the result of VOSE 4 (left) & VOSE 5 (right).

to integrate the prior language-specific knowledge easily.

Based on the evaluation on a real dataset, the system currently offers an acceptable performance (best result: detection accuracy 86%, correction accuracy 71%). With just an amount of small n-gram extraction data, the obtained result is very promising. Also, the detailed error analysis in previous section reveals that cases that current system **VOSE** cannot solve are extremely hard, referring to the problem of semantics-related ambiguity in Vietnamese language.

Further remarkable point of proposed approach is that it can perform the detection & correction processes in **real-time** manner.

Future works include some directions. First, we should crawl and add more textual data for n-gram extraction to improve the performance of current system. More data **VOSE** has, more accurate it performs. Second, we should investigate more on categories (as discussed earlier) that VOSE could not resolve well. Last, we also adapt this work for another language (like English) to assess the generalization and efficiency of proposed approach.

References

Fred J. Damerau. 1964. A technique for computer detection and correction of spelling errors. *Commun. ACM*, 7:171–176, March.

Victoria J. Hodge and Jim Austin. 2003. A comparison of standard spell checking algorithms and a novel binary neural approach. *IEEE Trans. on Knowl. and Data Eng.*, 15(5):1073–1081, September.

Aminul Islam and Diana Inkpen. 2009. Real-word spelling correction using google web it 3-grams. In *Proceedings of the 2009 Conference on Empirical Methods in Natural Language Processing: Volume 3 - Volume 3*, EMNLP '09, pages 1241–1249, Stroudsburg, PA, USA. Association for Computational Linguistics.

Daniel Jurafsky and James H. Martin. 2008. *Speech and Language Processing: An Introduction to Natural Language Processing, Computational Linguistics and Speech Recognition*. Prentice Hall, second edition, February.

Philipp Koehn. 2010. *Statistical Machine Translation*. Cambridge University Press.

Okan Kolak and Philip Resnik. 2002. Ocr error correction using a noisy channel model. In *Proceedings of the second international conference on Human Language Technology Research*, HLT '02, pages 257–262, San Francisco, CA, USA. Morgan Kaufmann Publishers Inc.

Dekang Lin. 1998. An information-theoretic definition of similarity. In *Proceedings of the Fifteenth International Conference on Machine Learning*, ICML '98, pages 296–304, San Francisco, CA, USA. Morgan Kaufmann Publishers Inc.

Walid Magdy and Kareem Darwish. 2006. Arabic ocr error correction using character segment correction, language modeling, and shallow morphology. In *Proceedings of the 2006 Conference on Empirical Methods in Natural Language Processing*, EMNLP '06, pages 408–414, Stroudsburg, PA, USA. Association for Computational Linguistics.

Walid Magdy and Kareem Darwish. 2008. Effect of ocr error correction on arabic retrieval. *Inf. Retr.*, 11:405–425, October.

Surapant Meknavin, Boonserm Kijsirikul, Ananlada Chotimongkol, and Cholwich Nuttee. 1998. Combining trigram and winnow in thai ocr error correction. In *Proceedings of the 36th Annual Meeting of the Association for Computational Linguistics and 17th International Conference on Computational Linguistics - Volume 2*, ACL '98, pages 836–842, Stroudsburg, PA, USA. Association for Computational Linguistics.

Masaaki Nagata. 1996. Context-based spelling correction for japanese ocr. In *Proceedings of the 16th conference on Computational linguistics - Volume 2*, COLING '96, pages 806–811, Stroudsburg, PA, USA. Association for Computational Linguistics.

Masaaki Nagata. 1998. Japanese ocr error correction using character shape similarity and statistical language model. In *Proceedings of the 36th Annual Meeting of the Association for Computational Linguistics and 17th International Conference on Computational Linguistics - Volume 2*, ACL '98, pages 922–928, Stroudsburg, PA, USA. Association for Computational Linguistics.

Gonzalo Navarro. 2001. A guided tour to approximate string matching. *ACM Comput. Surv.*, 33(1):31–88, March.

Kazem Taghva and Eric Stofsky. 2001. Ocrspell: an interactive spelling correction system for ocr errors in text. *International Journal of Document Analysis and Recognition*, 3:2001.

Xian Tong and David A. Evans. 1996. A statistical approach to automatic ocr error correction in context. In *Proceedings of the Fourth Workshop on Very Large Corpora (WVLC-4*, pages 88–100.

Yuen-Hsien Tseng. 2002. Error correction in a chinese ocr test collection. In *Proceedings of the 25th annual international ACM SIGIR conference on Research and development in information retrieval*, SIGIR '02, pages 429–430, New York, NY, USA. ACM.

Li Zhuang, Ta Bao, Xioyan Zhu, Chunheng Wang, and S. Naoi. 2004. A chinese ocr spelling check approach based on statistical language models. In *Systems, Man and Cybernetics, 2004 IEEE International Conference on*, volume 5, pages 4727 – 4732 vol.5.

Justin Zobel and Alistair Moffat. 2006. Inverted files for text search engines. *ACM Comput. Surv.*, 38, July.

Invited talk presentation
Multilingual Natural Language Processing

Rada Mihalcea
University of North Texas
USA
rada@cs.unt.edu

Title

Multilingual Natural Language Processing

Abstract

With rapidly growing online resources, such as Wikipedia, Twitter, or Facebook, there is an increasing number of languages that have a Web presence, and correspondingly there is a growing need for effective solutions for multilingual natural language processing. In this talk, I will explore the hypothesis that a multilingual representation can enrich the feature space for natural language processing tasks, and lead to significant improvements over traditional solutions that rely exclusively on a monolingual representation. Specifically, I will describe experiments performed on three different tasks: word sense disambiguation, subjectivity analysis, and text semantic similarity, and show how the use of a multilingual representation can leverage additional information from the languages in the multilingual space, and thus improve over the use of only one language at a time. This is joint work with Samer Hassan and Carmen Banea.

Bio

Rada Mihalcea is an Associate Professor in the Department of Computer Science and Engineering at the University of North Texas. Her research interests are in computational linguistics, with a focus on lexical semantics, graph-based algorithms for natural language processing, and multilingual natural language processing. She serves or has served on the editorial boards of the Journals of Computational Linguistics, Language Resources and Evaluations, Natural Language Engineering, and Research in Language in Computation. She was a program co-chair for the Conference of the Association for Computational Linguistics (2011), and the Conference on Empirical Methods in Natural Language Processing (2009). She is the recipient of a National Science Foundation CAREER award (2008) and a Presidential Early Career Award for Scientists and Engineers (2009).

Proceedings of the Workshop on Innovative Hybrid Approaches to the Processing of Textual Data (Hybrid2012), EACL 2012, page 45,
Avignon, France, April 23 2012.

Contrasting objective and subjective Portuguese texts from heterogeneous sources

Michel Généreux
Centro de Linguística da
Universidade de Lisboa (CLUL)
Av. Prof. Gama Pinto, 2
1649-003 Lisboa - Portugal
genereux@clul.ul.pt

William Martinez
Instituto de Linguística
Téorica e Computacional (ILTEC)
Avenida Elias Garcia, 147 - 5° direito
1050-099 Lisboa - Portugal
william@iltec.pt

Abstract

This paper contrasts the content and form of objective versus subjective texts. A collection of on-line newspaper news items serve as objective texts, while parliamentary speeches (debates) and blog posts form the basis of our subjective texts, all in Portuguese. The aim is to provide general linguistic patterns as used in objective written media and subjective speeches and blog posts, to help construct domain-independent templates for information extraction and opinion mining. Our hybrid approach combines statistical data along with linguistic knowledge to filter out irrelevant patterns. As resources for subjective classification are still limited for Portuguese, we use a parallel corpus and tools developed for English to build our subjective spoken corpus, through annotations produced for English projected onto a parallel corpus in Portuguese. A measure for the saliency of n-grams is used to extract relevant linguistic patterns deemed "objective" and "subjective". Perhaps unsurprisingly, our contrastive approach shows that, in Portuguese at least, subjective texts are characterized by markers such as descriptive, reactive and opinionated terms, while objective texts are characterized mainly by the absence of subjective markers.

1 Introduction

During the last few years there has been a growing interest in the automatic extraction of elements related to feelings and emotions in texts, and to provide tools that can be integrated into a more global treatment of languages and their subjective aspect. Most research so far has focused on English, and this is mainly due to the availability of resources for the analysis of subjectivity in this language, such as lexicons and manually annotated corpora. In this paper, we contrast the subjective and the objective aspects of language for Portuguese.

Essentially, our approach will extract linguistic patterns (hopefully "objective" for newspaper news items and "subjective" for parliamentary speeches and blog posts) by comparing frequencies against a reference corpus. Our method is relevant for hybrid approaches as it combines linguistic and statistic information. Our reference corpus, the Reference Corpus of Contemporary Portuguese (CRPC)[1], is an electronically based linguistic corpus of around 310 million tokens, taken by sampling from several types of written texts (literature, newspapers, science, economics, law, parliamentary debates, technical and didactic documents), pertaining to national and regional varieties of Portuguese. A random selection of 10,000 texts from the entire CRPC will be used for our experiment. The experiment flow-chart is shown in Figure 1. We define as objective short news items from newspapers that reports strictly a piece of news, without comments or analysis. A selection of blog post items and short verbal exchanges between member of the European parliament will serve as subjective texts.

2 Previous work

The task of extracting linguistic patterns for data mining is not new, albeit most research has so far dealt with English texts. Extracting subjective patterns represents a more recent and challenging task. For example, in the Text Analy-

[1] http://www.clul.ul.pt/en/resources/183-reference-corpus-of-contemporary-portuguese-crpc

Proceedings of the Workshop on Innovative Hybrid Approaches to the Processing of Textual Data (Hybrid2012), EACL 2012, pages 46–51, Avignon, France, April 23 2012. ©2012 Association for Computational Linguistics

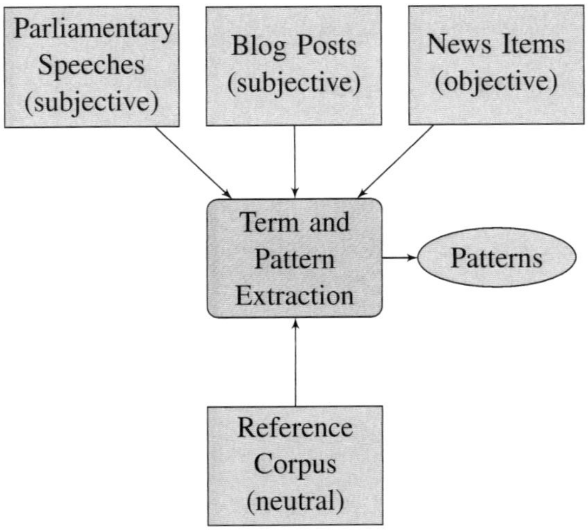

Figure 1: Experiment flow-chart.

sis Conference (TAC 2009), it was decided to withdraw the task of creating summaries of opinions, present at TAC 2008, the organizers having agreed on the difficulty of extracting subjective elements of a text and organize them appropriately to produce a summary. Yet, there is already some relevant work in this area which may be mentioned here. For opinions, previous studies have mainly focused in the detection and the gradation of their emotional level, and this involves three main subtasks. The first subtask is to distinguish subjective from objectives texts (Yu and Hatzivassiloglou, 2003). The second subtask focuses on the classification of subjective texts into positive or negative (Turney, 2002). The third level of refinement is trying to determine the extent to which texts are positive or negative (Wilson et al., 2004). The momentum for this type of research came through events such as TREC Blog Opinion Task since 2006. It is also worth mentioning recent efforts to reintroduce language and discursive approaches (e.g. taking into account the modality of the speaker) in this area (Asher and Mathieu, 2008). The approaches developed for automatic analysis of subjectivity have been used in a wide variety of applications, such as online monitoring of mood (Lloyd et al., 2005), the classification of opinions or comments (Pang et al., 2002) and their extraction (Hu an Liu, 2004) and the semantic analysis of texts (Esuli and Sebastiani, 2006). In (Mihalcea et al., 2007), a bilingual lexicon and a manually translated parallel corpus are used to generate a sentence classifier according to their level of subjectivity for Romanian. Although many recent studies in the analysis of subjectivity emphasize *sentiment* (a type of subjectivity, positive or negative), our work focuses on the recognition of subjectivity and objectivity in general. As stressed in some work (Banea et al., 2008), researchers have shown that in sentiment analysis, an approach in two steps is often beneficial, in which we first distinguish objective from subjective texts, and then classify subjective texts depending on their polarity (Kim and Hovy, 2006). In fact, the problem of distinguishing subjective versus objective texts has often been the most difficult of the two steps. Improvements in the first step will therefore necessarily have a beneficial impact on the second, which is also shown in some work (Takamura et al., 2006).

3 Creating a corpus of Subjective and Objective Portuguese Texts

To build our subjective spoken corpus (more than 2,000 texts), we used a parallel corpus of English-Portuguese speeches[2] and a tool to automatically classify sentences in English as objective or subjective (OpinionFinder (Riloff et al., 2003)). We then projected the labels obtained for the sentences in English on the Portuguese sentences. The original parallel corpus is made of 1,783,437 pairs of parallel sentences, and after removing pervasive short sentences (e.g. "the House adjourned at ...") or pairs of sentences with the ratio of their respective lengths far away from one (a sign of alignment or translation error), we are left with 1,153,875 pairs. A random selection of contiguous 20k pairs is selected for the experiment. The English sentences are submitted to OpinionFinder, which labels each of them as "unknown", "subjective" or "objective". OpinionFinder has labelled 11,694 of the 20k sentences as "subjective". As our experiment aims at comparing frequencies between texts, we have automatically created segments of texts showing lexical similarities using Textiling (Hearst, 1997), leading to 2,025 texts. We haven't made any attempt to improve or evaluate OpinionFinder and Textiling performance. This strategy is sensible as parliamentary speeches are a series of short opinionated interventions by members on specific

[2]European Parliament: `http://www.statmt.org/europarl/`

themes. The 11,694 subjective labels have been projected on each of the corresponding sentences of the Portuguese corpus to produce our final spoken corpus[3]. Note that apart from a bridge (here a parallel corpus) between the source language (here English) and the target language (here Portuguese), our approach does not require any manual annotation. Thus, given a bridge between English and the target language, this approach can be applied to other languages. The considerable amount of work involved in the creation of these resources for English can therefore serve as a leverage for creating similar resources for other languages.

We decided to include a collection of blog posts as an additional source of subjective texts. We gathered a corpus of 1,110 blog posts using BootCat[4], a tool that allows the harvesting and cleaning of web pages on the basis of a set of seed terms[5].

For our treatment of objectivity and how news are reported in Portuguese newspapers, we have collected and cleaned a corpus of nearly 1500 articles from over a dozen major websites (*Jornal de Notícias*, *Destak*, *Visão*, *A Bola*, etc.).

After tokenizing and POS-tagging all sentences, we collected all n-grams (n = 1, 2 and 3) along with their corresponding frequency for each corpus (reference (CRPC), objective (news items) and subjective (parliamentary speeches and blog posts)), each gram being a combination of a token with its part-of-speech tag (e.g. *falar*_V, "speak_V"). The list of POS tags is provided in appendix A.

[3]As our subjective spoken corpus has been built entirely automatically (Opinion Finder and Textiling), it is important to note that (Généreux and Poibeau, 2009) have verified that such a corpus correlates well with human judgements.

[4]`http://bootcat.sslmit.unibo.it/`

[5]In an attempt to collect as much opinionated pages in Portuguese as can be, we constraint BootCat to extract pages written in Portuguese from the following web domains: `communidades.net`, `blogspot.com`, `wordpress.com` and `myspace.com`. We used the following seed words, more or less strongly related to the Portuguese culture: *ribatejo*, *camões*, *queijo*, *vinho*, *cavaco*, *europa*, *sintra*, *praia*, *porto*, *fado*, *pasteis*, *bacalhau*, *lisboa*, *algarve*, *alentejo* and *coelho*.

4 Experiments and Results

4.1 POS and n-grams

In our experiments we have compared all the n-grams (n = 1, 2 and 3) from the objective and subjective texts with the n-grams from the reference corpus. This kind of analysis aims essentially at the identification of salient expressions (with high *log-odds* ratio scores). The log-odds ratio method (Baroni and Bernardini, 2004) compares the frequency of occurrence of each n-gram in a specialized corpus (news, parliamentary speeches or blogs) to its frequency of occurrence in a reference corpus (CRPC). Applying this method solely on POS, we found that objective texts used predominantly verbs with an emphasis on past participles (PPT/PPA, *adotado*, "adopted"), which is consistent with the nature of reported news. In general, we observed that subjective texts have a higher number of adjectives (ADJ, *ótimo*, "optimum"): parliamentary speeches also include many infinitives (INF, *felicitar* "congratulate"), while blogs make use of interjections (ITJ, *uau*, "wow"). Tables 1, 2 and 3 show salient expressions for each type of texts. These expressions do not always point to a distinction between subjectivity and objectivity, but also to topics normally associated with each type of texts, a situation particularly acute in the case of parliamentary speeches. Nevertheless, we can make some very general observations. There is no clear pattern in news items, except for a slight tendency towards the use of a quantitative terminology ("save", "spend"). Parliamentary speeches are concerned with societal issues ("socio-economic", "biodegradable") and forms of politeness ("wish to express/protest"). In blog posts we find terms related to opinions ("pinch of salt"), wishes ("I hope you enjoy"), reactions ("oups") and descriptions ("creamy").

4.2 Patterns around NPs

The n-gram approach can provide interesting patterns but it has its limits. In particular, it does not allow for generalization over larger constituents. One way to overcome this flaw is to chunk corpora into noun-phrases (NP). This is the approach taken in (Riloff and Wiebe, 2003) for English. In Riloff and Wiebe (2003), the patterns for English involved a very detailed linguistic analysis, such as the detection of grammatical functions as well

PORTUGUESE	ENGLISH
detetado_PPA	"detected"
empatado_PPT	"tied"
castigado_PPT	"punished"
ano_CN perdido_PPA	"lost year"
triunfa_ADJ	"triumph"
receção_CN	"recession"
podem_V poupar_INF	"can save"
vai_V salvar_INF	"will save"
deviam_V hoje_ADV	"must today"
ameaças_CN se_CL concretizem_INF	"threats materialize"
andam_V a_DA gastar_INF	"go to spend"
ano_CN de_PREP desafios_CN	"year of challenges"
contratações_CN de_PREP pessoal_CN	"hiring of staff"

Table 1: Salient expressions in news.

PORTUGUESE	ENGLISH
socioeconómicas_ADJ	"socio-economic"
biodegradveis_ADJ	"biodegradable"
infraestrutural_ADJ	"infra-structural"
base_CN jurídica_ADJ	"legal basis"
estado-membro_ADJ	"member state"
resolução_CN comun_ADJ	"common resolution"
gostaria_V de_PREP expressar_INF	"wish to express"
gostaria_V de_PREP manifestar_INF	"wish to protest"
adoptar_INF uma_UM abordagem_CN	"adopt an " approach"
agradecer_INF muito_ADV sinceramente_ADV	"thank very sincerely"
começar_INF por_PREP felicitar_INF	"start by congratulate"
senhora_CN comissária_CN	"Commissioner"
senhora_CN deputada_CN	"Deputy"
quitação_CN	"discharge"
governança_CN	"governance"

Table 2: Salient expressions in parliamentary speeches.

as active or passive forms. Without the proper resources needed to produce sophisticated linguistic annotations for Portuguese, we decided to simplify matters slightly by not making distinction of grammatical function or voice. That is, only NPs would matter for our analysis. We used the NP-chunker Yamcha[6] trained on 1,000 manually annotated (NPs and POS-tags) sentences. The main idea here remains the same and is to find a set of syntactic patterns that are relevant to each group of texts, as we did for n-grams previously, each NP becoming a single 1-gram for this purpose. It is worth mentioning that NP-chunking becomes particularly challenging in the case of blogs, which are linguistically heterogeneous and noisy. Finally, log-odds ratio once again serves as a discriminative measure to highlight relevant patterns around NPs. Tables 4, 5 and 6 illustrate salient expressions from the three specialized corpora, presenting some of them in context.

Although limited to relatively simple syntactic patterns, this approach reveals a number of salient linguistic structures for the subjective texts. In parliamentary speeches, forms of politeness are clearly predominant ("ladies and <NP>", "thank <NP>" and "<NP> wish to thank"). Unfortunately, the patterns extracted from blog posts are pervaded by "boiler-plate" material that were not filtered out during the cleaning phase and parasite the analysis: "published by <NP>", "share on <NP>" and "posted by <NP>". However, opinions ("<NP> is beautiful") and opinion primer ("currently, <NP>") remain present. News items are still characterized mainly by the absence of subjective structures (markers), albeit quantitative expressions can still be found ("spent").

Obviously, a statistical approach yields a certain number of irrelevant (or at best "counter-intuitive") expressions: our results are no exception to this reality. Clearly, in order to reveal insights or suggest meaningful implications, an external (human) evaluation of the patterns presented in this study would paint a clearer picture of the relevance of our results for information extraction and opinion mining, but we think they constitute a good starting point.

5 Conclusion and Future Work

We have presented a partly automated approach to extract subjective and objective patterns in se-

[6]`http://chasen.org/~taku/software/yamcha/`. Our evaluation of the trained chunker on Portuguese texts lead to an accuracy of 86% at word level.

PORTUGUESE	ENGLISH
direto_ADJ	"direct"
cremoso_ADJ	"creamy"
crocante_ADJ	"crispy"
atuais_ADJ	"current"
coletiva_ADJ	"collective"
muito_ADV legal_ADJ	"very legal"
redes_CN sociais_ADJ	"social networks"
ups_ITJ	"oups"
hum_ITJ	"hum"
eh_ITJ	"eh"
atualmente_ADV	"currently"
atrações_CN	"attractions"
tenho_V certeza_CN	"I am sure"
é_V exatamente_ADV	"this is exactly"
café_CN da_PREP+DA manhã_CN	"morning coffee"
pitada_CN de_PREP sal_CN	"pinch of salt"
espero_V que_CJ gostem_INF	"I hope you enjoy"

Table 3: Salient expressions in blogs.

Some NP-patterns in context
• *fiquemos_V à_PREP+DA <NP>* "we are waiting for <NP>" *E também não **fiquemos à <espera da Oposição**> mais interessada em chegar ao* Poder. "And also we are not waiting for an opposition more interested in coming to power."
• *revelam_V <NP> gastámos_V* "revealed by <NP> we spent" *O problema é que, como **revelam <os dados da SIBS, na semana do Natal> gastámos** quase 1300 euros por segundo.* "The problem is that as shown by the data of SIBS, in the Christmas week we spent nearly 1300 Euros per second."
• *<NP> deviam_V hoje_ADV* "<NP> must today" *E para evitar males maiores, **<todos os portugueses (ou quase todos)> deviam hoje** fazer . . .* "And to avoid greater evils, all the Portuguese (or almost all) should today make . . .
Other NP-patterns
• *<NP> gostámos_V quase_ADV* "<NP> spent almost"
• *precisa_V daqueles_PREP+DEM <NP>* "need those <NP>"

Table 4: NP-patterns in news

lected texts from the European Parliament, blog posts and on-line newspapers in Portuguese. Our work first shows that it is possible to built resources for Portuguese using resources (a parallel corpus) and tools (OpinionFinder) built for English. Our experiments also show that, despite our small specialised corpora, the resources are good enough to extract linguistic patterns that give a broad characterization of the language in use for reporting news items and expressing subjectivity in Portuguese. The approach could be favourably augmented with a more thorough cleaning phase, a parsing phase, the inclusion of larger n-grams (n > 3) and manual evaluation. A fully automated daily process to collect a large-scale Portuguese press (including editorials) and blog corpora is currently being developed.

Acknowledgments

We are grateful to Iris Hendrickx from CLUL for making available the POS-tagger used in our experiments.

References

Asher N., Benamara F. and Mathieu Y. Distilling opinion in discourse: A preliminary study. In Coling 2008, posters, pages 710, Manchester, UK.

Banea C., Mihalcea R., Wiebe J. and Hassan S. Multilingual subjectivity analysis using machine translation. In Conference on Empirical Methods in Natural Language Processing (EMNLP 2008), Honolulu, Hawaii, October 2008.

Baroni M. and Bernardini S. Bootcat : Bootstrapping corpora and terms from the web. In Proceedings of LREC 2004, p. 1313-1316.

Esuli A. and Sebastiani F. Determining term subjectivity and term orientation for opinion mining. In EACL 2006.

Généreux M. and Poibeau T. Approche mixte utilisant des outils et ressources pour l'anglais pour l'identification de fragments textuels subjectifs français. In DEFT'09, DÉfi Fouilles de Textes, Atelier de clôture, Paris, June 22nd, 2009.

Hearst M. TextTiling: Segmenting text into multi-paragraph subtopic passages. In Computational Linguistics, pages 33–64, 1997.

Hu M. and Liu B. Mining and summarizing customer reviews. In ACM SIGKDD.

Some NP-patterns in context
• *também_ADV <NP> gostaria_V* "also <NP> would like" *Senhor Presidente ,* ***também*** *<**eu**>* ***gostaria*** *de felicitar a relatora, ...* "Mr President, I would also like to congratulate the rapporteur, ..."
• *senhoras_ADJ e_CJ <NP>* "ladies and <NP>" *Senhor Presidente , Senhora Deputada McCarthy,* ***Senhoras e <Senhores Deputados>****, gostaria de começar ...* "Mr President, Mrs McCarthy, Ladies and gentlemen, let me begin ..."
• *agradecer_INF à_PREP+DA <NP>* "thank <NP>" *Gostaria de* ***agradecer à <minha colega, senhora deputada Echerer>****, pela ...* "I would like to thank my colleague, Mrs Echerer for ..."
Other NP-patterns
• *<NP> desejo_V agradecer_INF* "<NP> wish to thank"
• *aguardo_V com_PREP <NP>* "I look forward to <NP>"
• *associar_INF aos_PREP+DA <NP>* "associate with <NP>"
• *considero_V ,_PNT <NP>* "I consider, <NP>"

Table 5: NP-patterns in parliamentary speeches

Some NP-patterns in context
• *publicada_V por_PREP <NP>* "published by <NP>" ***Publicada por <Joaquim Trincheiras>*** *em 07:30* "Posted by Joaquim Trenches at 07:30"
• *partilhar_INF no_PREP+DA <NP>* "share on <NP>" ***Partilhar no <Twitter>*** *...* "Share on Twitter " ...
• *postado_PPA por_PREP <NP>* "posted by <NP>" ***Postado por <Assuntos de Polícia>*** *às 13:30.* "Posted by Police Affairs at 13:30."
Other NP-patterns
• *<NP> por_PREP lá_ADV* "<NP> over there"
• *<NP> deixe_V <NP>* "<NP> let <NP>"
• *atualmente_ADV ,_PNT <NP>* "currently, <NP>"
• *<NP> é_V linda_ADJ* "<NP> is beautiful"

Table 6: NP-patterns in blogs

Kim S.-M. and Hovy E. Identifying and analyzing judgment opinions. In HLT/NAACL 2006.

Lloyd L., Kechagias D. and Skiena S. Lydia: A system for large-scale news analysis. In SPIRE 2005.

Mihalcea R., Banea C. and Hassan S. Learning multilingual subjective language via cross-lingual projections. In ACL 2007.

Pang B., Lee L. and Vaithyanathan S. Thumbs up? Sentiment classification using machine learning techniques. In EMNLP 2002.

Riloff E. and Wiebe J. Learning extraction patterns for subjective expressions. In Proceedings of EMNLP-03, 8th Conference on Empirical Methods in Natural Language Processing, Sapporo, JP.

Riloff E., Wiebe J. and Wilson T. Learning subjective nouns using extraction pattern bootstrapping. In W. Daelemans & M. Osborne, Eds., Proceedings of CONLL-03, 7th Conference on Natural Language Learning, p. 2532, Edmonton, CA.

Takamura H., Inui T. and Okumura M. Latent variable models for semantic orientations of phrases. In EACL 2006.

Turney P. Thumbs up or thumbs down? Semantic orientation applied to unsupervised classification of reviews. In ACL 2002.

Wilson T., Wiebe J. and Hwa R. Just how mad are you? Finding strong and weak opinion clauses. In Proceedings of AAAI-04, 21st Conference of the American Association for Artificial Intelligence, p. 761-769, San Jose, US.

Yu H. and Hatzivassiloglou V. Towards answering opinion questions: Separating facts from opinions and identifying the polarity of opinion sentences. In EMNLP 2003.

A List of POS-tags

ADJ (adjectives), ADV (adverbs), CJ (conjunctions), CL (clitics), CN (common nouns), DA (definite articles), DEM (demonstratives), INF (infinitives), ITJ (interjections), NP (noun phrases), PNT (punctuation marks) PPA/PPT (past participles), PREP (prepositions), UM ("um" or "uma"), V (other verbs).

A Joint Named Entity Recognition and Entity Linking System

Rosa Stern,[1,2] **Benoît Sagot**[1] **and Frédéric Béchet**[3]
[1]Alpage, INRIA & Univ. Paris Diderot, Sorbonne Paris Cité / F-75013 Paris, France
[2]AFP-Medialab / F-75002 Paris, France
[3]Univ. Aix Marseille, LIF-CNRS / Marseille, France

Abstract

We present a joint system for named entity recognition (NER) and entity linking (EL), allowing for named entities mentions extracted from textual data to be matched to uniquely identifiable entities. Our approach relies on combined NER modules which transfer the disambiguation step to the EL component, where referential knowledge about entities can be used to select a correct entity reading. Hybridation is a main feature of our system, as we have performed experiments combining two types of NER, based respectively on symbolic and statistical techniques. Furthermore, the statistical EL module relies on entity knowledge acquired over a large news corpus using a simple rule-base disambiguation tool. An implementation of our system is described, along with experiments and evaluation results on French news wires. Linking accuracy reaches up to 87%, and the NER F-score up to 83%.

1 Introduction

1.1 Textual and Referential Aspects of Entities

In this work we present a system designed for the extraction of entities from textual data. Named entities (NEs), which include person, location, company or organization names[1] must therefore be detected using named entity recognition (NER) techniques. In addition to this detection based on their surface forms, NEs can be identified by mapping them to the actual entity they denote, in order for these extractions to constitute useful and complete information. However, because of name *variation*, which can be surfacic or encyclopedic, an entity can be denoted by several *mentions* (e.g., *Bruce Springsteen*, *Springsteen*, *the Boss*); conversely, due to name *ambiguity*, a single mention can denote several distinct entities (*Orange* is the name of 22 locations in the world; in French, *M. Obama* can denote both the US president *Barack Obama* (*M.* is an abbreviation of *Monsieur* 'Mr') or his spouse *Michelle Obama*; in this case ambiguity is caused by variation). Even in the case of unambiguous mentions, a clear link should be established between the surface mention and a uniquely identifiable entity, which is achieved by entity linking (EL) techniques.

1.2 Entity Approach and Related Work

In order to obtain referenced entities from raw textual input, we introduce a system based on the joint application of named entity recognition (NER) and entity linking (EL), where the NER output is given to the linking component as a set of possible mentions, preserving a number of ambiguous readings. The linking process must thereafter evaluate which readings are the most probable, based on the most likely entity matches inferred from a similarity measure with the context.

NER has been widely addressed by symbolic, statistical as well as hybrid approaches. Its major part in information extraction (IE) and other NLP applications has been stated and encouraged by several editions of evaluation campaigns such as MUC (Marsh and Perzanowski, 1998), the CoNLL-2003 NER shared task (Tjong Kim Sang and De Meulder, 2003) or ACE (Doddington et al., 2004), where NER systems show near-human performances for the English language. Our system aims at benefitting from both symbolic and statistical NER techniques, which have proven efficient

[1]The set of possible named entities varies from restrictive, as in our case, to wide definitions; it can also include dates, event names, historical periods, etc.

Proceedings of the Workshop on Innovative Hybrid Approaches to the Processing of Textual Data (Hybrid2012), EACL 2012, pages 52–60, Avignon, France, April 23 2012. ©2012 Association for Computational Linguistics

but not necessarily over the same type of data and with different precision/recall tradeoff. NER considers the surface form of entities; some type disambiguation and name normalization can follow the detection to improve the result precision but do not provide referential information, which can be useful in IE applications. EL achieves the association of NER results with uniquely identified entities, by relying on an entity repository, available to the extraction system and defined beforehand in order to serve as a target for mention linking. Knowledge about entities is gathered in a dedicated knowledge base (KB) to evaluate each entity's similarity to a given context. After the task of EL was initiated with Wikipedia-based works on entity disambiguation, in particular by Cucerzan (2007) and Bunescu and Pasca (2006), numerous systems have been developed, encouraged by the TAC 2009 KB population task (McNamee and Dang, 2009). Most often in EL, Wikipedia serves both as an entity repository (the set of articles referring to entities) and as a KB about entities (derived from Wikipedia infoboxes and articles which contain text, metadata such as categories and hyperlinks). Zhang et al. (2010) show how Wikipedia, by providing a large annotated corpus of linked ambiguous entity mentions, pertains efficiently to the EL task. Evaluated EL systems at TAC report a top accuracy rate of 0.80 on English data (McNamee et al., 2010).

Entities that are unknown to the reference database, called *out-of-base* entities, are also considered by EL, when a given mention refers to an entity absent from the available Wikipedia articles. This is addressed by various methods, such as setting a threshold of minimal similarity for an entity selection (Bunescu and Pasca, 2006), or training a separate binary classifier to judge whether the returned top candidate is the actual denotation (Zheng et al., 2010). Our approach of this issue is closely related to the method of Dredze et al. in (2010), where the *out-of-base* entity is considered as another entry to rank.

Our task differs from EL configurations outlined previously, in that its target is entity extraction from raw news wires from the news agency Agence France Presse (AFP), and not only linking relying on gold NER annotations: the input of the linking system is the result of an automatic NER step, which will produce errors of various kinds. In particular, spans erroneously detected as NEs will have to be discarded by our EL system. This case, which we call *not-an-entity*, contitute an additional type of special situations, together with *out-of-base* entities but specific to our setting. This issue, as well as others of our task specificities, will be discussed in this paper. In particular, we use resources partially based on Wikipedia but not limited to it, and we experiment on the building of a domain specific entity KB instead of Wikipedia.

Section 2 presents the resources used throughout our system, namely an entity repository and an entity KB acquired over a large corpus of news wires, used in the final linking step. Section 3 states the principles on which the NER components of our system relies, and introduces the two existing NER modules used in our joint architecture. The EL component and the methodology applied are presented in section 4. Section 5 illustrates this methodology with a number of experiments and evaluation results.

2 Entity Resources

Our system relies on two large-scale resources which are very different in nature:

- the entity database Aleda, automatically extracted from the French Wikipedia and `Geonames`;
- a knowledge base extracted from a large corpus of AFP news wires, with distributional and contextual information about automatically detected entites.

2.1 Aleda

The Aleda entity repository[2] is the result of an extraction process from freely available resources (Sagot and Stern, 2012). We used the French Aleda databased, extracted the French Wikipedia[3] and `Geonames`[4]. In its current development, it provides a generic and wide coverage entity resource accessible *via* a database. Each entity in Aleda is associated with a range of attributes, either referential (e.g., the type of the entity among *Person*, *Location*, *Organization* and *Company*, the population for a location or the gender of a person, etc.)

[2]Aleda is part of the Alexina project and freely available at `https://gforge.inria.fr/projects/alexina/`.

[3]`www.fr.wikipedia.org`

[4]`www.geonames.org`

or formal, like the entity's URI from Wikipedia or Geonames; this enables to uniquely identify each entry as a Web resource.

Moreover, a range of possible *variants* (*mentions* when used in textual content) are associated to entities entries. Aleda's variants include each entity's canonical name, Geonames location labels, Wikipedia redirection and disambiguation pages aliases, as well as dynamically computed variants for person names, based in particular on their first/middle/last name structure. The French Aleda used in this work comprises 870,000 entity references, associated with 1,885,000 variants.

The main informative attributes assigned to each entity in Aleda are listed and illustrated by examples of entries in Tab. 1. The popularity attribute is given by an approximation based on the length of the entity's article or the entity's population, from Wikipedia and Geonames entries respectively. Table 1 also details the structure of Aleda's variants entries, each of them associated with one or several entities in the base.

Unlike most EL systems, Wikipedia is not the entity base we use in the present work; rather, we rely on the autonomous Aleda database. The collect of knowledge about entities and their usage in context will also differ in that our target data are news wires, for which the adaptability of Wikipedia can be questioned.

2.2 Knowledge Acquisition over AFP news

The linking process relies on knowledge about entities, which can be acquired from their usage in context and stored in a dedicated KB. AFP news wires, like Wikipedia articles, have their own structure and formal metadata: while Wikipedia articles each have a title referring to an entity, object or notion, a set of *categories*, hyperlinks, etc., AFP news wires have a headline and are tagged with a *subject* (such as *Politics* or *Culture*) and several *keywords* (such as *cinema*, *inflation* or *G8*), as well as information about the date, time and location of production. Moreover, the distribution of entities over news wires can be expected to be significantly different from Wikipedia, in particular w.r.t. uniformity, since a small set of entities forms the majority of occurrences. Our particular context can thus justify the need for a domain specific KB.

As opposed to Wikipedia where entities are identifiable by hyperlinks, AFP corpora provide no such indications. Wikipedia is in fact a corpus where entity mentions are clearly and uniquely linked, whereas this is what we aim at achieving over AFP's raw textual data. The acquisition of domain specific knowledge about entities from AFP corpora must circumvent this lack of indications. In this perspective we use an implementation of a *naive linker* described in (Stern and Sagot, 2010). For the main part, this system is based on heuristics favoring popular entities in cases of ambiguities. An evaluation of this system showed good accuracy of entity linking (0.90) over the subset of correctly detected entity mentions:[5] on the evaluation data, the resulting NER reached a precision of 0.86 and a recall of 0.80. Therefore we rely on the good accuracy of this system to identify entities in our corpus, bearing in mind that it will however include cases of false detections, while knowledge will not be available on missed entities. It can be observed that by doing so, we aim at performing a form of co-training of a new system, based on supervised machine learning. In particular, we aim at providing a more portable and systematic method for EL than the heuristics-based naive linker which is highly dependent on a particular NER system, SXPipe/NP, described later on in section 3.2.

The knowledge acquisition was conducted over a large corpus of news wires (200,000 news items of the years 2009, 2010 and part of 2011). For each occurrence of an entity identified as such by the naive linker, the following features are collected, updated and stored in the KB at the entity level: (i) entity total occurrences and occurrences with a particular mention; (ii) entity occurrence with a news item topics and keywords, most salient words, date and location; (iii) entity co-occurrence with other entity mentions in the news item. These features are collected for both entities identified by the naive linker as Aleda's entities and mentions recognized by NER pattern based rules; the latter account for out-of-base entities, approximated by a cluster of all mentions whose normalization returns the same string. For instance, if the mentions *John Smith* and *J. Smith* were detected in a document but not linked to an entity in Aleda, it would be assumed

[5]This subset is defined by a strict span and type correct detection, and among the sole entities for which a match in Aleda or outside of it was identified; the evaluation data is presented in section 5.1.

Entities

ID	Type	CanonicalName	Popularity	URI
20013	Loc	Kingdom of Spain	46M	geon:2510769
10063	Per	Michael Jordan	245	wp:Michael_Jordan
20056	Loc	Orange (California)	136K	geon:5379513
10039	Comp	Orange	90	wp:Orange_(entreprise)

Variants

ID	Variant	FirstName	MidName	LastName
20013	Espagne	–	–	–
10063	Jordan	–	–	Jordan
10029	George Walker Bush	George	Walker	Bush
10039	Orange	–	–	–
20056	Orange	–	–	–

Table 1: Structure of Entities Entries and Variants in Aleda

that they co-refer to an entity whose normalized name would be *John Smith*; this *anonymous entity* would therefore be stored and identified *via* this normalized name in the KB, along with its occurrence information.

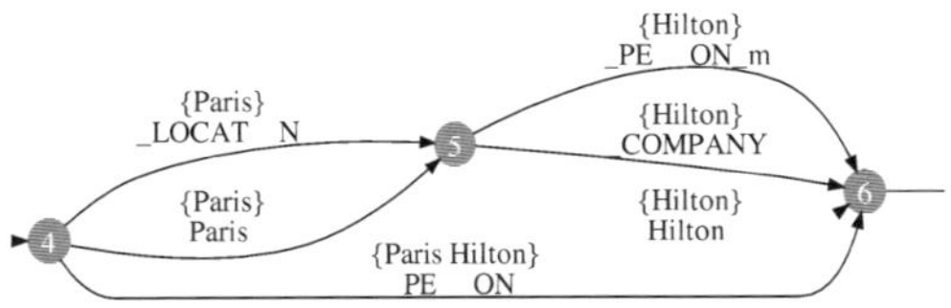

Figure 1: Ambiguous NER output for the segment *Paris Hilton* in SXPipe/NP

3 NER Component

3.1 Principles

One challenging subtask of NER is the correct detection of entity mentions *spans* among several ambiguous readings of a segment. The other usual subtask of NER consists in the labeling or classification of each identified mention with a *type*; in our system, this functionality is used as an indication rather than a final attribute of the denoted entity. The type assigned to each mention will in the end be the one associated with the matching entity. The segment *Paris Hilton* can for instance be split in two consecutive entity mentions, *Paris* and *Hilton*, or be read as a single one. Whether one reading or the other is more likely can be inferred from knowledge about entities possibly denoted by each of these three mentions: depending on the considered document's topic, it can be more probable for this segment to be read as the mention *Paris Hilton*, denoting the celebrity, rather than the sequence of two mentions denoting the capital of France and the hotel company. Based on this consideration, our system relies on the ability of the NER module to preserve multiple readings in its output, in order to postpone to the linker the appropriate decisions for ambiguous cases. Two NER systems fitted with this ability are used in our architecture.

3.2 Symbolic NER: SXPipe/NP

NP is part of the SXPipe surface processing chain (Sagot and Boullier, 2008). It is based on a series of recognition rules and on a large coverage lexicon of possible entity variants, derived from the Aleda entity repository presented in section 2.1. As an SXPipe component, NP formalizes the text input in the form of directed acyclic graphs (DAGs), in which each possible entity mention is represented as a distinct transition, as illustrated in Figure 1. Possible mentions are labeled with *types* among *Person, Location, Organization and Company*, based on the information available about the entity variant in Aleda and on the type of the rule applied for the recognition.

Figure 1 also shows how an alternative transition is added to each mention reading of a segment, in order to account for a possible non-entity reading (i.e., for a *false match* returned by the NER module). When evaluating the adequacy of each reading, the following EL module will in fact consider a special *not-an-entity* candidate as a possible match for each mention, and select it as the most probable if competing entity readings prove insufficiently adequate w.r.t. the considered context.

3.3 Statistical NER: LIANE

The statistical NER system LIANE (Bechet and Charton, 2010) is based on (i) a generative HMM-based process used to predict part-of-speech and semantic labels among *Person, Location, Organization and Product* for each input word[6], and (ii) a discriminative CRF-based process to determine the entity mentions' spans and overall type. The HMM and CRF models are learnt over the ESTER corpus, consisting in several hundreds of hours of transcribed radio broadcast (Galliano et al., 2009), annotated with the BIO format (table 2). The output of LIANE

investiture	NFS	O
aujourd'hui	ADV	B-TIME
à	PREPADE	O
Bamako	LOC	B-LOC
Mali	LOC	B-LOC

Table 2: BIO annotation for LIANE training

consists in an n-best lists of possible entity mentions, along with a confidence score assigned to each result. Therefore it also provides several readings of some text segments, with alternatives of entity mention readings.

As shown in (Bechet and Charton, 2010), the learning model of LIANE makes it particularly robust to difficult conditions such as non capitalization and allows for a good recall rate on various types of data. This is in opposition with manually handcrafted systems such as SXPipe/NP, which can reach high precision rates over the development data but prove less robust otherwise. These considerations, as well as the benefits of a cooperations between these two types of systems are explored in (Béchet et al., 2011).

By coupling LIANE and SXPipe/NP to perform the NER step of our architecture, we expect to benefit from each system's best predictions and improving the precision and recall rates. This is achieved by not enforcing disambiguation of spans and types at the NER level but by transferring this possible source of errors to the linking step, which will rely on entity knowledge rather than mere surface forms to determine the best readings, along with the association of mentions with entity references.

[6]For the purpose of type consistency across both NER modules, the NP type *Company* is merged with *Organization*, and the LIANE mentions typed as *Product* are ignored since they are not yet supported by the overall architecture.

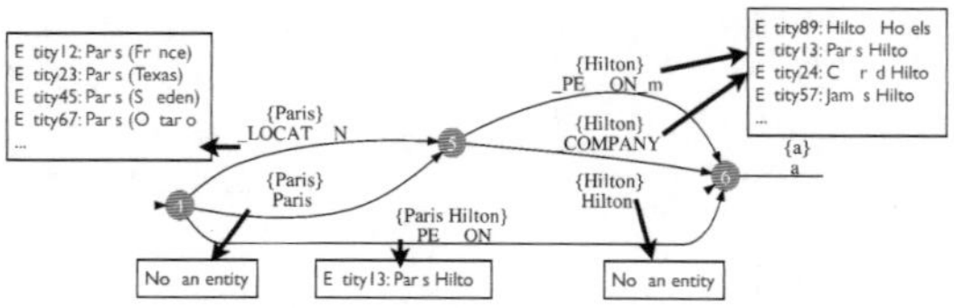

Figure 2: Possible readings of the segment *Paris Hilton* and ordered candidates

4 Linking Component

4.1 Methodology for Best Reading Selection

As previously outlined, the purpose of our joint architecture is to infer best entity readings from contextual similarity between entities and documents rather than at the surface level during NER. The linking component will therefore process ambiguous NER outputs in the following way, illustrated by Fig. 2.

1. For each mention returned by the NER module, we aim at finding the best fitting entity w.r.t. the context of the mention occurrence, i.e., at the document level. This results in a list of candidate entities associated with each mention. This candidates set always includes the *not-an-entity* candidate in order to account for possible false matches returned by the NER modules.

2. The list of candidates is ordered using a pointwise ranking model, based on the maximum entropy classifier `megam`.[7] The best scored candidate is returned as a match for the mention; it can be either an entity present in Aleda, i.e., a *known* entity, or an *anonymous* entity, seen during the KB acquisition but not resolved to a known reference and identified by a normalized name, or the special *not-an-entity* candidate, which discards the given mention as an entity denotation.

3. Each reading is assigned a score depending on the best candidates' scores in the reading.

The key steps of this process are the selection of candidates for each mention, which must reach a sufficient recall in order to ensure the reference resolution, and the building of the feature vector for each mention/entity pair, which will be evaluated by the candidate ranker to return the

[7]http://www.cs.utah.edu/~hal/megam/

most adequate entity as a match for the mention. Throughout this process, the issues usually raised by EL must be considered, in particular the ability for the model to learn cases of *out-of-base* entities, which our system addresses by forming a set of candidates not only from the entity reference base (i.e., Aleda), but also from the dedicated KB where anonymous entities are also collected. Furthermore, unlike the general configuration of EL tasks, such as the TAC KB population task (section 1.2), our input data does not consist in mentions to be linked but in multiple possibilities of mention readings, which adds to our particular case the need to identify false matches among the queries made to the linker module.

4.2 Candidates Selection

For each mention detected in the NER output, the mention string or *variant* is sent as a query to the Aleda database. Entity entries associated with the given variant are returned as candidates. The set of retrieved entities, possibly empty, constitutes the candidate set for the mention. Because the knowledge acquisition included the extraction of unreferenced entities identified by normalized names (section 2.2), we can send the normalization of the mention as an additional query to our KB. If a corresponding anonymous entity is returned, we can create an *anonymous* candidate and add it to the candidate set. *Anonymous* candidates account for the possibility of an *out-of-base* entity denoted by the given mention, with respectively some and no information about the potential entity they might stand for. Finally, the set is augmented with the special *not-an-entity* candidate.

4.3 Features for Candidates Ranking

For each pair formed by the considered mention and each entity from the candidate set, we compute a feature vector which will be used by our model for assessing the probability that it represents a correct mention/entity linking. The vector contains attributes pertaining to the mention, the candidate and the document themselves, and to the relations existing between them.

Entity attributes Entity attributes present in Aleda and the KB are used as features: Aleda provides the entity type, a popularity indication and the number of variants associated with the entity. We retrieve from the KB the entity frequency over the corpus used for knowledge acquisition.

Mention attributes At the mention level, the feature set considers the absence or presence of the mention as a variant in Aleda (for any entity), its occurrence frequency in the document, and whether similar variants, possibly indicating name variation of the same entity, are present in the document (similar variants can have a string equal to the mention's string, longer or shorter than the mention's string, included in the mention's string or including it). In the case of a mention returned by LIANE, the associated confidence score is also included in the feature set.

Entity/mention relation The comparison between the surface form of the entity's canonical name and the mention gives a similarity rate feature. Also considered as features are the relative occurrence frequency of the entity w.r.t. the whole candidate set, the existence of the mention as a variant for the entity in Aleda, the presence of the candidate's type (retrieved from Aleda) in the possible mention types provided by the NER. The KB indicates frequency of its occurrences with the considered mention, which adds another feature.

Document/entity similarity Document metadata (in particular topics and keywords) are inherited by the mention and can thus characterize the entity/mention pair. Equivalent information was collected for entities and stored in the KB, which allows to compute a cosine similarity between the document and the candidate. Moreover, the most salient words of the document are compared to the ones most frequently associated with the entity in the KB. Several atomic and combined features are derived from these similarity measures.

Other features pertain to the NER output configuration, as well as possible false matches:

NER combined information One of the two available NER modules is selected as the base provider for entity mentions. For each mention which is also returned by the second NER module, a feature is instanciated accordingly.

Non-entity features In order to predict cases of *not-an-entity* readings of a mention, we use a generic lexicon of French forms (Sagot, 2010) where we check for the existence of the mention's variant, both with and without capitalization. If the mention's variant is the first word of the sentence, this information is added as a feature.

These features represent attributes of the entity/mention pair which can either have a boolean value (such as variant presence or absence in

Aleda) or range throughout numerical values (e.g., entity frequencies vary from 0 to 201,599). In the latter case, values are discretized. All features in our model are therefore boolean.

4.4 Best Candidate Selection

Given the feature vector instanciated for an (candidate entity, mention) pair, our model assigns it a score. All candidates in the subset are then ranked accordingly and the first candidate is returned as the match for the current mention/entity linking. *Anonymous* and *not-an-entity* candidates, as defined earlier and accounting respectively for potential *out-of-base* entity linking and NER false matches, are included in this ranking process.

4.5 Ranking of Readings

The last step of our task consists in the ranking of multiple readings and has yet to be achieved in order to obtain an output where entity mentions are linked to adequate entities. In the case of a reading consisting in a single transition, i.e., a single mention, the score is equal to the best candidate's score. In case of multiple transitions and mentions, the score is the minimum among the best candidates' scores, which makes a low entity match probability in a mention sequence penalizing for the whole reading. Cases of false matches returned by the NER module can therefore be discarded as such in this step, if an overall non-entity reading of the whole path receives a higher score than the other entity predictions.

5 Experiments and Evaluation

5.1 Training and Evaluation Data

We use a gold corpus of 96 AFP news items intended for both NER and EL purposes: the manual annotation includes mention boundaries as well as an entity identifier for each mention, corresponding to an Aleda entry when present or the normalized name of the entity otherwise. This allows for the model learning to take into account cases of *out-of-base* entities. This corpus contains 1,476 mentions, 437 distinct Aleda's entries and 173 entities absent from Aleda. All news items in this corpus are dated May and June 2009.

In order for the model to learn from cases of *not-an-entity*, the training examples were augmented with false matches from the NER step, associated with this special candidate and the positive class prediction, while other possible candidates were associated with the negative class. Using a 10-fold cross-validation, we used this corpus for both training and evaluation of our joint NER and EL system.

It should be observed that the learning step concerns the ranking of candidates for a given mention and context, while the final purpose of our system is the ranking of multiple readings of sentences, which takes place after the application of our ranking model for mention candidates. Thus our system is evaluated according to its ability to choose the right reading, considering both NER recall and precision and EL accuracy, and not only the latter.

5.2 Task Specificities

As outlined in section 1.2, the input for the standard EL task consists in sets of entity mentions from a number of documents, sent as queries to a linking system. Our current task differs in that we aim at both the extraction and the linking of entities in our target corpus, which consists in unannotated news wires. Therefore, the results of our system are comparable to previous work when considering a setting where the NER output is in fact the gold annotation of our evaluation data, i.e., when all mention queries should be linked to an entity. Without modifying the parameters of our system (i.e., no deactivation of false matches predictions), we obtain an accuracy of 0.76, in comparison with a TAC top accuracy of 0.80 and a median accuracy of 0.70 on English data.[8]

It is important to observe that our data consists only in journalistic content, as opposed to the TAC dataset which included various types of corpora. This difference can lead to unequally difficulty levels w.r.t. the EL task, since NER and EL in journalistic texts, and in particular news wires, tend to be easier than on other types of corpora. This comes among other things from the fact that a small number of popular entities constitute the majority of NE mention occurrences.

In most systems, EL is performed over noisy

[8] As explained previously, these figures, as well as the ones presented later on, cannot be compared with the 0.90 score obtained by the naive linker which we used for the entity KB acquisition. This score is obtained only on mentions identified by the SXPipe/NP system with the correct span and type, whereas our system does not consider the mention type as a contraint for the linking process, and on correct identification of a match in or outside of Aleda.

Setting	NER			EL	Joint NER+EL		
	Precision	Recall	f-measure	Accuracy	Precision	Recall	f-measure
SXPipe/NP	0.849	0.768	0.806	*0.871*	0.669	0.740	0.702
LIANE	0.786	0.891	0.835	*0.820*	0.730	0.645	0.685
SXPipe/NP- NL	0.775	0.726	0.750	*0.875*	0.635	0.678	0.656
LIANE- NL	0.782	0.886	0.831	*0.818*	0.725	0.640	0.680
SXPipe/NP & 2	0.812	0.747	0.778	*0.869*	0.649	0.705	0.676
LIANE & SXPipe/NP	0.803	0.776	0.789	*0.859*	0.667	0.689	0.678

Table 3: Joint NER and EL results. *Each EL accuracy covers a different set of correctly detected mentions*

NER output and participates to the final decisions about NEs extractions. Therefore the ability of our system to correctly detect entity mentions in news content is estimated by computing its precision, recall and f-measure.[9] The EL accuracy, i.e., the rate of correctly linked mentions, is measured over the subset of mentions whose reading was adequately selected by the final ranking. The evaluation of our system has been conducted over the corpus described previously with settings presented in the next section.

5.3 Settings and results

We used each of the two available NER modules as a provider for entity mentions, either on its own or together with the second system, used as an indicator. For each of these settings, we tried a modified setting in which the prediction of the naive linker (NL) used to build the entity KB (section 2.2) was added as a feature to each mention/candidate pair (settings SXPipe/NP-NL and LIANE-NL). These experiments' results are reported in Table 3 and are given in terms of:

- NER precision, recall and f-measure;
- EL accuracy over correctly recognized entities; therefore, the different figures in column EL Accuracy are not directly comparable to one another, as they are not obtained over the same set of mentions;
- joint NER+EL precision, recall and f-measure; the precision/recall is computed as the product of the NER precision/recall by the EL accuracy.

[9]Only mention boundaries are considered for NER evaluation, while other settings require correct type identification for validating a fully correct detection. In our case, NER is not a final step, and entity typing is derived from the entity linking result.

As expected, SXPipe/NP performs better as far as NER precision is concerned, and LIANE performs better as far as NER recall is concerned. However, the way we implemented hybridation at the NER level does not seem to bring improvements. Using the output of the naive linker as a feature leads to similar or slightly lower NER precision and recall. Finally, it is difficult to draw clear-cut comparative conclusions at this stage concerning the joint NER +EL task.

6 Conclusion and Future Work

We have described and evaluated various settings for a joint NER and EL system which relies on the NER systems SXPipe/NP and LIANE for the NER step. The EL step relies on a hybrid model, i.e., a statistical model trained on a manually annotated corpus. It uses features extracted from a large corpus automatically annotated and where entity disambiguations and matches were computed using a basic heuristic tool. The results given in the previous section show that the joint model allows for good NER results over French data. The impact of the hybridation of the two NER modules over the EL task should be further evaluated. In particular, we should investigate the situations where an mention was incorrectly detected (e.g., the span is not fully correct) although the EL module linked it with the correct entity. Moreover, a detailed evaluation of out-of-base linkings vs. linking in Aleda remains to be performed.

In the future, we aim at exploring various additional features in the EL system, in particular more combinations of the current features. The adaptation of our learning model to NER combinations should also be improved. Finally, a larger set of training data should be considered. This shall become possible with the recent manual annotation of a half-million word French journalistic corpus.

References

F. Bechet and E Charton. 2010. Unsupervised knowledge acquisition for extracting named entities from speech. In *2010 IEEE International Conference on Acoustics, Speech and Signal Processing*.

R. Bunescu and M. Pasca. 2006. Using encyclopedic knowledge for named entity disambiguation. In *Proceedings of EACL*, volume 6, pages 9–16.

F. Béchet, B. Sagot, and R. Stern. 2011. Coopération de méthodes statistiques et symboliques pour l'adaptation non-supervisée d'un système d'étiquetage en entités nommées. In *Actes de la Conférence TALN 2011*, Montpellier, France.

S. Cucerzan. 2007. Large-scale named entity disambiguation based on wikipedia data. In *Proceedings of EMNLP-CoNLL*, volume 2007, pages 708–716.

G. Doddington, A. Mitchell, M. Przybocki, L. Ramshaw, S. Strassel, and R. Weischedel. 2004. The automatic content extraction (ace) program-tasks, data, and evaluation. In *Proceedings of LREC - Volume 4*, pages 837–840.

M. Dredze, P. McNamee, D. Rao, A. Gerber, and T. Finin. 2010. Entity disambiguation for knowledge base population. In *Proceedings of the 23rd International Conference on Computational Linguistics*, pages 277–285.

S. Galliano, G. Gravier, and L. Chaubard. 2009. The Ester 2 Evaluation Campaign for the Rich Transcription of French Radio Broadcasts. In *Interspeech 2009*.

E. Marsh and D. Perzanowski. 1998. Muc-7 evaluation of ie technology: Overview of results. In *Proceedings of the Seventh Message Understanding Conference (MUC-7) - Volume 20*.

P. McNamee and H.T. Dang. 2009. Overview of the tac 2009 knowledge base population track. In *Text Analysis Conference (TAC)*.

P. McNamee, H.T. Dang, H. Simpson, P. Schone, and S.M. Strassel. 2010. An evaluation of technologies for knowledge base population. *Proc. LREC2010*.

B. Sagot and P. Boullier. 2008. SXPipe 2 : architecture pour le traitement présyntaxique de corpus bruts. *Traitement Automatique des Langues (T.A.L.)*, 49(2):155–188.

B. Sagot and R. Stern. 2012. Aleda, a free large-scale entity database for French. In *Proceedings of LREC*. To appear.

B. Sagot. 2010. The L*efff*, a freely available and large-coverage morphological and syntactic lexicon for French. In *Proceedings of the 7th Language Resources and Evaluation Conference (LREC'10)*, Vallette, Malta.

R. Stern and B. Sagot. 2010. Détection et résolution d'entités nommées dans des dépêches d'agence. In *Actes de la Conférence TALN 2010*, Montréal, Canada.

E. F. Tjong Kim Sang and F. De Meulder. 2003. Introduction to the conll-2003 shared task: Language-independent named entity recognition. In *Proceedings of CoNLL*, pages 142–147, Edmonton, Canada.

W. Zhang, J. Su, C.L. Tan, and W.T. Wang. 2010. Entity linking leveraging: automatically generated annotation. In *Proceedings of the 23rd International Conference on Computational Linguistics*, pages 1290–1298.

Z. Zheng, F. Li, M. Huang, and X. Zhu. 2010. Learning to link entities with knowledge base. In *Human Language Technologies: The 2010 Annual Conference of the North American Chapter of the Association for Computational Linguistics*, pages 483–491.

Collaborative Annotation of Dialogue Acts: Application of a New ISO Standard to the Switchboard Corpus

Alex C. Fang[1], Harry Bunt[2], Jing Cao[3], and Xiaoyue Liu[4]

[1,3,4]The Dialogue Systems Group, Department of Chinese, Translation and Linguistics
City University of Hong Kong, Hong Kong, SAR
[2]Tilburg Centre for Cognition and Communication
Tilburg University, The Netherlands
[3]School of Foreign Languages, Zhongnan University of Economics and Law, China
E-mail: {[1]acfang, [3]cjing3, [4]xyliu0}@cityu.edu.hk, [2]harry.bunt@uvt.nl

Abstract

This article reports some initial results from the collaborative work on converting SWBD-DAMSL annotation scheme used in the Switchboard Dialogue Act Corpus to ISO DA annotation framework, as part of our on-going research on the interoperability of standardized linguistic annotations. A qualitative assessment of the conversion between the two annotation schemes was performed to verify the applicability of the new ISO standard using authentic transcribed speech. The results show that in addition to a major part of the SWBD-DAMSL tag set that can be converted to the ISO DA scheme automatically, some problematic SWBD-DAMSL tags still need to be handled manually. We shall report the evaluation of such an application based on the preliminary results from automatic mapping via machine learning techniques. The paper will also describe a user-friendly graphical interface that was designed for manual manipulation. The paper concludes with discussions and suggestions for future work.

1. Introduction

This article describes the collaborative work on applying the newly proposed ISO standard for dialogue act annotation to the Switchboard Dialogue Act (SWBD-DA) Corpus, as part of our on-going effort to promote interoperability of standardized linguistic annotations with the ultimate goal of developing shared and open language resources.

Dialogue acts (DA) play a key role in the interpretation of the communicative behaviour of dialogue participants and offer valuable insight into the design of human-machine dialogue systems (Bunt et al., 2010). More recently, the emerging ISO DIS 24617-2 (2010) standard for dialogue act annotation defines dialogue acts as the 'communicative activity of a participant in dialogue interpreted as having a certain communicative function and semantic content, and possibly also having certain functional dependence relations, rhetorical relations and feedback dependence relations' (p. 3). The semantic content specifies the objects, relations, events, etc. that the dialogue act is about; the communicative function can be viewed as a specification of the way an addressee uses the semantic content to update his or her information state when he or she understands the corresponding stretch of dialogue.

Continuing efforts have been made to identify and classify the dialogue acts expressed in dialogue utterances taking into account the empirically proven multifunctionality of utterances, i.e., the fact that utterances often express more than one dialogue act (see Bunt, 2009 and 2011). In other words, an utterance in dialogue typically serves several functions. See Example (1) taken from the SWBD-DA Corpus (`sw_0097_3798.utt`).

(1) A: *Well, Michael, what do you think about, uh, funding for AIDS research? Do you…*
B: *Well, uh, uh, that's something I've thought a lot about.*

With the first utterance, Speaker A performs two dialogue acts: he (a) assigns the next turn to the participant Michael, and (b) formulates an open question. Speaker B, in his response, (a) accepts the turn, (b) stalls for time, and (c) answers the question by making a statement.

Our concern in this paper is to explore the applicability of the new ISO Standard to the existing Switchboard corpus with joint efforts of automatic and manual mapping. In the rest of the paper, we shall first describe the Switchboard Dialogue Act (SWBD-DA) Corpus and its annotation scheme (i.e. SWBD-DAMSL). We shall then describe the new ISO Standard and explain our mapping of SWBD-DAMSL to the ISO DIS 24617-2 DA tag set. In addition, machine learning techniques are employed for automatic DA classification on the basis of lexical features to evaluate the application of the new ISO DA scheme using authentic transcribed speech. We shall then introduce the user interface designed for manual mapping and explain the annotation guidelines. Finally, the paper will conclude with discussions and suggestions for future work.

2. Corpus Resource

This study uses the Switchboard Dialog Act (SWBD-DA) Corpus as the corpus resource, which is available online from the Linguistic Data Consortium [1]. The corpus

[1] http://www.ldc.upenn.edu/

Proceedings of the Workshop on Innovative Hybrid Approaches to the Processing of Textual Data (Hybrid2012), EACL 2012, pages 61–68,
Avignon, France, April 23 2012. ©2012 Association for Computational Linguistics

contains 1,155 5-minute conversations[2], orthographically transcribed in about 1.5 million word tokens. It should be noted that the minimal unit of utterances for DA annotation in the SWBD Corpus is the so called "slash unit" (Meteer and Taylor, 1995), defined as "maximally a sentence but can be smaller unit" (p. 16), and "slash-units below the sentence level correspond to those parts of the narrative which are not sentential but which the annotator interprets as complete" (p. 16). See Table 1 for the basic statistics of the SWBD-DA Corpus.

Folder	*# of Conversations*	*# of Slash-units*	*# of Tokens*
sw00	99	14,277	103,045
sw01	100	17,430	119,864
sw02	100	20,032	132,889
sw03	100	18,514	127,050
sw04	100	19,592	132,553
sw05	100	20,056	131,783
sw06	100	19,696	135,588
sw07	100	20,345	136,630
sw08	100	19,970	134,802
sw09	100	20,159	133,676
sw10	100	22,230	143,205
sw11	16	3,213	20,493
sw12	11	2,773	18,164
sw13	29	5,319	37,337
Total	1,155	223,606	1,507,079

Table 1: Basic Statistics of the SWBD-DA Corpus

Altogether, the corpus comprises 223,606 slash-units and each is annotated for its communicative function according to a set of dialogue acts specified in the SWBD-DAMSL scheme (Jurafsky et al., 1997) and assigned a DA tag. See Example (2) taken from `sw_0002_4330.utt`, where `qy` is the DA tag for yes/no questions.

(2) qy A.1 utt1: *{D Well, } {F uh, } does the company you work for test for drugs? /*

A total of 303 different DA tags are identified throughout the corpus, which is different from the total number of 220 tags mentioned in Jurafsky et al. (1997: 3). To ensure enough instances for the different DA tags, we also conflated the DA tags together with their secondary carat-dimensions, and yet we did not use the seven special groupings by Jurafsky et al. (1997) as we kept them as separate DA types (see Section 4 for further explanations). In the end, the 303 tags were clustered into 60 different individual communicative functions. See Table 2 for the basic statistics of the 60 DA clusters.

According to Table 2, we observe that the 60 DA clusters range from 780,570 word tokens for the top-ranking `statement-non-opinion` to only 4 word tokens for `you're-welcome`. In Table 2, the *Token %* column lists the relative importance of DA types measured as the proportion of the word tokens in the SWBD-DA corpus as whole. It can be observed that, as yet another example to illustrate the uneven use of DA types, `statement-opinion` accounts for 21.04% of the total number of word tokens in the corpus.

60 DAs	*Tokens*	*Token %*	*Cum %*
Statement-non-opinion	780,570	51.79	51.79
Statement-opinion	317,021	21.04	72.83
Segment-(multi-utterance)	135,632	9.00	81.83
Acknowledge-(backchannel)	40,696	2.70	84.53
Abandoned	35,214	2.34	86.87
Yes-no-question	34,817	2.31	89.18
Accept	20,670	1.37	90.55
Statement-expanding-y/n-answer	14,479	0.96	91.51
Wh-question	14,207	0.94	92.45
Appreciation	13,957	0.93	93.38
Declarative-yes-no-question	10,062	0.67	94.05
Conventional-closing	9,017	0.60	94.65
Quoted-material	7,591	0.50	95.15
Summarize/reformulate	6,750	0.45	95.60
Action-directive	5,860	0.39	95.99
Rhetorical-questions	5,759	0.38	96.37
Hedge	5,636	0.37	96.74
Open-question	4,884	0.32	97.06
Affirmative-non-yes-answers	4,199	0.28	97.34
Uninterpretable	4,138	0.27	97.61
Yes-answers	3,512	0.23	97.84
Completion	2,906	0.19	98.03
Hold-before-answer/agreement	2,860	0.19	98.22
Or-question	2,589	0.17	98.39
Backchannel-in-question-form	2,384	0.16	98.55
Acknowledge-answer	2,038	0.14	98.69
Negative-non-no-answers	1,828	0.12	98.81
Other-answers	1,727	0.11	98.92
No-answers	1,632	0.11	99.03
Or-clause	1,623	0.11	99.14
Other	1,578	0.10	99.24
Dispreferred-answers	1,531	0.10	99.34
Repeat-phrase	1,410	0.09	99.43
Reject	891	0.06	99.49
Transcription-errors:-slash-units	873	0.06	99.55
Declarative-wh-question	855	0.06	99.61
Signal-non-understanding	770	0.05	99.66
Self-talk	605	0.04	99.70
Offer	522	0.03	99.73
Conventional-opening	521	0.03	99.76
3rd-party-talk	458	0.03	99.79
Accept-part	399	0.03	99.82
Downplayer	341	0.02	99.84
Apology	316	0.02	99.86
Exclamation	274	0.02	99.88
Commit	267	0.02	99.90
Thanking	213	0.01	99.91
Double-quote	183	0.01	99.92
Reject-part	164	0.01	99.93
Tag-question	143	0.01	99.94
Maybe	140	0.01	99.95
Sympathy	80	0.01	99.96
Explicit-performative	78	0.01	99.97
Open-option	76	0.01	99.98
Other-forward-function	42	0.00	99.98
Correct-misspeaking	37	0.00	99.98
No-plus-expansion	26	0.00	99.98
Yes-plus-expansion	22	0.00	99.98
You're-welcome	4	0.00	99.98
Double-labels	2	0.00	100.00
Total	1,507,079	100.00	100.00

Table 2: Basic Statistics of the 60 DAs

If the cumulative proportion (*Cum%*) is considered, we

[2] Past studies (e.g. Stolcke et al., 2000; Jurafsky et al., 1997; Jurafsky et al., 1998a; Jurafsky et al., 1998b) have been focused on only 1115 conversations in the SWBD-DA Corpus as the training set. As there is no clear description which 40 conversations have been used as the testing set or for future use, we use all the 1155 conversations.

see that the top 10 DA types alone account for 93.38% of the whole corpus, suggesting again the uneven occurrence of DA types in the corpus and hence the disproportional use of communication functions in conversational discourse.

It is particularly worth mentioning that `segment-(multi-utterance)` is not really a DA type indicating communicative function and yet it is the third most frequent DA tag in SWBD-DAMSL. As a matter of fact, the SWBD-DAMSL annotation scheme contains quite a number of such non-communicative DA tags, such as `abandoned`, and `quoted-material`.

3. ISO DIS 24617-2 (2010)

A basic premise of the emerging ISO standard for dialogue act annotation, i.e., ISO DIS 24617-2 (2010), is that utterances in dialogue are often multifunctional; hence the standard supports so-called 'multidimensional tagging', i.e., the tagging of utterances with multiple DA tags. It does so in two ways: First of all, it defines nine dimensions to which a dialogue act can belong:

- Task
- Auto-Feedback
- Allo-Feedback
- Turn Management
- Time Management
- Discourse Structuring
- Social Obligations Management
- Own Communication Management
- Partner Communication Management

Secondly, it takes a so-called 'functional segment' as the unit in dialogue to be tagged with DA information, defined as a 'minimal stretch of communicative behavior that has one or more communicative functions' (Bunt et al., 2010). A functional segment is allowed to be discontinuous, and to overlap with or be included in another functional segment. A functional segment may be tagged with at most one DA tag for each dimension.

Another important feature is that an ISO DA tag consists not only of a communicative function encoding, but also of a dimension indication, with optional attributes for representing certainty, conditionality, sentiment, and links to other dialogue units expressing semantic, rhetorical and feedback relations.

Thus, two broad differences can be observed between SWBD-DAMSL and ISO. The first concerns the treatment of the basic unit of analysis. While in SWBD-DAMSL this is the slash-unit, ISO DIS 24617-2 (2010) employs the functional segment, which serves well to emphasise the multifunctionality of dialogue utterances. An important difference here is that the ISO scheme identifies multiple DAs per segment and assigns multiple tags via the stand-off annotation mechanism.

The second difference is that each slash-unit (or utterance) in the SWBD-DA Corpus is annotated with one SWBD-DAMSL label, while each DA tag in the ISO scheme is additionally associated with a dimension tag and, when appropriate, with function qualifiers and relations to other dialogue units. See the following example taken from the Schiphol Corpus.

`sw00-0052-0010-B007-01.txt`	the original utterance
`sw00-0052-0010-B007-01-S.da`	SWBD-DAMSL tag

In the .txt file, there is the original utterance:

{C And,} {F uh,} <inhaling> we've done <sigh> lots to it. /

While the *-S.da file only contains the DA label: sd^t. Still another one or more files (depending on the number of dimensions) will be added to this set after converting the SWBD-DAMSL to the ISO tag sets. Take Example (4) for instance. Two more files will be created, namely,

`sw00-0052-0010-B007-01-ISO-0.da`	ISO DA tag
`sw00-0052-0010-B007-01-ISO-1.da`	ISO DA tag

The *-ISO-0.da file will contain in this case:

```
communicativeFunction = "inform"
dimension = "task"
```
[3]

and the *-ISO-1.da file will contain[4]:

```
communicativeFunction = "stalling"
dimension = "timeManagement"
```

[3] The same function `Inform` have been observed to occur in different dimensions. See ISO DIS 24617-2 (2010) for detailed description.

[4] See Section 4.2 for more explanation of the multi-layer annotations in ISO standard.

4.2 Assessment of the Conversion

When mapping SWBD-DAMSL tags to functional ISO tags, it is achieved in terms of semantic contents rather than the surface labels. To be more exact, four situations were identified in the matching process.

The first is what is named as "exact matches". It is worth mentioning that since we are not matching the labels in the two annotation schemes, even for the exact matches, the naming in SWBD-DAMSL is not always the same as that in the ISO scheme, but they have the same or very similar meaning. Table 3 lists the exact matches.

SWBD-DAMSL	*ISO*
Open-question	Question
Dispreferred answers	Disconfirm
Offer	Offer
Commit	Promise
Open-option	Suggest
Hold before answer/ agreement	Stalling
Completion	Completion
Correct-misspeaking	CorrectMisspeaking
Apology	Apology
Downplayer	AcceptApology
Thanking	Thanking
You're-welcome	AcceptThanking
Signal-non-understanding	AutoNegative
Conventional-closing	InitialGoodbye

Table 3: Exact Matches

It can also be noted that in the previous study on the 42 DA types in SWBD-DAMSL, `open-option` (`oo`), `offer` (`co`), `commit` (`cc`) are treated as one DA type. In the current study, they are treated as individual DA types, which makes more sense especially when mapping to the ISO DA tag sets since each of them corresponds to a different ISO tag, `suggest`, `offer`, and `promise` respectively. The same is also true for the `you're-welcome` (`fw`) and `correct-misspeaking` (`bc`), which are combined together in SWBD-DAMSL and correspond to different ISO DA label.

SWBD-DAMSL	*ISO*
Wh-question; Declarative wh-question	SetQuestion
Or-question; Or-clause	ChoiceQuestion
Yes-no-question; Backchannel in question form	PropositionalQuestion
Tag-question; Declarative Yes-no-question	CheckQuestion
Statement-non-opinion; Statement-opinion; Rhetorical-question; Statement expanding y/n answer; Hedge	Inform
Maybe; Yes-answer; Affirmative non-yes answers; Yes plus expansion; No-answer; Negative non-no answers; No plus expansion	Answer
Acknowledge (backchannel); Acknowledge answer; Appreciation; Sympathy; Summarize/reformulate; Repeat-phrase	AutoPositive
Accept-part; Reject-part	Correction

Table 4: Many-to-one Matches

The second situation is where more than one SWBD-DAMSL tags can be matched to the one ISO DA type, as defined as many-to-one matches. Table 4 shows the many-to-one matches. Such matches occur because semantically identical functions are sometimes given different names in SWBD-DAMSL in order to distinguish differences in lexical or syntactic form. For example, an `affirmative non-yes answer` is defined as an affirmative answer that does not contain the word `yes` or one of its variants (like `yeah` and `yep`).

The most complex issue is with the one-to-many matches, where a DA function in SWBD-DAMSL is too general and corresponds to a set of different DAs in the ISO scheme. Consider the DA type of `accept` in SWBD-DAMSL. It is a broad function applicable to a range of different situations. For instance, accept annotated as `aa` in Example (5) taken from `sw_0005_4646.utt` corresponds to `Agreement` in ISO DIS 24617-2 (2010).

(5) sd A.25 utt1: *{C Or } people send you there as a last resort. /*
aa B.26 utt1: *Right, /*

However, `accept` (`aa`) in Example (6) taken from `sw_0098_3830.utt` actually corresponds to `acceptOffer` in ISO/DIS 24617-2 (2010).

(6) co B.26 utt1: *I can tell you my last job or --/*
aa A.27 utt1: *Okay, /*

As a matter of fact, `accept` in SWBD-DAMSL may correspond to several different DAs in the ISO tag set such as:

- Agreement
- AcceptRequest (addressRequest)
- AccpetSuggestion (addressSuggestion)
- AcceptOffer (addressOffer)
- etc.

Other cases include `reject`, `action-directive` and `other answers`.

Finally, the remaining tags are unique to SWBD-DAMSL, including

- quoted material
- uninterpretable
- abandoned
- self-talk
- 3rd-party-talk
- double labels
- explicit-performative
- exclamation
- other-forward-function

It is not difficult to notice that 6 out of the 9 DA types mainly concern the marking up of other phenomena than dialogue acts. The last three unique DA types only account for a marginal portion of the whole set, about 0.03% all together (See Table 2).

In addition, multi-layer annotations of ISO can be added to the original markup of SWBD (Meteer and Taylor 1995), especially in cases such as Stalling and Self-Correction. See Example (7) taken from `sw_0052_4378.utt`.

(7) sd A.12 utt2 : *[I, + {F uh, } two months ago I] went to Massachusetts -- /*

According to Meteer and Taylor (1995), the *{F ...}* is used to mark up "filler" in utterances, which corresponds to Stalling in ISO DIS 24617-2 (2010). In addition, the markup of *[... + ...]* indicates the repairs (Meteer and Taylor, 1995), which suits well the definition of Self-correction in the ISO standard. As a result, the utterance in Example (7) is thus annotated in three dimensions:

```
communicativeFunction = "inform"
dimension = "task"

communicativeFunction = "stalling"
dimension = "timeManagement"

communicativeFunction = "self-correction"
dimension = "ownCommManagement"
```

4.3 Mapping Principles

Given the four setting of the matching, there major principles were made:

1) Cases in both "exact matches" and "many-to-one matches" can be automatically mapped to ISO tags by programming.

2) Tags that are unique to SWBD-DAMSL would not be considered at the current stage due to the absence of ISO counterparts and their marginal proportion.

3) Cases in "one-to-many matches" are more complex and call for manual mapping, which will be further discussed in Section 6.

4) Different DA dimensions will be also automatically added accordingly to each utterance in the format of stand-off annotation.

5. Application Verification

To evaluate the applicability of mapping SWBD-DAMSL tag set to the new ISO standard (ISO DIS 24617-2, 2010), machine learning techniques are employed, based on the preliminary results from the automatic mapping, to see how well the SWBD-ISO DA tags can be automatically identified and classified based on lexical features. The result is also compared with that obtained from the Top-15 SWBD-DAMSL tags. It will be particularly interesting to find out whether the emerging ISO DA annotation standard will produce better automatic prediction accuracy. In this paper, we evaluate the performance of automatic DA classification in the two DA annotation schemes by employing the unigrams as the feature set.

Two classification tasks were then identified according to the two DA annotation schemes. Task 1 is to automatically classify the DA types in the SWBD-DAMSL. Based on the observations mentioned above, it was decided to use the top 15 DA types to investigate the distribution of word types in order to ascertain the lexical characteristics of DAs. Furthermore, since `segment-(multi-utterance)`, `abandoned`, and `quoted-material` do not relate to dialogue acts per se, these three were replaced with `rhetorical-questions`, `open-question` and `affirmative-non-yes-answers`. We thus derive Table 6 below, showing that the revised list of top 15 DA types account for 85.13% of the SWBD corpus. The DA types are arranged according to *Token%* in descending order.

Top-15 SWBD-DAMSL DAs	*Tokens*	*Token %*	*Cum %*
Statement-non-opinion	780,570	51.79	51.79
Statement-opinion	317,021	21.04	72.83
Acknowledge-(backchannel)	40,696	2.70	75.53
Yes-no-question	34,817	2.31	77.84
Accept	20,670	1.37	79.21
Statement-expanding-y/n-answer	14,479	0.96	80.17
Wh-question	14,207	0.94	81.11
Appreciation	13,957	0.93	82.04
Declarative-yes-no-question	10,062	0.67	82.71
Conventional-closing	9,017	0.60	83.31
Summarize/reformulate	6,750	0.45	83.76
Action-directive	5,860	0.39	84.15
Rhetorical-questions	5,759	0.38	84.53
Open-question	4,884	0.32	84.85
Affirmative-non-yes-answers	4,199	0.28	85.13
Total	1,282,948	85.13	

Table 6: Top-15 SWBD-DAMSL DA types

Next, accordingly, task 2 is to classify the top 15 ISO DAs based on the results from the automatic mapping. It should be pointed out that only one layer of annotation in the ISO DA tags is considered in order to make the result comparable to that from SWBD-DAMSL, and the dimension of `task` is the priority when it comes to multi-layer annotations.

Top-15 SWBD-ISO DAs	*Tokens*	*Token %*	*Cum %*
Inform	1,117,829	74.17	74.17
AutoPositive	64,851	4.30	78.47
PropositionalQuestion	37,201	2.47	80.94
SetQuestion	15,062	1.00	81.94
Answer	11,171	0.74	82.68
CheckQuestion	10,062	0.67	83.35
InitialGoodbye	9,017	0.60	83.95
Question	4,884	0.32	84.27
ChoiceQuestion	4,212	0.28	84.55
Completion	2,906	0.19	84.75
Stalling	2,860	0.19	84.94
Disconfirm	1,531	0.10	85.04
AutoNegative	770	0.05	85.09
Offer	522	0.03	85.12
AcceptApology	341	0.02	85.15
Total	1,283,219	85.15	

Table 7: Top-15 SWBD-ISO DA types

The Naïve Bayes Multinomial classifier was employed, which is available from Waikato Environment for Knowledge Analysis, known as Weka (Hall et al., 2009). 10-fold cross validation was performed and the results evaluated in terms of precision, recall and F-score (*F1*).

Table 8 presents the results for classification task 1. The SWBD-DAMSL DAs are arranged according to F-score in descending order.

Top 15 SWBD-DAMSL DAs	*Precision*	*Recall*	*F1*
Acknowledge-(backchannel)	0.821	0.968	0.888
Statement-non-opinion	0.732	0.862	0.792
Appreciation	0.859	0.541	0.664
Statement-opinion	0.538	0.584	0.560
Conventional-closing	0.980	0.384	0.552
Accept	0.717	0.246	0.367
Yes-no-question	0.644	0.204	0.309
Wh-question	0.760	0.189	0.303
Open-question	0.932	0.084	0.154
Action-directive	1.000	0.007	0.013
Statement-expanding-y/n-answer	0.017	0	0.001
Declarative-yes-no-question	0	0	0
Summarize/reformulate	0	0	0
Rhetorical-questions	0	0	0
Affirmative-non-yes-answers	0	0	0
Weighted Average	0.704	0.725	0.692

Table 8: Results from Task 1

As can be noted, the weighted average F-score is 69.2%. To be more specific, `acknowledge-(backchannel)` achieves the best F-score of 0.888, followed by `statement-non-opinion` with an F-score of 0.792. Surprisingly, the `action-directive` has the highest precision of 100%, but has the second lowest recall of over 0.7%. It can also be noted that the last four types of DAs cannot be classified with the F-score of 0%.

Top 15 SWBD-ISO DAs	*Precision*	*Recall*	*F1*
Inform	0.879	0.987	0.930
Answer	0.782	0.767	0.775
AutoPositive	0.711	0.507	0.592
InitialGoodbye	0.972	0.351	0.516
PropositionalQuestion	0.521	0.143	0.224
SetQuestion	0.668	0.120	0.203
Question	0.854	0.051	0.097
AutoNegative	0.889	0.026	0.051
ChoiceQuestion	0.286	0.008	0.015
Stalling	0.400	0.003	0.007
CheckQuestion	0.042	0.001	0.001
AcceptApology	0	0	0
Completion	0	0	0
Disconfirm	0	0	0
Offer	0	0	0
Weighted Average	0.832	0.865	0.831

Table 9: Results from Task 2

Table 9 presents the results for classification task 2. The DAs are arranged according to F-score in descending order. As can be noted, the weighted average F-score is 83.1%, over 10% higher than task 1. To be more specific, `Inform` achieves the best F-score of 0.93, followed by `Answer` with an F-score of 0.775. The DA `InitialGoodbye` has the highest precision, of about 97%, whereas `Inform` has the highest recall of over 98%. Similar to the results obtained in Task 1, the last four types of DAs in Task 2 also cannot be classified with the F-score of 0%.

Meanwhile, as mentioned earlier, when the data size for each DA type is taken into consideration, Task 2 may be more challenging than Task 1 in that 6 out of the 15 SWBD-ISO DA types has a total number of word tokens fewer than 4,000 whereas all the 15 SWBD-DAMSL DA types has a total number of over 4,000. Therefore, the much higher average F-score suggests that the application of ISO standard DA scheme could lead to better classification performance, suggesting that the ISO DA standard represents a better option for automatic DA classification.

To sum up, with a comparable version of the SWBD-DA Corpus, results from the automatic DA classification tasks show that the ISO DA annotation scheme produces better automatic prediction accuracy, which encourages the completion of the manual mapping.

6. Manual Mapping

6.1 Analysis of Problematic DA Types

As mentioned earlier, there are mainly four problematic SWBD-DAMSL tags, namely, `accept (aa)`, `reject (ar)`, `action-directive (ad)` and `other answers (no)`. They are problematic in that they carry a broad function applicable to a range of different situations according to the new ISO standard, as evidenced in the case of `accept` discussed in Section 4.2. Consequently, to map the problematic SWBD-DAMSL tags to the ISO tags calls for manual manipulation.

A close look into those four types shows that the mapping could be further divided into two setting. Again, take `accept (aa)` for example. In the first setting, a sub-division of `accept (aa)` can also be automatically matched according to the previous utterance by the other speaker in the adjacent pair. See Example (8) taken from `sw_0001_4325.utt`.

(8) sv A.49 utt3: *take a long time to find the right place /*
x A.49 utt4: *<laughter>.*
aa B.50 utt1: *Yeah, /*

Here `accept (aa)` corresponds to `Agreement` because of the DA type in `A.49 utt3` but not the immediate previous DA as in `A.49 utt4`. With this principle, the particular sub-groups for automatic mapping were identified for `accept (aa)`. See Table 10.

SWBD-DAMSL		*ISO*
Previous DA	*Current DA*	
Statement-non-opinion; Statement-opinion; Hedge Rhetorical-question; Statement expanding y/n answer,	accept	Agreement
Offer		AcceptOffer
Open-option		AcceptRequest
Thanking		AcceptThanking
Apology		AcceptApology

Table 10: Sub-groups of `accept` for Auto Mapping

The remaining cases, in the second setting, call for manual annotation. For instance, when the previous DA type is also a problematic one, annotators need to decide the corresponding ISO DA tag for the previous SWBD-DAMSL one before converting the `accept` (`aa`). See Example (9) taken from `sw_0423_3325.utt`.

(9) ad B.128 utt2: *{C so } we'll just wait. /*
   aa A.129 utt1: *Okay, /*

Here, `action-directive` (`ad`) is first decided as a suggestion, and therefore `accept` (`aa`) turns out to actually correspond to `acceptSuggestion` (`addressSuggestion`) in ISO/DIS 24617-2 (2010).

6.2 Design of a User Interface

Given the analysis of those four DA tags, a user-friendly interface was then designed to assist annotators to maximize the inter-annotator agreement. See Figure 1.

Figure 1: User Interface

Figure 1 shows the screenshot when the targeted SWBD-DAMSL type is `accept` (`aa`). As can be noted above, the basic functional bars have been designed, including:

- *Input*: the path of the input
- *Automatch*: to filter out the sub-groups that can be automatically matched
- *DA Tag*: the targeted problematic DAs, namely,
  - `aa` (`accept`)
  - `ar` (`reject`)
  - `ad` (`action-directive`) and
  - `no` (`other answers`)
- *Previous*: to go back to the previous instance of the targeted DA type
- *Next*: to move on to the next instance of the targeted DA type
- *Current*: the extraction of the adjacent turns
- Previous5T: the extraction of the previous five turns when necessary
- *PreviousAll*: the extraction of all the previous turns when necessary
- *MatchInfo*: Bars for mapping information with five options:
  - ➢ Four pre-defined ISO DA types
  - ➢ Other: a user-defined mapping with a two-fold function: for user defined ISO DA type and for extra pre-defined ISO DA types (since the pre-defined DA types differ for the four targeted SWBD-DAMSL types).
- *Output*: the path of the output
- *Result*: export the results to the chosen path

With this computer-aided interface, three annotators are invited to carry out the manual mapping. They are all postgraduates with linguistic background. After a month of training on the understanding of the two annotation schemes (in process), they will work on the SWBD-DAMSL DA instances from 115 randomly chosen files, and map them into ISO DA tags independently. The kappa value will be calculated to measure the inter-annotator agreement.

7. Conclusion

In this paper, we reported our efforts in applying the ISO-standardized dialogue act annotations to the Switchboard Dialogue Act (SWBD-DA) Corpus. In particular, the SWBD-DAMSL tags employed in the SWBD-DA Corpus were analyzed and mapped onto the ISO DA tag set (ISO DIS 24617-2 2010) according to their communicative functions and semantic contents. Such a conversion is a collaborative process involving both automatic mapping and manual manipulation. With the results from the automatic mapping, machine learning techniques were employed to evaluate the applicability of the new ISO standard for dialogue act annotation in practice. With the encouraging results from the evaluation, the manual mapping was carried out. A user-friendly interface was designed to assist annotators. The immediate future work would be finish the manual mapping and thus to produce a comparable version of the SWBD-DA Corpus was produced so that the two annotation schemes (i.e. SWBD-DAMSL vs. SWBD-ISO) can be effectively compared on the basis of empirical data. Furthermore, with the newly built resource, i.e., SWBD-ISO, we plan to examine the effect of grammatical and syntactic cues on the performance of DA classification, with a specific view on whether dialogue acts exhibit differentiating preferences for grammatical and syntactic constructions that have been overlooked before.

8. Acknowledgements

Research described in this article was supported in part by grants received from City University of Hong Kong (Project Nos 7008002, 9610188, 7008062 and 6454005). It was also partially supported by the General Research Fund of the Research Grants Council of Hong Kong (Project No 142711).

9. References

Bunt, H. (2009). Multifunctionality and multidimensional dialogue semantics. In *Proceedings of DiaHolmia Workshop on the Semantics and Pragmatics of*

Dialogue, Stockholm, 2009.

Bunt, H. (2011). Multifunctionality in dialogue and its interpretation. *Computer, Speech and Language,* 25 (2), pp. 225--245.

Bunt, H., Alexandersson, J., Carletta, J., Choe, J.-W., Fang, A.C., Hasida, K., Lee, K., Petukhova, V., Popescu-Belis, A., Romary, L., Soria, C. and Traum, D. (2010). Towards an ISO standard for dialogue act annotation. In *Proceedings of the Seventh International Conference on Language Resources and Evaluation*. Valletta, MALTA, 17-23 May 2010.

Hall, M., Frank, E., Holmes, G., Pfahringer, B., Reutemann, P. and Witten, I. H. (2009). The WEKA data mining software: an update. *SIGKDD Explorations*, 11 (1), pp. 10--18.

ISO DIS 24617-2. (2010). *Language resource management – Semantic annotation framework (SemAF), Part 2: Dialogue acts*. ISO, Geneva, January 2010.

Jurafsky, D., Shriberg, E. and Biasca, D. (1997). Switchboard SWBD-DAMSL shallow-discourse-function annotation coders manual, Draft 13. University of Colorado, Boulder Institute of Cognitive Science Technical Report 97-02.

Jurafsky, D., Bates, R., Coccaro, N., Martin, R., Meteer, M., Ries, K., Shriberg, E., Stolcke, A., Taylor, P. and Ess-Dykema, C. V. (1998a). Switchbaod Discourse Language Modeling Project and Report. *Research Note 30, Center for Language and Speech Processing*, Johns Hopkins University, Baltimore, MD, January.

Jurafsky, D., Shriberg, E., Fox B. and Curl, T. (1998b). Lexical, prosodic, and syntactic cues for dialog acts. *ACL/COLING-98 Workshop on Discourse Relations and Discourse Markers*.

Meeter, M., Taylor, A. (1995). Dysfluency annotation stylebook for the Switchboard Corpus. Available at ftp://ftp.cis.upenn.edu/pub/treebank/swbd/doc/DFL-book.ps.

Stolcke, A., Ries, K., Coccaro, N., Shriberg, E., Bates, R., Jurfsky, D., Taylor, P., Martin, R., Ess-Dykema, C.V. and Meteer, M. (2000). Dialogue Act Modeling for Automatic Tagging and Recognition of Conversational Speech. *Computational Linguistics*, 26 (3), pp. 339--373.

Coupling Knowledge-Based and Data-Driven Systems for Named Entity Recognition

Damien Nouvel **Jean-Yves Antoine** **Nathalie Friburger** **Arnaud Soulet**
Université François Rabelais Tours, Laboratoire d'Informatique
3, place Jean Jaures, 41000 Blois, France
{damien.nouvel, jean-yves.antoine, nathalie.friburger, arnaud.soulet}@univ-tours.fr

Abstract

Within Information Extraction tasks, Named Entity Recognition has received much attention over latest decades. From symbolic / knowledge-based to data-driven / machine-learning systems, many approaches have been experimented. Our work may be viewed as an attempt to bridge the gap from the data-driven perspective back to the knowledge-based one. We use a knowledge-based system, based on manually implemented transducers, that reaches satisfactory performances. It has the undisputable advantage of being modular. However, such a hand-crafted system requires substantial efforts to cope with dedicated tasks. In this context, we implemented a pattern extractor that extracts symbolic knowledge, using hierarchical sequential pattern mining over annotated corpora. To assess the accuracy of mined patterns, we designed a module that recognizes Named Entities in texts by determining their most probable boundaries. Instead of considering Named Entity Recognition as a labeling task, it relies on complex context-aware features provided by lower-level systems and considers the tagging task as a markovian process. Using thos systems, coupling knowledge-based system with extracted patterns is straightforward and leads to a competitive hybrid NE-tagger. We report experiments using this system and compare it to other hybridization strategies along with a baseline CRF model.

1 Introduction

Named Entity Recognition (NER) is an information extraction (IE) task that aims at extracting and categorizing specific entities (proper names or dedicated linguistic units as time expressions, amounts, etc.) in texts. These texts can be produced in diverse conditions. In particular, they may correspond to either electronic written documents (Marsh & Perzanowski, 1998) or more recently speech transcripts provided by a human expert or an automatic speech recognition (ASR) system (Galliano et al., 2009). The recognized entities may later be used by higher-level tasks for different purposes such as Information Retrieval or Open-Domain Question-Answering (Voorhees & Harman, 2000).

While NER is often considered as quite a simple task, there is still room for improvement when it is confronted to difficult contexts. For instance, NER systems may have to cope with noisy data such as word sequences containing speech recognition errors in ASR. In addition, NER is no more circumscribed to proper names, but may also involve common nouns (e.g., *"the judge"*) or complex multi-word expressions (e.g. *"the Computer Science department of the New York University"*). These complementary needs for robust and detailed processing explain that knowledge-based and data-driven approaches remain equally competitive on NER tasks as shown by numerous evaluation campaigns. For instance, the French-speaking Ester2 evaluation campaign on radio broadcasts (Galliano et al., 2009) has shown that knowledge-based approaches outperformed data-driven ones on manual transcriptions while a system based on Conditional Random Fields (CRFs, participant LIA) is ranked first on noisy ASR transcripts. This is why the development of hybrid systems has been investigated by the NER community.

Proceedings of the Workshop on Innovative Hybrid Approaches to the Processing of Textual Data (Hybrid2012), EACL 2012, pages 69–77,
Avignon, France, April 23 2012.

In this paper, we present a strategy of hybridization benefiting from features produced by a knowledge-based system (CasEN) and a data-driven pattern extractor (mineXtract). CasEN has been manually implemented based on *finite-state transducers*. Such a hand-crafted system requires substantial efforts to be adapted to dedicated tasks. We developed mineXtract, a text-mining system that automatically extracts *informative rules*, based on hierarchical sequential pattern mining. Both implement processings that are context-aware and use lexicons. Finally, to recognize NEs, we propose mStruct, a light multi-purpose automatic annotator, parameterized using logistic regression over available features. It takes into account features provided by lower-level systems and annotation scheme constraints to output a valid annotation maximizing likelihood. Our experiments show that the resulting hybrid system outperforms standalone systems and reaches performances comparable to a baseline hybrid CRF system. We consider this as a step forward towards a tighter integration of knowledge-based and data-driven approaches for NER.

The paper is organized as follows. Section 2 describes the context of this work and reviews related work. Section 3 describes CasEN, the knowledge-based NE-tagger. Section 4 details the process of extracting patterns from annotated data as informative rules. We then introduce the automatic annotator mStruct in Section 5. Section 6 describes how to gather features from systems and present diverse hybridization strategies. Corpora, metrics used and evaluation results are reported in Section 7. We conclude in Section 8.

2 Context and Related Work

2.1 Ester2 Evaluation Campaign

This paper focuses on NER in the context of the Ester2 evaluation campaign (Galliano et al., 2009). This campaign assesses system's performance for IE tasks over ASR outputs and manual transcriptions of radio broadcast news (see details in Section 7). The annotation guidelines specified 7 kinds of entities to be detected and categorized: persons ('pers'), organizations ('org'), locations ('loc'), amounts ('amount'), time expressions ('time'), functions ('func'), products ('prod'). Technically, the annotation scheme is quite simple: only one annotation per entity, almost no nesting (except for persons collocated with their function: both should be embedded in an encompassing 'pers' NE).

$\mathcal{D}$	
Sent.	Tokens and NEs
s_1	<pers> Isaac Newton </pers> was admitted in <time> June 1661 </time> to <org> Cambridge </org>.
s_2	<time> In 1696 </time>, he moved to <loc> London </loc> as <func> warden of the Royal Mint </func>.
s_3	He was buried in <loc> Westminster Abbey </loc>.

Table 1: Sentences from an annotated corpus

We illustrate the annotation scheme using a running example. Table 1 presents the expected annotation in the context of Ester2 from *"Isaac Newton was admitted in June 1661 to Cambridge. In 1696, he moved to London as warden of the Royal Mint. He was buried in Westminster Abbey."*. This example illustrates frequent problems for NER task. Determining the extent of a NE may be difficult. For instance, NER should consider here either "Westminster" (city) or "Westminster Abbey" (church, building). Categorizing NEs is confronted to words ambiguities, for instance "Cambridge" may be considered as a city ('loc') or a university ('org'). In addition, oral transcripts may contain disfluencies, repetitions, hesitations, speech recognition errors: overall difficulty is significantly increased. For these reasons, NER over such noisy data is a challenging task.

2.2 State of the Art

Knowledge-based approaches Most of the symbolic systems rely on shallow parsing techniques, applying regular expressions or linguistic patterns over Part-Of-Speech (POS), in addition to proper name lists checking. Some of them handle a deep syntactic analysis which has proven its ability to reach outstanding levels of performances (Brun & Hagège, 2004; Brun & Hagège, 2009; van Shooten et al., 2009).

Data-driven approaches A large diversity of data-driven approaches have been proposed during the last decade for NER. Generative models such as Hidden Markov Models or stochastic finite state transducers (Miller et al., 1998; Favre et al., 2005) benefit from their ability to take into account the sequential nature of language. On the other hand, discriminative classifiers such as

Support Vector Machines (SVMs) are very effective when a large variety of features (Isozaki & Kazawa, 2002) is used, but lack the ability to take a global decision over an entire sentence. Context Random Fields (CRFs) (Lafferty et al., 2001) have enabled NER to benefit from the advantages of both generative and discriminative approaches (McCallum & Li, 2003; Zidouni et al., 2010; Béchet & Charton, 2010). Besides, the robustness of data-driven / machine-learning approaches explains that the latter are more appropriate on noisy data such as ASR transcripts.

Hybrid systems Considering the complementary behaviors of knowledge-based and data-driven systems for NER, projects have been conducted to investigate how to conciliate both approaches. Work has been done to automatically induce symbolic knowledge (Hingston, 2002; Kushmerick et al., 1997) that may be used as NE taggers. But in most cases, hybridization for NER relies a much simpler principle: outputs of knowledge-based systems are considered as features by a machine learning algorithm. For instance, maximum entropy may be used when a high diversity of knowledge sources are to be taken into account (Borthwick et al., 1998). CRFs also have demonstrated their ability to merge symbolic and statistic processes in a machine learning framework (Zidouni et al., 2010).

We propose an approach to combine knowledge-based and data-driven approaches in a modular way. Our first concern is to implement a module that automatically extracts knowledge that should be interoperable with the existing system's transducers. This is done by focusing, in annotated corpora, more on '*markers*' (tags) that are to be inserted between tokens (e.g. `<pers>`, `</pers>`, `<org>`, `</org>`, etc.), than on 'labels' assigned to each token, as transducer do. By doing so, we expect to establish a better grounding for hybriding manually implemented and automatically extracted patterns. Afterwards, another module is responsible of annotating NEs by using those context-aware patterns and standard machine-learning techniques.

3 CasEN: a knowledge-based system

The knowledge-based system is based on CasSys (Friburger & Maurel, 2004), a finite-state cascade system that implements processings on texts at diverse levels (morphology, lexicon, chunking). It may be used for various IE tasks, or simply to transform or prepare a text for further processings. The principle of this finite-state processor is to first consider islands of certainty (Abney, 2011), so as to give priority to most confident rules. Each transducer describes local patterns corresponding to NEs or interesting linguistic units available to subsequent transducers within the cascade.

Casen is the set of NE recognition transducers. It was initially designed to process written texts, taking into account diverse linguistic clues, proper noun lists (covering a broad range of first names, countries, cities, etc.) and lexical evidences (expressions that may trigger recognition of a named entity).

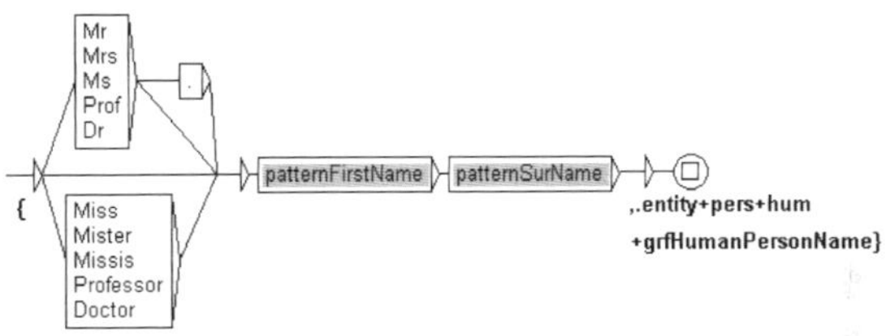

Figure 1: A transducer recognizing person names

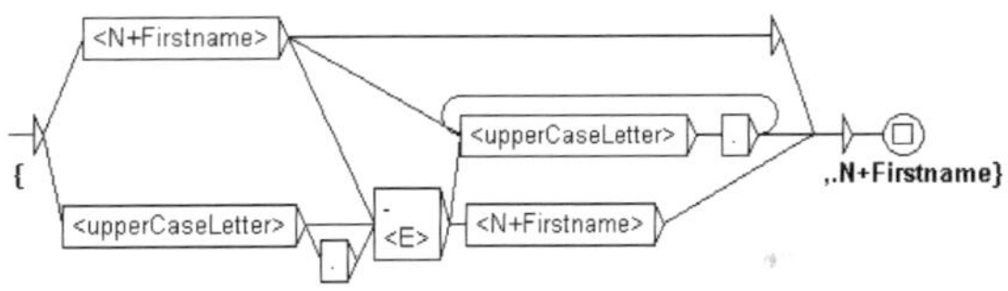

Figure 2: Transducer 'patternFirstName'

As an illustration, Figure 1 presents a very simple transducer tagging person names made of an optional title, a first name and a surname. The boxes contain the transitions of the transducer as items to be matched for recognizing a person's name. Grayed boxes contain inclusions of other transducers (e.g. box 'patternFirstName' in Figure 1 is to be replaced by the transducer depicted in Figure 2). Other boxes can contain lists of words or diverse tags (e.g. `<N+firstname>` for a word tagged as first name by lexicon). The outputs of transducers are displayed below boxes (e.g. '{' and '*,.entity+pers+hum*}' in Figure 1).

For instance, that transducer matches the word sequence '*Isaac Newton*' and outputs: '{{*Isaac ,.firstname*} {*Newton ,.surname*} *,.entity+pers+hum*}'. By applying multiple transducers on a text sequence, CasEN can provide several (possibly nested) annotations on a NE and its components. This has the advantage of providing detailed information about CasEN internal processings for NER.

Finally, the processing of examples in Table 1 leads to annotations such as:

- { { *June ,.month*} { *1661 ,.year*} *,entity+time+date+rel*}
- { *Westminster ,.entity+loc+city*} { *Abbey ,buildingName*} *,.entity+loc+buildingCityName* }

In standalone mode, post-processing steps convert outputs into Ester2 annotation scheme (e.g. <pers> *Isaac Newton* </pers>).

Experiments conducted on newspaper documents for recognizing persons, organizations and locations on an extract of the Le Monde corpus have shown that CasEN reaches 93.2% of recall and 91.1% of f-score (Friburger, 2002). During the Ester2 evaluation campaign, CasEN ("LI Tours" participant in (Galliano et al., 2009)) obtained 33.7% SER (Slot Error Rate, see section about metrics description) and a f-score of 75%. This may be considered as satisfying when one knows the lack of adaptation of Casen to specificities of oral transcribed texts.

4 mineXtract: Pattern Mining Method

4.1 Enriching an Annotated Corpus

We investigate the use of data mining techniques in order to supplement our knowledge-based system. To this end, we use an annotated corpus to mine patterns related to NEs. Sentences are considered as sequences of *items* (this precludes extraction of patterns accross sentences). An item is either a word from natural language (e.g. "admitted", "Newton") or a tag delimiting NE categories (e.g., <pers>, </pers> or <loc>). The annotated corpus $\mathcal{D}$ is a multiset of sequences.

Preprocessing steps enrich the corpus by (1) using lexical resources (lists of toponyms, anthroponyms and so on) and (2) lemmatizing and applying a POS tagger. This results in a *multi-dimensional corpus* where a token may gradually be generalized to its lemma, POS or lexical category. Figure 3 illustrates this process on the words sequence 'moved to <loc> London </loc>'.

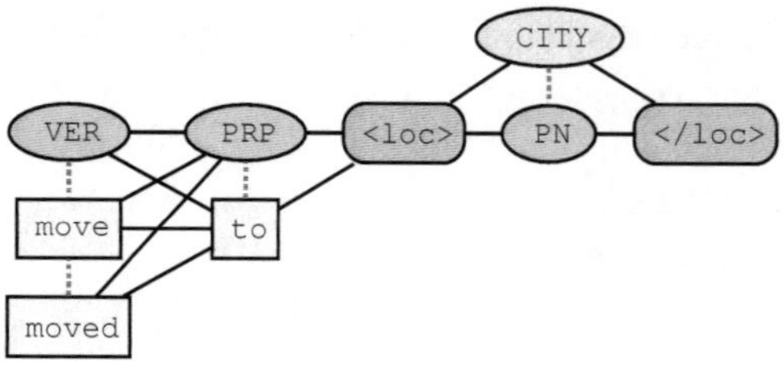

Figure 3: Multi-dimensional representation of the phrase 'moved to <loc> London </loc>'

The first preprocessing step consists in considering lexical resources to assign tokens to lexical categories (e.g., CITY for "London") whenever possible. Note that those resources contain multi-word expressions. Figure 4 provides a short extract limited to tokens of Table 1) of lexical ressources (totalizing 201,057 entries). This assignment should be ambiguous. For instance, processing "Westminster Abbey" would lead to categorizing 'Westminster' as CITY and the whole as INST.

Afterwards, a POS tagger based on TreeTagger (Schmid, 1994) distinguishes common nouns (NN) from proper names (PN). Besides, token is deleted (only PN category is kept) to avoid extraction of patterns that would be specific to a given proper name (on Figure 3, "London" is removed). Figure 5 shows how POS, tokens and lemmas are organized as a hierarchy.

Category	Tokens
ANTHRO	Newton, Royal ...
CITY	Cambridge, London, Westminster ...
INST	Cambridge, Royal Mint, Westminster Abbey ...
METRIC	Newton ...
...	...

Figure 4: Lexical Ressources

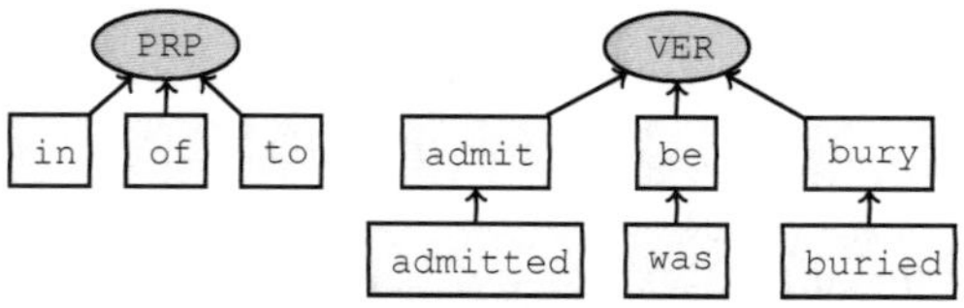

Figure 5: Items Hierarchy

4.2 Discovering Informative Rules

We mine this large enriched annotated corpus to find generalized patterns correlated to NE markers. It consists in exhaustively enumerating *all* the contiguous patterns mixing words, POS and categories. This provides a very broad spectrum of patterns, diversely accurate to recognize NEs. As an illustration, if you consider the words sequence "moved to <loc> London </loc>" in Figure 3 leads to examining patterns as:

- 'VER PRP <loc> PN </loc>'
- 'VER to <loc> PN </loc>'
- 'moved PRP <loc> CITY </loc>'

The most relevant patterns will be filtered by considering two thresholds which are usual in data mining: support and confidence (Agrawal & Srikant, 1994). The *support* of a pattern P is its number of occurrences in $\mathcal{D}$, denoted by $supp(P, \mathcal{D})$. The greater the support of P, the more general the pattern P. As we are only interested in patterns sufficiently correlated to markers, a *transduction rule* R is defined as a pattern containing at least one marker. To estimate empirically how much R is accurate to detect markers, we calculate its *confidence*. A dedicated function $suppNoMark(R, \mathcal{D})$ returns the support of R when markers are omitted both in the rule and in the data. The confidence of R is:

$$conf(R, \mathcal{D}) = \frac{supp(R, \mathcal{D})}{suppNoMark(R, \mathcal{D})}$$

For instance, consider the rule $R =$ 'VER PRP <loc>' in Table 1. Its support is 2 (sentences s_2 and s_3). But its support without considering markers is 3, since sentence s_1 matches the rule when markers are not taken in consideration. The confidence of R is 2/3.

In practice, the whole collection of transduction rules exceeding minimal support and confidence thresholds remains too large, especially when searching for less frequent patterns. Consequently, we filter-out "redundant rules": those for which a more specific rule exists with same support (both cover same examples in corpus). For instance, the rules $R_1 =$ 'VER VER in <loc>' and $R_2 =$ 'VER in <loc>' are more general and have same support than $R_3 =$ ' was VER in <loc>': we only retain the latter.

The system mineXtract implements those processing using a level-wise algorithm (Mannila & Toivonen, 1997).

5 mStruct: Stochastic Model for NER

We have established a common ground for the systems to interact with a higher level model. Our assumption is that lower level systems examine the input (sentences) and provide valuable clues playing a key role in the recognition of NEs. In that context, the annotator is implemented as an abstracted view of sentences. Decisions will only have to be taken whenever one of the lower-level systems provides information. Formally, beginning or ending a NE at a given position i may be viewed as the affectation of a random variable $P(Mi = m_{j_i})$ where the value of m_{j_i} is one of the markers ($\{\emptyset$, <pers>, </pers>, <loc>, <org>, ...$\}$).

For a given sentence, we use binary features triggered by lower-level systems at a given position (see section 6.1) for predicting what marker would be the most probable at that very position. This may be viewed as an instance of a classification problem (more precisely multilabel classification since several markers may appear at a single position, but we won't enter into that level of detail due to lack of space). Empirical experiments with diverse machine learning algorithms using Scikit-learn (Pedregosa et al., 2011) lead us to consider logistic regression as the most effective on the considered task.

Considering those probabilities, it is now possible to estimate the likelihood of a given annotation over a sentence. Here, markers are assumed to be independent. With this approximation, the likehood of an annotation is computed by a simple product:

$$P(M_1 = m_{j_1}, M_2 = m_{j_2}, \ldots, M_n = m_{j_n}) \approx \prod_{i=1\ldots n} P(M_i = m_{j_i})$$

As an illustration, Figure 6 details the computation of an annotation given the probability of every markers, using the Ester2 annotation scheme. For clarity purposes, only sufficiently probable markers (including $\emptyset$) are displayed at each position. A possible <func> is discarded (crossed out), being less probable than a previous one. An annotation solution <org>...</org> is evaluated, but is less likely ($0.3*0.4*0.9*0.4*0.4*0.1 = 0.0017$) than *warden of the Royal Mint* as a function ($0.6*0.4*0.9*0.3*0.5*0.4 = 0.0129$)

which will be retained (and is the expected annotation).

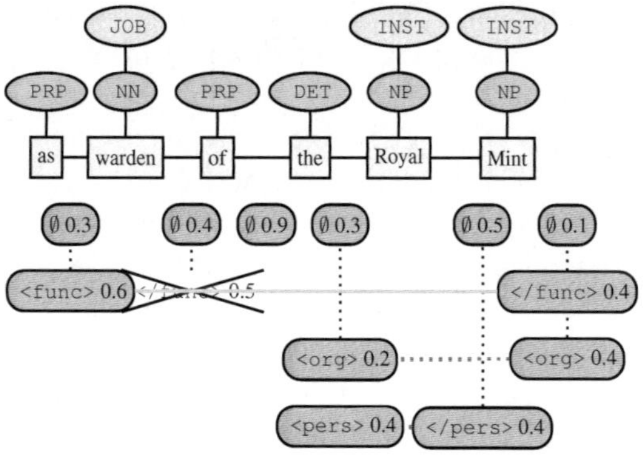

Figure 6: Stochastic Annotation of a Sequence

Estimating markers probabilities allows the model to combine evidences from separate knowledge sources when recognizing starting or ending boundaries. For instance, CasEN may recongize intermediary structures but not the whole entity (e.g. when unexpected words appear inside it) while extracted rules may propose markers that are not necessarily paired. The separate detection of markers enables the system to recognize named entities without modeling all their tokens. This may be useful when NER has to face noisy data or speech disfluences.

Finally, it is not necessary to compute likelihoods over all possible combination of markers, since the annotation scheme is much constrained. As the sentence is processed, some annotation solutions are to be discarded. It is straightforward to see that this problem may be resolved using dynamic programming, as did Borthwick et al. (1998). Depending on the annotation scheme, constraints are provided to the annotator which outputs an annotation for a given sentence that is valid and that maximizes likelihood. Our system mStruct (micro-Structure) implements this (potentially multi-purpose) automatic annotation process as a separate module.

6 Hybriding systems

6.1 Gathering Clues from Systems

Figure 7 describes the diverse resources and algorithms that are plugged together. The knowledge-based system uses lists that recognize lexical patterns useful for NER (e.g. proper names, but also automata to detect time expressions, functions, etc.). Those resources are exported and available to the data mining software as lexical resources (see section 4) and (as binary features) to the baseline CRF model.

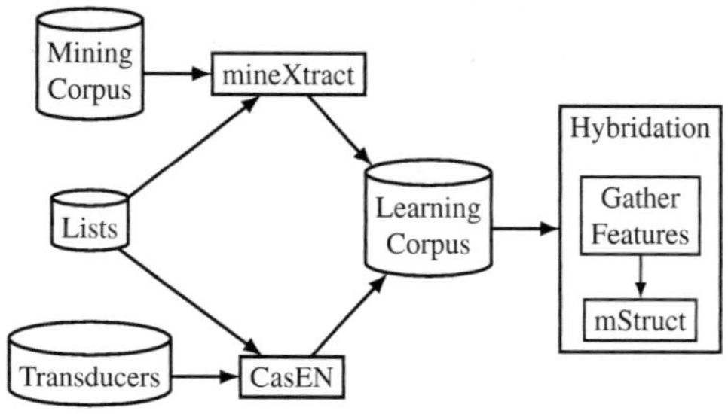

Figure 7: Systems Modules (Hybrid data flow)

Each system processes input text and provides features used by the Stochastic Model mStruct. It is quite simple to take in consideration mined informative rules: each time a rule i proposes its jth marker, a Boolean feature M_{ij} is activated. What is provided by CasEN is more sophisticated, since each transducer is able to indicate more detailed information (see section 3), as multiple features separated by '+' (e.g. 'entity+pers+hum'). We want to benefit as much as possible from this richness: whenever a CasEN tag begins or ends, we activate a boolean feature for each mentioned feature plus one for each prefixes of features (e.g. 'entity', 'pers', 'hum' but also 'entity.pers' and 'entity.pers.hum').

6.2 Coupling Strategies

We report results for the following hybridizations and CRF-based system using Wapiti (Lavergne et al., 2010).

- CasEN: knowledge-based system standalone
- mXS: mineXtract extracts, mStruct annotates
- Hybrid: gather features from CasEN and mineXtract, mStruct annotates
- Hybrid-sel: as Hybrid, but features are selected
- CasEN-mXS-mine: as mXS, but text is preprocessed by CasEN (adding a higher generalization level above lexical lists)
- mXS-CasEN-vote: as mXS, plus a postprocessing step as a majority vote based on mXS and CasEN outputs
- CRF: baseline CRF, using BIO and common features (unigrams: lemma and lexical lists, bigrams: previous, current and next POS)

Corpus	Tokens	Sentences	NEs
Ester2-Train	1 269 138	44 211	80 227
Ester2-Dev	73 375	2 491	5 326
Ester2-Test-corr	39 704	1 300	2 798
Ester2-Test-held	47 446	1 683	3 067

Table 2: Characteristics of Corpora

- CasEN-CRF: same as CRF, but the output of CasEN is added as a single feature (concatenation of CasEN features)

7 Experimentations

7.1 Corpora and Metrics

For experimentations, we use the corpus that has been made available after the Ester2 evaluation campaign. Table 2 gives statistics on diverse subparts of this corpus. Unfortunately, many inconsistencies where noted for manual annotation, especially for 'Ester2-Train' part that won't be used for training.

There were fewer irregularities in other parts of the corpus. Although, manual corrections were done on half of the Test corpus (Nouvel et al., 2010) (Ester2-Test-corr in Table 2), to obtain a gold standard that we will use to evaluate our approach. The remaining part of the Test corpus (Ester2-Test-held in Table 2) merged with the Dev part constitute our training set (Ester2-Dev in Table 2), used as well to extract rules with mineXtract, to estimate stochastic model probabilities of mStruct and to learn CRF models.

We evaluate systems using following metrics:

- *detect*: rate of detection of the presence of any marker (binary decision) at any position
- *desamb*: f-score of markers when comparing N actual markers to N most probable markers, computed over positions where k markers are expected (N=k) or the most probable marker is not ∅ (N=1)
- *precision, recall, f-score*: evaluation of NER by categories by examining labels assigned to tokens (similarly to Ester2 results)
- *SER* (Slot Error Rate): weighted error rate of NER (official Ester2 performance metric, to be lowered), where errors are discounted per entity as Galliano et al. (2009) (deletion and insertion errors are weighted 1 whereas type and boundary errors, 0.5)

System	support	confidence	detect	disamb	f-score	SER
CasEN	∅	∅	∅	∅	78	30.8
mXS	5	0.1	97	73	76	28.4
	5	0.5	96	71	74	31.2
	15	0.1	96	72	73	30.1
Hybrid	5	0.1	97	78	79	26.3
	5	0.5	97	77	77	28.3
	15	0.1	97	78	76	28.2
	inf	inf	96	71	70	42.0

Table 3: Performance of Systems

7.2 Comparing Hybridation with Systems

First, we separately evaluate systems. While CasEN is not to be parameterized, mineXtract has to be given minimum frequency and support thresholds. Table 3 shows results for each system separately and for the combination of systems. Results obtained by mXS show that even less confident rules are improving performances. Generally speaking, the *detect* score is very high, but this mainly due to the fact that the ∅ case is very frequent. The *disamb* score is much correlated to the SER. This reflects the fact that the challenge is for mStruct to determine the correct markers to insert.

Comparing systems shows that the hybridization strategy is competitive. The knowledge-based system yields to satisfying results. mXS obtains slightly better SER and the hybrid system outperforms both in most cases. Considering SER, the only exception to this is the 'inf' line (mStruct uses only CasEN features) where performances are degraded. We note that mStruct obtains better results as more rules are extracted.

7.3 Assessing Hybridation Strategies

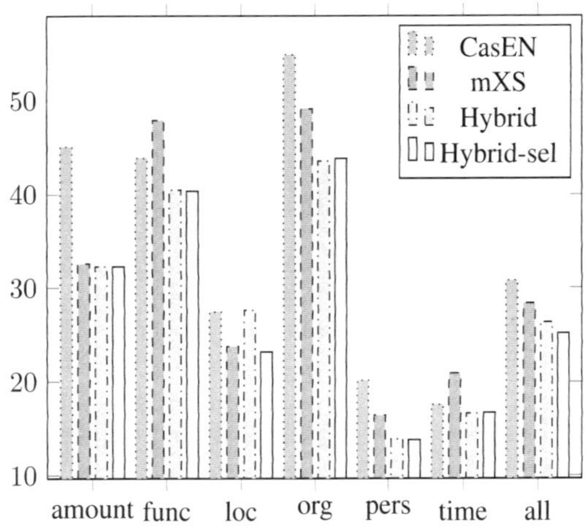

Figure 8: SER of Systems by NE types

System	precision	recall	f-score	SER
Hybrid-sel	83.1	74.8	79	25.2
CasEN-mXS-mine	76.8	75.5	76	29.4
mXS-CasEN-vote	78.7	79.0	79	26.9
CRF	83.8	77.3	80	26.1
CasEN-CRF	84.1	77.5	81	26.0

Table 4: Comparing performances of systems

System	NE type	insert	delet	type	SER	f-score
Hybrid-sel	func	8	21	7	40.3	65
	all	103	205	210	25.2	79
CasEN-CRF	func	9	37	0	53.5	64
	all	77	251	196	26.0	81

Table 5: Impact of 'func' over SER and f-score

In a second step, we look in detail what NE types are the most accurately recognized. Those results are reported in Figure 8, where is depicted the error rates (to be lowered) for main types ('prod', being rare, is not reported). This revealed that features provided by CasEN for 'loc' type appeared to be unreliable for mStruct. Therefore, we filtered-out related features, so as to couple systems in a more efficient fashion. This leads to a 1.1 SER gain (from 26.3 to 25.2) when running the so-called 'Hybrid-sel' system, and demonstrates that the hybridation is very sensitive to what is provided by CasEN.

With this constrained hybridization, we compare previous results to other hybridization strategies and a baseline CRF system as described in section 6. Those experiments are reported in Table 4. We see that, when considering SER, the hybridization strategy using CasEN features within mStruct stochastic model slightly outperforms 'simpler' hybridizations schemes (pre-processing or post-processing with CasEN) and the CRF model (even when it uses CasEN preprocessing as a single unigram feature).

However the f-score metric gives advantage to CasEN-CRF, especially when considering recall. By looking indepth into errors and when reminded that SER is a weighted metric based on slots (entities) while f-score is based on tokens (see section 7.1), we noted that on longest NEs (mainly 'func'), Hybrid-sel does type errors (discounted as 0.5 in SER) while CasEN-CRF does deletion errors (1 in SER). This is pointed out by Table 5. The influence of error's type is clear when considering the SER for 'func' type for which Hybrid-sel is better while f-score doesn't measure such a difference.

7.4 Discussion and Perspectives

Assessment of performances using a baseline CRF pre-processed by CasEN and the hybrided strategy system shows that our approach is competitive, but do not allow to draw definitive conclusions. We keep in mind that the evaluated CRF could be further improved. Other methods have been successfully experimented to couple more efficiently that kind of data-driven approach with a knowledge-based one (for instance Zidouni et al. (2010) reports 20.3% SER on Ester2 test corpus, but they leverage training corpus).

Nevertheless, the CRFs models do not allow to directly extract symbolic knowledge from data. We aim at organizing our NER system in a modular way, so as to be able to adapt it to dedicated tasks, even if no training data is available. Results show that this proposed hybridization reaches a satisfactory level of performances.

This kind of hybridization, focusing on "markers", is especially relevant for annotation tasks. As a next step, experiments are to be conducted on other tasks, especially those involving nested annotations that our current system is able to process. We will also consider how to better organize and integrate automatically extracted informative rules into our existing knowledge-based system.

8 Conclusion

In this paper, we consider Named Entity Recognition task as the ability to detect boundaries of Named Entities. We use CasEN, a knowledge-based system based on transducers, and mineXtract, a text-mining approach, to extract informative rules from annotated texts. To test these rules, we propose mStruct, a light multi-purpose annotator that has the originality to focus on boundaries of Named Entities ("markers"), without considering the labels associated to tokens. The extraction module and the stochastic model are plugged together, resulting in mXS, a NE-tagger that gives satisfactory results. Those systems altogether may be hybridized in an efficient fashion. We assess performances of our approach by reporting results of our system compared to other baseline hybridization strategies and CRF systems.

References

Steven P. Abney. 1991. Parsing by Chunks. *Principle-Based Parsing*, 257–278.

Rakesh Agrawal and Ramakrishnan Srikant. 1994. Fast algorithms for mining association rules in large databases. *Very Large Data Bases*, 487–499.

Frédéric Bechet and Eric Charton. 2010. Unsupervised knowledge acquisition for Extracting Named Entities from speech. *Acoustics, Speech, and Signal Processing (ICASSP'10)*, Dallas, USA.

Andrew Borthwick, John Sterling, Eugene Agichtein and Ralph Grishman. 1998. Exploiting Diverse Knowledge Sources via Maximum Entropy in Named Entity Recognition. *Very Large Corpora (VLC'98)*, Montreal, Canada.

Caroline Brun and Caroline Hagège. 2004. Intertwining Deep Syntactic Processing and Named Entity Detection. *Advances in Natural Language Processing*, 3230:195-206.

Caroline Brun and Maud Ehrmann. 2009. Adaptation of a named entity recognition system for the ester 2 evaluation campaign. *Natural Language Processing and Knowledge Engineering (NLPK'09)*, Dalian, China.

Benoît Favre, Frédéric Béchet, and Pascal Nocera. 2005. Robust Named Entity Extraction from Large Spoken Archives. *Human Language Technology and Empirical Methods in Natural Language Processing (HLT/EMNLP'05)*, Vancouver, Canada.

Nathalie Friburger. 2002. Reconnaissance automatique des noms propres: Application à la classification automatique de textes journalistiques. *PhD*.

Nathalie Friburger and Denis Maurel. 2004. Finite-state transducer cascades to extract named entities. *Theoretical Computer Sciences (TCS)*, 313:93–104.

Sylvain Galliano, Guillaume Gravier and Laura Chaubard. 2009. The ESTER 2 evaluation campaign for the rich transcription of French radio broadcasts. *International Speech Communication Association (INTERSPEECH'09)*, Brighton, UK.

Philip Hingston. 2002. Using Finite State Automata for Sequence Mining. *Australasian Computer Science Conference (ACSC'02)*, Melbourne, Australia.

Hideki Isozaki and Hideto Kazawa. 2002. Efficient support vector classifiers for named entity recognition. *Conference on Computational linguistics (COLING'02)*, Taipei, Taiwan.

Nicholas Kushmerick and Daniel S. Weld and Robert Doorenbos. 1997. Wrapper Induction for Information Extraction. *International Joint Conference on Artificial Intelligence (IJCAI'97)*, Nagoya, Japan.

John D. Lafferty, Andrew McCallum and Fernando C. N. Pereira. 2001. Conditional Random Fields: Probabilistic Models for Segmenting and Labeling Sequence Data. *International Conference on Machine Learning (ICML'01)*, Massachusetts, USA.

Thomas Lavergne and Olivier Cappé and François Yvon 2010. Practical Very Large Scale CRFs. *Association for Computational Linguistics (ACL'10)*, Uppsala, Sweden.

Heikki Mannila and Hannu Toivonen. 1997. Level-wise search and borders of theories in knowledge discovery. *Data Mining and Knowledge Discovery*, 1(3):241–258.

Elaine Marsh and Dennis Perzanowski. 1998. MUC-7 Evaluation of IE Technology: Overview of Results. *Message Understanding Conference (MUC-7)*.

Andrew McCallum and Wei Li. 2003. Early results for named entity recognition with conditional random fields, feature induction and web-enhanced lexicons. *Computational Natural Language Learning (CONLL'03)*, Edmonton, Canada.

Scott Miller, Michael Crystal, Heidi Fox, Lance Ramshaw, Richard Schwartz, Rebecca Stone and Ralph Weischedel. 1998. Algorithms That Learn To Extract Information BBN: Description Of The Sift System As Used For MUC-7. *Message Understanding Conference (MUC-7)*.

Damien Nouvel, Jean-Yves Antoine, Nathalie Friburger and Denis Maurel. 2010. An Analysis of the Performances of the CasEN Named Entities Recognition System in the Ester2 Evaluation Campaign. *Language Resources and Evaluation (LREC'10)*, Valetta, Malta.

Fabian Pedregosa, Gaël Varoquaux, Alexandre Gramfort, Vincent Michel, Bertrand Thirion, Olivier Grisel, Mathieu Blondel, Peter Prettenhofer, Ron Weiss, Vincent Dubourg, Jake Vanderplas, Alexandre Passos, David Cournapeau, Matthieu Brucher, Matthieu Perrot and Édouard Duchesnay. 2011. Scikit-learn: Machine Learning in Python. *Journal of Machine Learning Research*, 12:2825–2830.

Helmut Schmid. 1994. Probabilistic POS Tagging Using Decision Trees. *New Methods in Language Processing (NEMLP'94*, Manchester, UK.

Boris W. van Schooten, Sophie Rosset, Olivier Galibert, Aurélien Max, Rieks op den Akker, and Gabriel Illouz. 2009. Handling speech in the ritel QA dialogue system. *International Speech Communication Association (INTERSPEECH'09)*, Brighton, UK.

Ellen M. Voorhees and Donna Harman. 2000. Overview of the Ninth Text REtrieval Conference (TREC-9). *International Speech Communication Association (INTERSPEECH'09)*, Brighton, UK.

Azeddine Zidouni and Sophie Rosset and Hervé Glotin 2010. Efficient combined approach for named entity recognition in spoken language. *International Speech Communication Association (INTERSPEECH'10)*, Makuhari, Japan.

A random forest system combination approach for error detection in digital dictionaries

Michael Bloodgood and **Peng Ye** and **Paul Rodrigues**
and **David Zajic** and **David Doermann**
University of Maryland
College Park, MD
meb@umd.edu, pengye@umiacs.umd.edu, prr@umd.edu,
dzajic@casl.umd.edu, doermann@umiacs.umd.edu

Abstract

When digitizing a print bilingual dictionary, whether via optical character recognition or manual entry, it is inevitable that errors are introduced into the electronic version that is created. We investigate automating the process of detecting errors in an XML representation of a digitized print dictionary using a hybrid approach that combines rule-based, feature-based, and language model-based methods. We investigate combining methods and show that using random forests is a promising approach. We find that in isolation, unsupervised methods rival the performance of supervised methods. Random forests typically require training data so we investigate how we can apply random forests to combine individual base methods that are themselves unsupervised without requiring large amounts of training data. Experiments reveal empirically that a relatively small amount of data is sufficient and can potentially be further reduced through specific selection criteria.

1 Introduction

Digital versions of bilingual dictionaries often have errors that need to be fixed. For example, Figures 1 through 5 show an example of an error that occurred in one of our development dictionaries and how the error should be corrected. Figure 1 shows the entry for the word "turfah" as it appeared in the original print copy of (Qureshi and Haq, 1991). We see this word has three senses with slightly different meanings. The third sense is "rare". In the original digitized XML version of (Qureshi and Haq, 1991) depicted in Figure 2, this was misrepresented as not being the meaning of "turfah" but instead being a usage note that frequency of use of the third sense was rare. Figure 3 shows the tree corresponding to this XML representation. The corrected digital XML representation is depicted in Figure 4 and the corresponding corrected tree is shown in Figure 5.

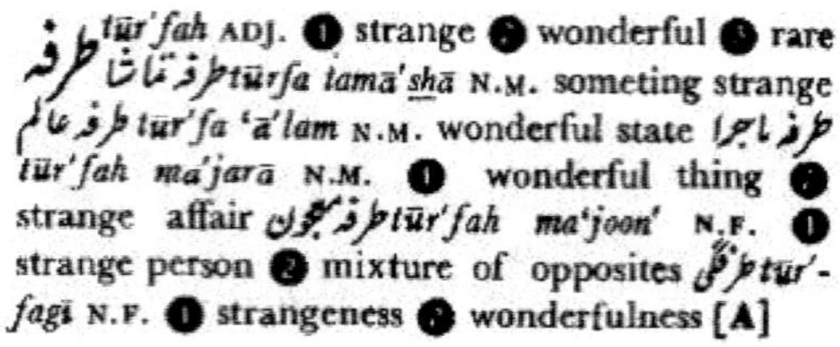

Figure 1: Example dictionary entry

```
<ENTRY ID="351782">
    <FORM ID="351783">
      <ORTH ID="351784">طرفه</ORTH>
      <PRON ID="351785">tūr'fah</PRON>
    </FORM>
    ...
    <SENSE N="3" ID="351794">
      <USG TYPE="time" ID="351795">rare</USG>
    </SENSE>
    ...
</ENTRY>
```

Figure 2: Example of error in XML

Zajic et al. (2011) presented a method for repairing a digital dictionary in an XML format using a dictionary markup language called DML. It remains time-consuming and error-prone however to have a human read through and manually correct a digital version of a dictionary, even with languages such as DML available. We therefore investigate automating the detection of errors.

We investigate the use of three individual methods. The first is a supervised feature-based method trained using SVMs (Support Vector Machines). The second is a language-modeling

Proceedings of the Workshop on Innovative Hybrid Approaches to the Processing of Textual Data (Hybrid2012), EACL 2012, pages 78–86,
Avignon, France, April 23 2012.

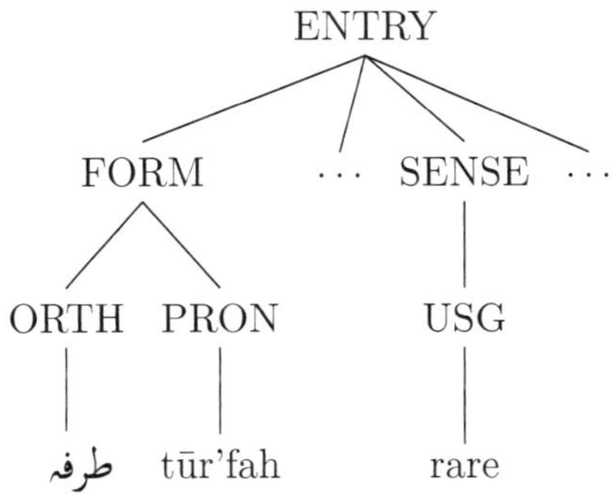

Figure 3: Tree structure of error

```
<ENTRY ID="351782">
    <FORM ID="351783">
      <ORTH ID="351784">طرفه</ORTH>
      <PRON ID="351785">tūr'fah</PRON>
    </FORM>
    ...
    <SENSE N="3" ID="351794">
      <TRANS ID="351794+1">
        <TR ID="351795">rare</TR>
      </TRANS>
    </SENSE>
    ...
</ENTRY>
```

Figure 4: Example of error in XML, fixed

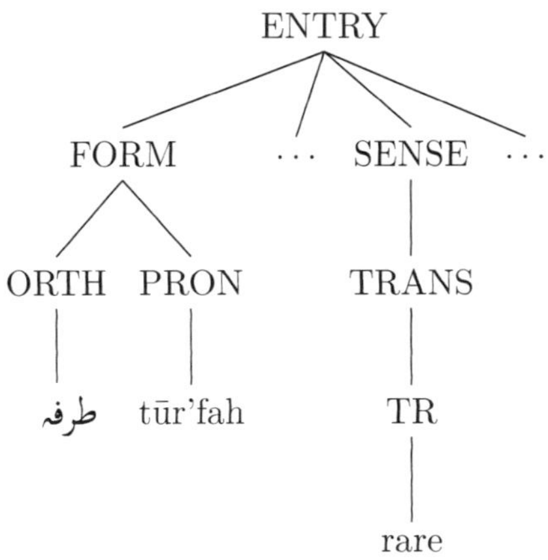

Figure 5: Tree structure of error, fixed

method that replicates the method presented in (Rodrigues et al., 2011). The third is a simple rule inference method. The three individual methods have different performances. So we investigate how we can combine the methods most effectively. We experiment with majority vote, score combination, and random forest methods and find that random forest combinations work the best.

For many dictionaries, training data will not be available in large quantities a priori and therefore methods that require only small amounts of training data are desirable. Interestingly, for automatically detecting errors in dictionaries, we find that the unsupervised methods have performance that rivals that of the supervised feature-based method trained using SVMs. Moreover, when we combine methods using the random forest method, the combination of unsupervised methods works better than the supervised method in isolation and almost as well as the combination of all available methods. A potential drawback of using the random forest combination method however is that it requires training data. We investigated how much training data is needed and find that the amount of training data required is modest. Furthermore, by selecting the training data to be labeled with the use of specific selection methods reminiscent of active learning, it may be possible to train the random forest system combination method with even less data without sacrificing performance.

In section 2 we discuss previous related work and in section 3 we explain the three individual methods we use for our application. In section 4 we explain the three methods we explored for combining methods; in section 5 we present and discuss experimental results and in section 6 we conclude and discuss future work.

2 Related Work

Classifier combination techniques can be broadly classified into two categories: mathematical and behavioral (Tulyakov et al., 2008). In the first category, functions or rules combine normalized classifier scores from individual classifiers. Examples of techniques in this category include Majority Voting (Lam and Suen, 1997), as well as simple score combination rules such as: sum rule, min rule, max rule and product rule (Kittler et al., 1998; Ross and Jain, 2003; Jain et al., 2005). In the second category, the output of individual classifiers are combined to form a feature vector as the input to a generic classifier such as classification trees (P. and Chollet, 1999; Ross and Jain, 2003) or the k-nearest neighbors classifier (P. and Chollet, 1999). Our method falls into the second category, where we use a random forest for system combination.

The random forest method is described in (Breiman, 2001). It is an ensemble classifier consisting of a collection of decision trees (called a random forest) and the output of the random forest is the mode of the classes output by the individual trees. Each single tree is trained as follows: 1) a random set of samples from the initial training set is selected as a training set and 2) at each node of the tree, a random subset of the features is selected, and the locally optimal split is based on only this feature subset. The tree is fully grown without pruning. Ma et al. (2005) used random forests for combining scores of several biometric devices for identity verification and have shown encouraging results. They use all fully supervised methods. In contrast, we explore minimizing the amount of training data needed to train a random forest of unsupervised methods.

The use of active learning in order to reduce training data requirements without sacrificing model performance has been reported on extensively in the literature (e.g., (Seung et al., 1992; Cohn et al., 1994; Lewis and Gale, 1994; Cohn et al., 1996; Freund et al., 1997)). When training our random forest combination of individual methods that are themselves unsupervised, we explore how to select the data so that only small amounts of training data are needed because for many dictionaries, gathering training data may be expensive and labor-intensive.

3 Three Single Method Approaches for Error Detection

Before we discuss our approaches for combining systems, we briefly explain the three individual systems that form the foundation of our combined system.

First, we use a supervised approach where we train a model using SVM^{light} (Joachims, 1999) with a linear kernel and default regularization parameters. We use a depth first traversal of the XML tree and use unigrams and bigrams of the tags that occur as features for each subtree to make a classification decision.

We also explore two unsupervised approaches. The first unsupervised approach learns rules for when to classify nodes as errors or not. The rule-based method computes an anomaly score based on the probability of subtree structures. Given a structure A and its probability P(A), the event that A occurs has anomaly score 1-P(A) and the event that A does not occur has anomaly score P(A). The basic idea is if a certain structure happens rarely, i.e. P(A) is very small, then the occurrence of A should have a high anomaly score. On the other hand, if A occurs frequently, then the absence of A indicates anomaly. To obtain the anomaly score of a tree, we simply take the maximal scores of all events induced by subtrees within this tree.

The second unsupervised approach uses a reimplementation of the language modeling method described in (Rodrigues et al., 2011). Briefly, this methods works by calculating the probability a flattened XML branch can occur, given a probability model trained on the XML branches from the original dictionary. We used (Stolcke, 2002) to generate bigram models using Good Turing smoothing and Katz back off, and evaluated the log probability of the XML branches, ranking the likelihood. The first 1000 branches were submitted to the hybrid system marked as an error, and the remaining were submitted as a non-error. Results for the individual classifiers are presented in section 5.

4 Three Methods for Combining Systems

We investigate three methods for combining the three individual methods. As a baseline, we investigate simple majority vote. This method takes the classification decisions of the three methods and assigns the final classification as the classification that the majority of the methods predicted.

A drawback of majority vote is that it does not weight the votes at all. However, it might make sense to weight the votes according to factors such as the strength of the classification score. For example, all of our classifiers make binary decisions but output scores that are indicative of the confidence of their classifications. Therefore we also explore a score combination method that considers these scores. Since measures from the different systems are in different ranges, we normalize these measurements before combining them (Jain et al., 2005). We use z-score which computes the arithmetic mean and standard deviation of the given data for score normalization. We then take the summation of normalized measures as the final measure. Classification is performed by thresholding this final measure.[1]

Another approach would be to weight them by the performance level of the various constituent classifiers in the ensemble. Weighting based on performance level of the individual classifiers is difficult because it would require extra labeled data to estimate the various performance levels. It is not clear how to translate the different performance estimates into weights, or how to have those weights interact with weights based on strengths of classification. Therefore, we did not weigh based on performance level explicitly.

We believe that our third combination method, the use of random forests, implicitly captures weighting based on performance level and strengths of classifications. Our random forest approach uses three features, one for each of the individual systems we use. With random forests, strengths of classification are taken into account because they form the values of the three features we use. In addition, the performance level is taken into account because the training data used to train the decision trees that form the forest help to guide binning of the feature values into appropriate ranges where classification decisions are made correctly. This will be discussed further in section 5.

5 Experiments

This section explains the details of the experiments we conducted testing the performance of the various individual and combined systems. Subsection 5.1 explains the details of the data we experiment on; subsection 5.2 provides a summary of the main results of our experiments; and subsection 5.3 discusses the results.

5.1 Experimental Setup

We obtained the data for our experiments using a digitized version of (Qureshi and Haq, 1991), the same Urdu-English dictionary that Zajic et al. (2011) had used. Zajic et al. (2011) presented DML, a programming language used to fix errors in XML documents that contain lexicographic data. A team of language experts used DML to correct errors in a digital, XML representation of the Kitabistan Urdu dictionary. The current research compared the source XML document and the DML commands to identify the elements that the language experts decided to modify. We consider those elements to be errors. This is the ground truth used for training and evaluation. We evaluate at two tiers, corresponding to two node types in the XML representation of the dictionary: ENTRY and SENSE. The example depicted in Figures 1 through 5 shows an example of SENSE. The intuition of the tier is that errors are detectable (or learnable) from observing the elements within a tier, and do not cross tier boundaries. These tiers are specific to the Kitabistan Urdu dictionary, and we selected them by observing the data. A limitation of our work is that we do not know at this time whether they are generally useful across dictionaries. Future work will be to automatically discover the meaningful evaluation tiers for a new dictionary. After this process, we have a dataset with 15,808 Entries, of which 47.53% are marked as errors and 78,919 Senses, of which 10.79% are marked as errors. We perform tenfold cross-validation in all experiments. In our random forest experiments, we use 12 decision trees, each with only 1 feature.

[1]In our experiments we used 0 as the threshold.

	Recall	Precision	F1-Measure	Accuracy
LM	11.97	89.90	21.13	57.53
RULE	99.79	70.83	82.85	80.37
FV	35.34	93.68	51.32	68.14

Table 1: Performance of individual systems at ENTRY tier.

5.2 Results

This section presents experimental results, first for individual systems and then for combined systems.

5.2.1 Performance of individual systems

Tables 1 and 2 show the performance of language modeling-based method (LM), rule-based method (RULE) and the supervised feature-based method (FV) at different tiers. As can be seen, at the ENTRY tier, RULE obtains the highest F1-Measure and accuracy, while at the SENSE tier, FV performs the best.

	Recall	Precision	F1-Measure	Accuracy
LM	9.85	94.00	17.83	90.20
RULE	84.59	58.86	69.42	91.96
FV	72.44	98.66	83.54	96.92

Table 2: Performance of individual systems at SENSE tier.

5.2.2 Improving individual systems using random forests

In this section, we show that by applying random forests on top of the output of individual systems, we can have gains (absolute gains, not relative) in accuracy of 4.34% to 6.39% and gains (again absolute, not relative) in F1-measure of 3.64% to 11.39%. Tables 3 and 4 show our experimental results at ENTRY and SENSE tiers when applying random forests with the rule-based method.[2] These results are all obtained from 100 iterations of the experiments with different partitions of the training data chosen at each iteration. Mean values of different evaluation measures and their standard deviations are shown in these tables. We change the percentage of training data and repeat the experiments to see how the amount of training data affects performance.

It might be surprising to see the gains in performance that can be achieved by using a random forest of decision trees created using only the rule-based scores as features. To shed light on why this is so, we show the distribution of RULE-based output scores for anomaly nodes and clean nodes in Figure 6. They are well separated and this explains why RULE alone can have good performance. Recall RULE classifies nodes with anomaly scores larger than 0.9 as errors. However, in Figure 6, we can see that there are many clean nodes with anomaly scores larger than 0.9. Thus, the simple thresholding strategy will bring in errors. Applying random forest will help us identify these errorful regions to improve the performance. Another method for helping to identify these errorful regions and classify them correctly is to apply random forest of RULE combined with the other methods, which we will see will even further boost the performance.

[2]We also applied random forests to our language modeling and feature-based methods, and saw similar gains in performance.

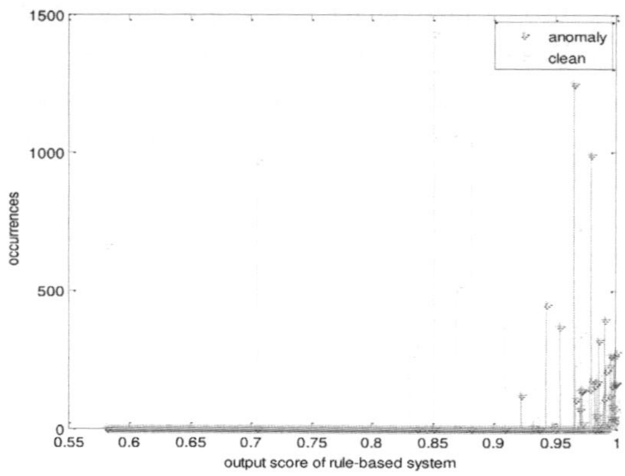

Figure 6: Output anomalies score from RULE (ENTRY tier).

5.2.3 System combination

In this section, we explore different methods for combining measures from the three systems. Table 5 shows the results of majority voting and score combination at the ENTRY tier. As can be seen, majority voting performs poorly. This may be due to the fact that the performances of the three systems are very different. RULE significantly outperforms the other two systems, and as discussed in Section 4 neither majority voting nor score combination weights this higher performance appropriately.

Tables 6 and 7 show the results of combining RULE and LM. This is of particular interest since these two systems are unsupervised. Combining these two unsupervised systems works better than the individual methods, including supervised methods. Tables 8 and 9 show the results for combinations of all available systems. This yields the highest performance, but only slightly higher than the combination of only unsupervised base methods.

The random forest combination technique does require labeled data even if the underlying base methods are unsupervised. Based on the observation in Figure 6, we further study whether choosing more training data from the most errorful regions will help to improve the performance. Experimental results in Table 10 show how the choice of training data affects performance. It appears that there may be a weak trend toward higher performance when we force the selection of the majority of the training data to be from ENTRY nodes whose RULE anomaly scores are

Training %	Recall	Precision	F1-Measure	Accuracy
0.1	78.17(14.83)	75.87(3.96)	76.18(7.99)	77.68(5.11)
1	82.46(4.81)	81.34(2.14)	81.79(2.20)	82.61(1.69)
10	87.30(1.96)	84.11(1.29)	85.64(0.46)	86.10(0.35)
50	89.19(1.75)	83.99(1.20)	86.49(0.34)	86.76(0.28)

Table 3: Mean and std of evaluation measures from 100 iterations of experiments using RULE+RF. (ENTRY tier)

Training %	Recall	Precision	F1-Measure	Accuracy
0.1	60.22(12.95)	69.66(9.54)	63.29(7.92)	92.61(1.57)
1	70.28(3.48)	86.26(3.69)	77.31(1.39)	95.55(0.25)
10	71.52(1.23)	91.26(1.39)	80.18(0.41)	96.18(0.07)
50	72.11(0.75)	91.90(0.64)	80.81(0.39)	96.30(0.06)

Table 4: Mean and std of evaluation measures from 100 iterations of experiments using RULE+RF. (SENSE tier)

larger than 0.9. However, the magnitudes of the observed differences in performance are within a single standard deviation so it remains for future work to determine if there are ways to select the training data for our random forest combination in ways that substantially improve upon random selection.

5.3 Discussion

Majority voting (at the entry level) performs poorly, since the performance of the three individual systems are very different and majority voting does not weight votes at all. Score combination is a type of weighted voting. It takes into account the confidence level of output from different systems, which enables it to perform better than majority voting. However, score combination does not take into account the performance levels of the different systems, and we believe this limits its performance compared with random forest combinations.

Random forest combinations perform the best, but the cost is that it is a supervised combination method. We investigated how the amount of training data affects the performance, and found that a small amount of labeled data is all that the random forest needs in order to be successful. Moreover, although this requires further exploration, there is weak evidence that the size of the labeled data can potentially be reduced by choosing it carefully from the region that is expected to be most errorful. For our application with a rule-based system, this is the high-anomaly scoring region because although it is true that anomalies are often errors, it is also the case that some structures occur rarely but are not errorful.

RULE+LM with random forest is a little better than RULE with random forest, with gain of about 0.7% on F1-measure when evaluated at the ENTRY level using 10% data for training.

An examination of examples that are marked as being errors in our ground truth but that were not detected to be errors by any of our systems suggests that some examples are decided on the basis of features not yet considered by any system. For example, in Figure 7 the second FORM is well-formed structurally, but the Urdu text in the first FORM is the beginning of the phrase transliterated in the second FORM. Automatic systems detected that the first FORM was an error, however did not mark the second FORM as an error whereas our ground truth marked both as errors.

Examination of false negatives also revealed cases where the systems were correct that there was no error but our ground truth wrongly indicated that there was an error. These were due to our semi-automated method for producing ground truth that considers elements mentioned in DML commands to be errors. We discovered instances in which merely mentioning an element in a DML command does not imply that the element is an error. These cases are useful for making refinements to how ground truth is generated from DML commands.

Examination of false positives revealed two categories. One was where the element is indeed an error but was not marked as an element in our ground truth because it was part of a larger error

Method	Recall	Precision	F1-Measure	Accuracy
Majority voting	36.71	90.90	52.30	68.18
Score combination	76.48	75.82	76.15	77.23

Table 5: LM+RULE+FV (ENTRY tier)

Training %	Recall	Precision	F1-Measure	Accuracy
0.1	77.43(15.14)	72.77(6.03)	74.26(8.68)	75.32(6.71)
1	86.50(3.59)	80.41(1.95)	83.27(1.33)	83.51(1.11)
10	88.12(1.12)	84.65(0.57)	86.34(0.46)	86.76(0.39)
50	89.12(0.62)	87.39(0.56)	88.25(0.30)	88.72(0.29)

Table 6: System combination based on random forest (LM+RULE). (ENTRY tier, mean (std))

Training %	Recall	Precision	F1-Measure	Accuracy
0.1	65.85(12.70)	71.96(7.63)	67.68(7.06)	93.38(1.03)
1	80.29(3.58)	84.97(3.13)	82.45(1.36)	96.31(0.28)
10	82.68(2.49)	90.91(2.37)	86.53(0.41)	97.22(0.07)
50	83.22(2.43)	92.21(2.29)	87.42(0.35)	97.42(0.04)

Table 7: System combination based on random forest (LM+RULE). (SENSE tier, mean (std))

Training %	Recall	Precision	F1-Measure	Accuracy
20	91.57(0.55)	87.77(0.43)	89.63(0.23)	89.93(0.22)
50	92.04(0.54)	88.85(0.48)	90.41(0.29)	90.72(0.28)

Table 8: System combination based on random forest (LM+RULE+FV). (ENTRY tier, mean (std))

Training %	Recall	Precision	F1-Measure	Accuracy
20	86.47(1.01)	90.67(1.02)	88.51(0.26)	97.58(0.06)
50	86.50(0.81)	92.04(0.85)	89.18(0.30)	97.73(0.06)

Table 9: System combination based on random forest (LM+RULE+FV). (SENSE tier, mean (std))

	Recall	Precision	F1-Measure	Accuracy
50%	85.40(4.65)	80.71(3.49)	82.82(1.57)	82.63(1.54)
70%	86.13(3.94)	80.97(2.64)	83.36(1.33)	83.30(1.21)
90%	85.77(3.61)	81.82(2.72)	83.65(1.45)	83.69(1.35)
95%	85.93(3.46)	82.14(2.98)	83.89(1.32)	83.94(1.18)
random	86.50(3.59)	80.41(1.95)	83.27(1.33)	83.51(1.11)

Table 10: Effect of choice of training data based on rule based method (Mean evaluation measures from 100 iterations of experiments using RULE+LM at ENTRY tier). We choose 1% of the data for training and the first column in the table specifies the percentage of training data chosen from Entries with anomalous score larger than 0.9.

```
<FORM><ORTH>آپ ہی</ORTH></FORM>
<FORM><ORTH>آپ ہی کی جوتیوں کاصدقہ ہے</ORTH>
   <PRON>āp'hI kI joo'tiyoṅ
         kā sad'qah hai</PRON>
</FORM>
```

Figure 7: Example of error in XML

that got deleted and therefore no DML command ever mentioned the smaller element but lexicographers upon inspection agree that the smaller element is indeed errorful. The other category was where there were actual errors that the dictionary editors didn't repair with DML but that should have been repaired.

A major limitation of our work is testing how well it generalizes to detecting errors in other dictionaries besides the Urdu-English one (Qureshi and Haq, 1991) that we conducted our experiments on.

6 Conclusions

We explored hybrid approaches for the application of automatically detecting errors in digitized copies of dictionaries. The base methods we explored consisted of a variety of unsupervised and supervised methods. The combination methods we explored also consisted of some methods which required labeled data and some which did not.

We found that our base methods had different levels of performance and with this scenario majority voting and score combination methods, though appealing since they require no labeled data, did not perform well since they do not weight votes well.

We found that random forests of decision trees was the best combination method. We hypothesize that this is due to the nature of our task and base systems. Random forests were able to help tease apart the high-error region (where anomalies take place). A drawback of random forests as a combination method is that they require labeled data. However, experiments reveal empirically that a relatively small amount of data is sufficient and the amount might be able to be further reduced through specific selection criteria.

Acknowledgments

This material is based upon work supported, in whole or in part, with funding from the United States Government. Any opinions, findings and conclusions, or recommendations expressed in this material are those of the author(s) and do not necessarily reflect the views of the University of Maryland, College Park and/or any agency or entity of the United States Government. Nothing in this report is intended to be and shall not be treated or construed as an endorsement or recommendation by the University of Maryland, United States Government, or the authors of the product, process, or service that is the subject of this report. No one may use any information contained or based on this report in advertisements or promotional materials related to any company product, process, or service or in support of other commercial purposes.

References

Leo Breiman. 2001. Random forests. *Machine Learning*, 45:5–32. 10.1023/A:1010933404324.

David A. Cohn, Les Atlas, and Richard Ladner. 1994. Improving generalization with active learning. *Machine Learning*, 15:201–221.

David A. Cohn, Zoubin Ghahramani, and Michael I. Jordan. 1996. Active learning with statistical models. *Journal of Artificial Intelligence Research*, 4:129–145.

Yoav Freund, H. Sebastian Seung, Eli Shamir, and Naftali Tishby. 1997. Selective sampling using the query by committee algorithm. *Machine Learning*, 28:133–168.

Anil K. Jain, Karthik Nandakumar, and Arun Ross. 2005. Score normalization in multimodal biometric systems. *Pattern Recognition*, pages 2270–2285.

Thorsten Joachims. 1999. Making large-scale SVM learning practical. In Bernhard Schölkopf, Christopher J. Burges, and Alexander J. Smola, editors, *Advances in Kernel Methods – Support Vector Learning*, chapter 11, pages 169–184. The MIT Press, Cambridge, US.

J. Kittler, M. Hatef, R.P.W. Duin, and J. Matas. 1998. On combining classifiers. *Pattern Analysis and Machine Intelligence, IEEE Transactions on*, 20(3):226 –239, mar.

L. Lam and S.Y. Suen. 1997. Application of majority voting to pattern recognition: an analysis of its behavior and performance. *Systems, Man and Cybernetics, Part A: Systems and Humans, IEEE Transactions on*, 27(5):553 –568, sep.

David D. Lewis and William A. Gale. 1994. A sequential algorithm for training text classifiers. In *SIGIR '94: Proceedings of the 17th annual international ACM SIGIR conference on Research and development in information retrieval*, pages 3–12,

New York, NY, USA. Springer-Verlag New York, Inc.

Yan Ma, Bojan Cukic, and Harshinder Singh. 2005. A classification approach to multi-biometric score fusion. In *AVBPA'05*, pages 484–493.

Verlinde P. and G. Chollet. 1999. Comparing decision fusion paradigms using k-nn based classifiers, decision trees and logistic regression in a multimodal identity verification application. In *Proceedings of the 2nd International Conference on Audio and Video-Based Biometric Person Authentication (AVBPA)*, pages 189–193.

Bashir Ahmad Qureshi and Abdul Haq. 1991. *Standard Twenty First Century Urdu-English Dictionary*. Educational Publishing House, Delhi.

Paul Rodrigues, David Zajic, David Doermann, Michael Bloodgood, and Peng Ye. 2011. Detecting structural irregularity in electronic dictionaries using language modeling. In *Proceedings of the Conference on Electronic Lexicography in the 21st Century*, pages 227–232, Bled, Slovenia, November. Trojina, Institute for Applied Slovene Studies.

Arun Ross and Anil Jain. 2003. Information fusion in biometrics. *Pattern Recognition Letters*, 24:2115–2125.

H. S. Seung, M. Opper, and H. Sompolinsky. 1992. Query by committee. In *COLT '92: Proceedings of the fifth annual workshop on Computational learning theory*, pages 287–294, New York, NY, USA. ACM.

Andreas Stolcke. 2002. Srilm - an extensible language modeling toolkit. In *Proceedings of the International Conference on Spoken Language Processing*.

Sergey Tulyakov, Stefan Jaeger, Venu Govindaraju, and David Doermann. 2008. Review of classifier combination methods. In *Machine Learning in Document Analysis and Recognition*, volume 90 of *Studies in Computational Intelligence*, pages 361–386. Springer Berlin / Heidelberg.

David Zajic, Michael Maxwell, David Doermann, Paul Rodrigues, and Michael Bloodgood. 2011. Correcting errors in digital lexicographic resources using a dictionary manipulation language. In *Proceedings of the Conference on Electronic Lexicography in the 21st Century*, pages 297–301, Bled, Slovenia, November. Trojina, Institute for Applied Slovene Studies.

Methods Combination and ML-based Re-ranking of Multiple Hypothesis for Question-Answering Systems

Arnaud Grappy
LIMSI-CNRS
arnaud.grappy@limsi.fr

Brigitte Grau
LIMSI-CNRS
ENSIIE
brigitte.grau@limsi.fr

Sophie Rosset
LIMSI-CNRS
sophie.rosset@limsi.fr

Abstract

Question answering systems answer correctly to different questions because they are based on different strategies. In order to increase the number of questions which can be answered by a single process, we propose solutions to combine two question answering systems, QAVAL and RITEL. QAVAL proceeds by selecting short passages, annotates them by question terms, and then extracts from them answers which are ordered by a machine learning validation process. RITEL develops a multi-level analysis of questions and documents. Answers are extracted and ordered according to two strategies: by exploiting the redundancy of candidates and a Bayesian model. In order to merge the system results, we developed different methods either by merging passages before answer ordering, or by merging end-results. The fusion of end-results is realized by voting, merging, and by a machine learning process on answer characteristics, which lead to an improvement of the best system results of 19 %.

1 Introduction

Question-answering systems aim at giving short and precise answers to natural language questions. These systems are quite complex, and include many different components. Question-Answering systems are generally organized within a pipeline which includes at a high level at least three components: questions processing, snippets selection and answers extraction. But each module of these systems is quite different. They are based on different knowledge sources and processing. Even if the global performance of these systems are similar, they show great disparity when examining local results. Moreover there is no question-answering system able to answer correctly to all possible questions. Considering all QA evaluation campaigns in French like CLEF, EQUER or Quæro, or for other languages like TREC, no system obtained 100% correct answers at first rank. A new direction of research was built upon these observations: how can we combine correct answers provided by different systems?

This work deals with this issue[1] . In this paper we describe different experiments concerning the combination of QA systems. We used two different available systems, QAVAL and RITEL, while RITEL includes two different answer extraction strategies. We propose to merge the results of these systems at different levels. First, at an intermediary step (for example, between snippet selection and answer extraction). This approach allows to evaluate a fusion process based on the integration of different strategies. Another way to proceed is to execute the fusion at the end of each system. The aim is then to choose between all the candidate answers the best one for each question. Such an approach has been successfully applied in the information retrieval field, with the definition of different functions for combining results of search engines (Shaw and Fox, 1994). However, in QA, the problem is different as answers to questions are not made of a list of answers, but are made of excerpts of texts, which may be different in their writing, but which correspond to a unique and same answer. Thus, we propose fusion methods that rely on the information generally computed by QA systems, such as score, rank, an-

[1]This work was partially financed by OSEO under the Quro program

Proceedings of the Workshop on Innovative Hybrid Approaches to the Processing of Textual Data (Hybrid2012), EACL 2012, pages 87–96,
Avignon, France, April 23 2012.

swer redundancy, etc. We defined new voting and scoring functions, and a machine learning system to combine these features. Most of the strategies presented here allow a clear improvement (up to 19 %) on the first ranked correct answers.

In the following, related work is presented in the section 2. We then describe the different systems used in this work (Section 3.1 and 3.2). The proposed approach are presented (Section 4 and 5). The methods and the different systems are then evaluated on the same corpus.

2 Related work

QA system hybridization often consists in merging end-results. The first studies presented here aim at merging the results of different strategies for finding answers in the same set of documents. (Jijkoun and Rijke, 2004) developed several strategies for answering questions, based on different paradigms for extracting answers. They search for answers in a knowledge base or by applying extraction patterns or by selecting the n-grams the closest to the question words. They defined different methods for recognizing the similarity of two answers: equality, inclusion and an edit distance. The merging of answers is realized by summing the confidence scores of similar answers and leads to improve the number of right answers at first rank of 31 %.

(Tellez-Valero et al., 2010) combine the output of QA systems, whose strategy is not known. They only dispose of the provided answers associated with a supporting snippet. Merging is done by a machine learning approach, which combines different criteria such as the question category, the expected answer type, the compatibility between the provided answer and the question, the system which was applied and the rate of question terms in the snippet. When applying this module on the CLEF QA systems which were run on the Spanish data, they obtain a better MRR[2] value than the best system from 0.62 up to 0.73.

In place of diversifying the answering strategies, another possibility is to apply a same strategy on different collections. (Aceves-Pérez et al., 2008) apply classical merging strategies to multilingual QA systems, by merging answers according to their rank or by combining their confidence scores, normalized or not. They show that the combination of normalized scores obtains results which are better than a monolingual system (MRR from 0.64 up to 0.75). They also tested hybridization at the passage level by extracting answers from the overall set of passages which proved to be less relevant than answer merging.

(Chalendar et al.,) combine results obtained by searching the Web in parallel to a given collection. The combination which consists in boosting answers if they are found by the two systems is very effective, as it is less probable to find same incorrect answers on different documents.

The hybridization we are interested in concerns the merging of different strategies and different system capabilities in order to improve the final result. We tested different hybridization levels, and different merging methods. One is closed to (Tellez-Valero et al., 2010) as it is based on a validation module. Other are voting and scoring methods which have been defined according to our task, and are compared to classical merging scheme which have been proposed in information retrieval (Shaw and Fox, 1994), ComSum and CombMNZ.

3 The Question-Answering systems

3.1 The QAVAL system

3.1.1 General overview

QAVAL(Grappy et al., 2011) is made of sequential modules, corresponding to five main steps (see Fig. 1). The question analysis provides main characteristics for retrieving passages and for guiding the validation process. Short passages of about 300-character long are obtained directly from the search engine Lucene and are annotated with question terms and their weighted variants. They are then parsed by a syntactic parser and enriched with the question characteristics, which allows QAVAL to compute the different features for validating or discarding candidate answers.

A specificity of QAVAL relies on its validation module. Candidate answers are extracted according to the expected answer type, i.e. a named entity or not. In case of a named entity, all the named entities corresponding to the expected type are extracted while, in the second case, QAVAL extracts all the noun phrases which are not question phrases. As many candidate answers can be extracted, a first step consists in recognizing obvious false answers. Answers from a passage that does

[2] Mean Reciprocal Rank

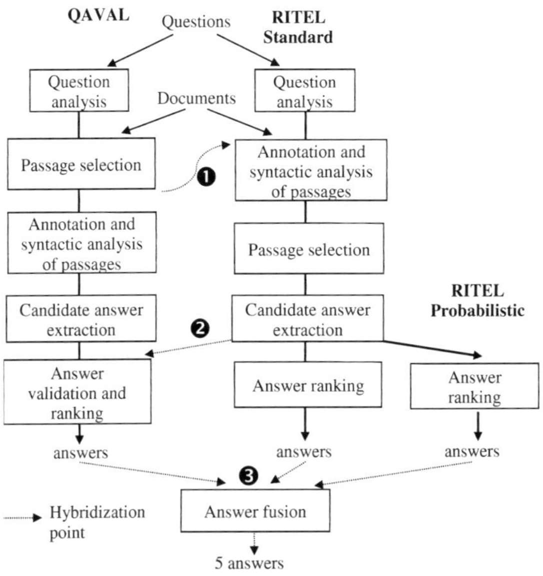

Figure 1: The QAVAL and RITEL systems and their possible hybridizations

not contain all the named entities of the question are discarded. The remaining answers are then ranked based on a learning method which combines features characterizing the passage and the candidate answer it provides. The QAVAL system has been evaluated on factual questions and obtains good results.

3.1.2 Answer ranking by validation

A machine based learning validation module provides scores to each candidate answer. Features relative to passages aim at evaluating in which part a passage conveys the same meaning as the question. They are based on lexical features, as the rate of question words in the passage, their POS tag, the main terms of the question, etc.

Features relative to the answer represent the property that an answer has to be of an expected type, if explicitly required, and to be related to the question terms. Another kind of criterion concerns the answer redundancy: the most frequent an answer is, the most relevant it is. Answer type verification is applied for questions which give an explicit type for the answer, as in "Which president succeeded Georges W. Bush?" that expects as answer the name of a president, more specific than the named entity type PERSON. This module (Grappy and Grau, 2010) combines results given by different kinds of verifications, based on named entity recognizers and searches in corpora. To evaluate the relation degree of an answer with the question terms, QAVAL computes i) the longest chain of consecutive common words between the question plus the answer and the passage; ii) the average distance between the answer and each of the question words in the passage.

Other criteria are the passage rank given by using results of the passage analysis, the question category, i.e. definition, characterization of an entity, verb modifier or verb complement, etc.

3.2 The RITEL systems

3.3 General overview

The RITEL system (see Figure 1) which we used in these experiments is fully described in (Bernard et al., 2009). This system has been developed within the framework of the Ritel project which aimed at building a human-machine dialogue system for question-answering in open domain (Toney et al., 2008).

The same multilevel analysis is carried out on both queries and documents. The objective of this analysis is to find the bits of information that may be of use for search and extraction, called *pertinent information chunks*. These can be of different categories: named entities, linguistic entities (e.g., verbs, prepositions), or specific entities (e.g., scores). All words that do not fall into such chunks are automatically grouped into chunks via a longest-match strategy. The analysis is hierarchical, resulting in a set of trees. Both answers and important elements of the questions are supposed to be annotated as one of these entities.

The first step of the QA system itself is to build a search descriptor (SD) that contains the important elements of the question, and the possible answer types with associated weights. Answer types are predicted through rules based on combinations of elements of the question. On all secondary and mandatory chunks, the possible transformations (synonym, morphological derivation, etc.) are indicated and weighted in the SD. Documents are selected using this SD. Each element of the document is scored with the geometric mean of the number of occurrences of all the SD elements that appear in it, and sorted by score, keeping the n-best. Snippets are extracted from the document using fixed-size windows and scored using the geometrical mean of the number of occurrences of all the SD elements that appear in the snippet, smoothed by the document score.

3.3.1 Answer selection and ranking

Two different strategies are implemented in RITEL. The first one is based on distance between question words and candidate answer, named RITEL Standard. The second one is based on a Bayesian model, named RITEL Probabilistic.

Distance-based answer scoring The snippets are sorted by score and examined one by one independently. Every element in a snippet with a type found in the list of expected answer types of the SD is considered an answer candidate. RITEL associates to each candidate answer a score which is the sum of the distances between itself and the elements of the SD. That score is smoothed with the snippet score through a δ-ponderated geometric mean. All the scores for the different instances of the same element are added together. The entities with the best scores then win. The scores for identical (type,value) pairs are added together and give the final scoring to the candidate answers.

Answer scoring through Bayesian modeling This method of answer scoring is built upon a Bayesian modeling of the process of estimating the quality of an answer candidate. This approach relies on multiple elementary models including element co-occurrence probabilities, question element appearance probability in the context of a correct answer and out of context answer probability. The model parameters are either estimated on the documents or are set empirically. This system has not better result than the distance-based one but is interesting because it allows to obtain different correct answers.

3.4 Systems combination

The systems we used in these experiments are very different especially with respect to the passage selection and the answer extraction and scoring methods. The QAVAL system proceeds to the passage selection before any analysis while the two RITEL systems do a complete and multilevel analysis on the documents before the passage selection. Concerning the answer extraction and scoring, the QAVAL system uses an answer validation process based on machine learning approach while the answer extraction of the RITEL-S system uses a distance-based scoring and the RITEL-P Bayesian models. It seems then interesting to combine these various approaches in a in-system way (see Section 4): (1) the passages selected by the QAVAL system are provided as document collection to the RITEL systems; (2) the candidate answers provided by the RITEL systems are given to the answer validation module of the QAVAL system.

We also worked, in a more classical way, on interleaving results of answer selection methods (see Section 5 and 6). These methods make use of the various information provided by the different systems along with all candidate answers.

4 Internal combination

4.1 QAVAL snippets used by RITEL

The RITEL system proceeds to a complete analysis of the document which is used during the document and selection extraction procedure and obtains 80.3% of the questions having a correct answer in at least one passage. The QAVAL system extracts short passages (150) using Lucene and obtains a score of 88%. We hypothesized that the RITEL's fine-grained analysis could better work on small collection than on the overall document collection (combination 1 Fig. 1). We consider the passages extracted by the QAVAL system being a new collection for the RITEL system. First, the analysis is done on this new collection and the analysis result is indexed. Then the general question-answering procedures are applied: question analysis, SD construction, document and snippet extraction and then answer selection and ranking. The two answer extraction methods have been applied and the results are presented in the Table 1. This simple approach does not allow any

	All documents		QAVAL' snippets	
	Ritel-S	Ritel-P	Ritel-S	Ritel-P
top-1	34.0%	22.4%	29.9%	22.4%
MRR	0.41	0.29	0.38	0.32
top-20	61.2%	48.7%	54.4%	49.7%

Table 1: Results of Ritel systems (Ritel-S used the distance-based answer scoring, Ritel-P used the Bayesian modeling) working on the QAVAL' snippets.

improvement. Actually all the results are worsening, except maybe for the Ritel-P systems (which is actually not the best one). One of our hypothesis is that the QAVAL snippets are too short and do not fit the criteria used by the RITEL system.

4.2 Answer validation

In QAVAL, answer ranking is done by an answer validation module (fully described in section 3.1). The candidate answers ranked by this module are associated to a confidence score. The objective of this answer validation module is to decide whether the candidate answer is correct or not given an associated snippet. The objective is to use this answer validation module on the candidate answers and the snippets provided by all the systems (combination 2 Fig. 1). Unfortunately, this method did not obtain better results than the best system. We assume that this module being learnt on the QAVAL data only is not robust to different data and more specifically to the passage length which is larger in RITEL than in QAVAL. A possible improvement could be to add answers found by the RITEL system in the training base.

5 Voting methods and scores combination

These methods are based on a comparison between the candidate answers: are they identical ? An observation that can be made concerning the use of a strict equality between answers is that in some cases, 2 different answers can be more or less identical. For example if one system returns "Sarkozy" and another one "Nicolas Sarkozy" we may want to consider these two answers as identical. We based the comparison of answers on the notion of *extended equality*. For that, we used morpho-syntactic information such as the lemmas and the part of speech of each words of the answers. The TreeTagger tool[3] has been used. An answer R_1 is then considered as included in an answer R_2 if all non-empty words of R_1 are included in R_2. Two words having the same lemma are considered as identical. For example "chanta" and "chanterons" are identical because they share the same lemma "chanter". Adjectives, proper names and substantives are considered as non-empty words. Following this definition, two answers R_1 and R_2 are considered identical if R_1 is included in R_2 and R_2 in R_1.

[3]www.ims.uni-stuttgart.de/projekte/corplex/TreeTagger

5.1 Merge based on candidate answer rank

The first information we used takes into account the rank of the candidate answers. The hypothesis beyond this is that the systems often provide the correct answer at first position, if they found it.

5.1.1 Simple interleaving

The first method, and probably the simplest, is to merge the candidate answers provided by all the systems: the first candidate answer of the first system is ranked in the first position; the first answer of the second system is ranked in the second position; the second answer of the first system is ranked in the third position, and so on. If one answer was already merged (because ranked at a higher rank by another system), it is not used. We choose to base the systems order given their individual score. The first system is QAVAL, the second RITEL-S and the third RITEL-P. Following that method, the accuracy (percentage of correct answers at first rank) is the one obtained by the best system. But we assume that the MRR at the top-n (with $n > 1$) would be improved.

5.1.2 Sum of the inverse of the rank

The simple interleaving method does not take into account the answer rank provided by the different systems. However, this information may be relevant and was used in order to merge candidate answer extracted from different document collection, Web articles and news paper (Chalendar et al.,). In our case, answers are extracted from the same document collection by the different systems. Then it is possible that the same wrong answers will be extracted by the different systems.

A first possible method to take into account the rank provided by the systems is to weight the candidate answer using this information. For a same answer provided by the different systems, the weight is the sum of the inverse of the rank given by the systems. To compare the answers the strict equality is applied. If a system ranks an answer at the first position and another system ranks the same answer at the second position, the weight is 1.5 ($1 + \frac{1}{2}$). The following equation express in a more formalized way this method.

$$weight = \sum \frac{1}{rank}$$

Comparing to the previous method, that one should allow to place more correct answers at the first rank.

5.2 Using confidence scores

In order to rank all their candidate answers, the systems used a confidence score associated to each candidate answer. We then wanted to use these confidence scores in order to re-rank all the candidate answers provided by all the systems. But this is only possible if all systems produce comparable scores. This is not the case. QAVAL produces scores ranging from -1 to +1. RITEL-P, being probabilistic, produces a score between 0 and +1. And RITEL-S does not use strict interval and the scores are potentially ranged from $-\infty$ to $+\infty$. The following normalization (a linear regression) has been applied to the RITEL-S and RITEL-P scores in order to place it in the range -1 to 1.

$$value_{normalized} = \frac{2 * value_{origin}}{val_{Min} - val_{Max}} - 1$$

5.2.1 Sum of confidence scores

In order to compare our methods with classical approaches, we used two methods presented in (Shaw and Fox, 1994):

- **CombSum** which adds the different confidence scores of an answer given by the different systems;
- **CombMNZ** which adds the confidence scores of the different systems and multiply the obtained value by the number of systems having found the considered answer.

5.2.2 Hybrid method

An hybrid method combining the rank and the confidence score has been defined. The weight is the sum of two elements: the higher confidence score and a value taking into account the rank given by the different systems. This value is dependent on the number of answers, the type of the equality (the answers are included or equal) which results in the form of a bonus, and the rank of the different considered answers. The weight of an answer *a* to a question *q* is then:

$$w(a) = s(a) + \prod be * (|a(q)| - \sum r(a)) \quad (1)$$

with *be* the equality bonus, *w* the weight, *s*, the score and *r* the rank.

The equality bonus, *found empirically*, is given for each systems pair. The value is 3 if the two answers are equal, 2 if an answer is included in the other and 1 otherwise. When an answer is found by two or more systems, the higher confidence score is kept. The result of this method is that the answers extracted by more than one system are favored. An answer found by only one system, even with a very high confidence score, may be downgraded.

6 Machine-learning-based method for answer re-ranking

To solve a re-ranking problem, machine learning approaches can be used (for example (Moschitti et al., 2007)). But in most of the cases, the objective is to re-rank answers provided by one system, that means to re-rank multiple hypotheses from one system. In our case, we want to re-rank multiple answers from different systems. We decided to use an SVM-based approach, namely SVMrank (Joachims, 2006), which is well adapted to our problem. An important aspect is then to choose the pertinent features for such a task. Our objective is to consider robust enough features to deal with different systems' answers without introducing biases. Two classes of characteristic should be able to give a useful representation of the answers: those related to the answer itself and those related to the question.

6.1 Answer characteristics

First of all, we should use the rank and the score as we did in the preceding merging methods. The problem may appear here because not all candidate answers are found by the different systems. In that case, the score and the rank given to these systems is then -2. It guarantees us that the features are out of the considered range $[-1, +1]$. Considering that, it may be useful to know which system provided the considered answer. For each answer all systems having found that answer are indicated. Moreover this information may help to distinguish answers coming from for example QAVAL and RITEL-S or RITEL-P from answers coming from RITEL-S and RITEL-P. The two RITEL systems share most of the modules and their answers may have the same problems. Concerning the answer, another aspect may be of interest: how many time this answer has been found? The question is not, how many times the answer appears in the documents but how many times the answer appears in a context allowing this answer to be considered as a candidate answer. We used the number of different snippets selected by the systems in which that answer was found.

6.2 Question characteristics

When observing the results obtained by the systems on different questions, we observed that the "kind" of the question has an impact on the systems' performance. More specifically, it is largely accepted in the community that at least two criteria are of importance: the length of the question, and the type of the expected answer (EAT).

Question length We may consider that the length of the questions is more or less a good indicator for the complexity level of the question. The number of non-empty words of the question can then be a interesting feature.

Expected answer type One of the task of the question processing, in a classical Question-Answering system, is to decide of which type will be the answer. For example, for a question like *Who is the president of France?* the type of the expected answer will be a named entity of the class *person* and for a question like *what wine to drink with seafood?* that the EAT is not a named entity. (Grappy, 2009) observed that the QAVAL system is better when the EAT is of a named entity class. It is possible that adding this information will, during the learning phase, positively weight an answer coming from RITEL when the EAT is not a named entity.

The value of this feature indicates the compatibility of the answer and the EAT. We used the method presented in (Grappy and Grau, 2010) and already used for the answer validation module of the QAVAL system. This method is based on a ML-based combination of different methods using named entity dictionaries, wikipedia knowledge, etc. This system gives a confidence score, ranging from -1 to +1 which indicates the confidence the system has in compatibility between the answer and the EAT. In some cases, the question processing module may indicate if the EAT is of a more fine-grained entity. For example, the question *Who is the president of France?* is not only waiting for a *person* but more precisely for a person having the function of a *president*. A new feature is then added. If the EAT is a fine-grained named entity, then the value is 1 and -1 otherwise.

7 Experiments and results

7.1 Data and observations

For the training of the SVM model, we used the answers to 104 questions provided by the 2009 Quaero evaluation campaign (Quintard et al., 2010). Only 104 questions have been used because we need to have at least one correct answer provided by at least one system in the training base for each question. Models have been trained using 5, 10, 15 and 20 answers for each system.

For the evaluation, we used 147 factoid questions used in the 2010 Quaero[4] evaluation campaign. The document collection is made of 500,000 Web pages[5]. We used the Mean Reciprocal Rank (MRR) as it is a usual metric in Question-Answering on the first five candidate answers. The MRR is the average of the reciprocal ranks of all considered answers. We also used the top-1 metric which indicates the number of correct answers ranked at the first position.

The baseline results, provided by each of the three systems, are presented in Table 2. QAVAL and RITEL-S have quite similar results which are higher than those obtained by the RITEL-P system. We can observe that, within the 20 top ranks, 38% of the questions have an answer given by all the systems, 76 % by at least 2 systems and 21% receive no correct answers. The best possible result that could be obtained by a perfect fusion method is also indicated in this table (0.79 of MRR and 79% for top-1). Such a method would lead to rank first each correct answer found by at least a system. Figure 2 presents the answer repartition between ranks 2 and 20 (the numbers of correct answers in first rank are given in Table 2). This figure shows that the systems ranked the correct answer mostly in the first positions. That means that these systems are relatively effective for re-ranking their own candidate answers. Very

System	MRR	% top-1 (#)
QAVAL	0.45	36 (53)
RITEL-S	0.41	32 (47)
RITEL-P	0.26	18 (27)
Perfect fusion	0.79	79 (115)

Table 2: Baseline results

[4] http://www.quaero.org

[5] crawled by Exalead http://www.exalead.com/

few correct answers are ranked after the tenth position. Following these observations, the evaluations are done on the first 10 candidate answers.

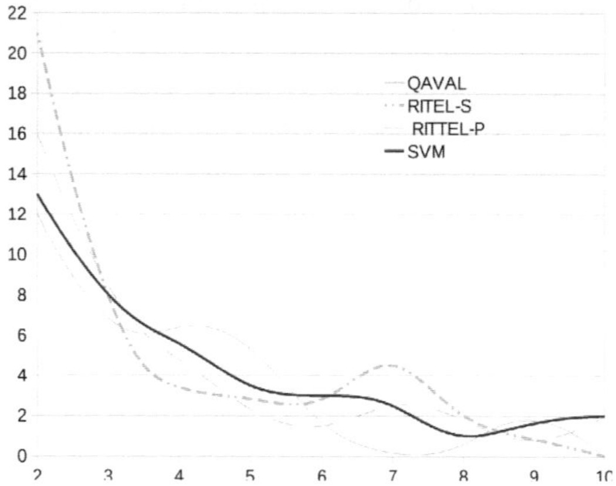

Figure 2: Answer repartition

7.2 Results and analysis

Table 3 presents the results obtained with the different merging methods: simple interleaving (*Inter.*), Sum of the inverse of the rank, CombSum, CombMNZ, hybrid method (*Hyb. Meth.*) and SVM model. In order to evaluate the impact of the RITEL-P (which achieved less good results), the results are given using two (QAVAL and RITEL-S) or three systems.

Method	MRR (2 sys. / 3 sys.)	% Top-1 (#) (2 sys. / 3 sys.)
Inter.	0.47 / 0.45	36 (53) / 36 (53)
$\sum \frac{1}{rang}$	0.48 / 0.46	38 (56)/ 36 (53)
CombSum	0.46 / 0.44	38 (56) / 34 (50)
CombMNZ	0.46/ 0.44	38 (56) / 35 (51)
Hyb. meth.	0.49 /0.44	40 (58) / 34 (50)
SVM	0.48 / **0.51**	39 (57) / **42** (62)
QAVAL	0.44	36 (53)

Table 3: General results.

As shown in Table 3, the different methods improve the results and the best method is the SVM-based model which allows an improvement of 19% of correct answer at first rank. This result is significantly better than the baseline result and this method can be considered as very effective. Figure 2 shows the results of this model. In order to validate our choice of using the SVM-Rank model, we also tested the use of a combination of decision trees, as QAVAL obtained good results with this classifier in the validation module. We obtained a MRR of 0.44 which is obviously lower than the result obtained by the SVM method. Generally speaking, the methods taking into account the answer rank allow better results than the methods using the answer confidence score. Another interesting observation is that the interleaving methods obtained better results when not using the RITEL-P system while the SVM one obtained better results when using the three systems. We assume that these two systems, RITEL-S and RITEL-P are too similar to provide strict useful information, but that a ML-based approach is able to generalize such information.

# candidate answers	% Top-1 (#)
20	39 (58)
15	39 (58)
10	43 (63)
5	37 (55)

Table 4: Impact of the number of candidate answers

normalization	MRR	# Top-1
without	0.49	58 (39%)
with	0.51	63 (43%)

Table 5: Impact of the normalization

In order to validate our choice of using only the first ten candidate answers, we did some more tests using 5, 10, 15 and 20 candidate answers. Table 4 shows the results obtained with the SVM model. We can see that is is better to consider 10 candidate answers. Beyond the first 10 candidate answers it is difficult to re-rank the correct answer without adding unsustainable noise. Moreover most of the correct answers are in the first ten candidates.

In order to validate the confidence score normalization, we did experiments with and without this normalization. Table 5 presents results which validate our choice.

To better understand how the fusion is made, we observed the repartition of the correct answers at the first rank and at the top five ranks according to the number of systems which extracted them (figure 3 and figure 4). We do this for the three best fusion approaches: the ML method with 3 systems, the hybrid method and the sum of the inverse of the ranks with two systems. As we can

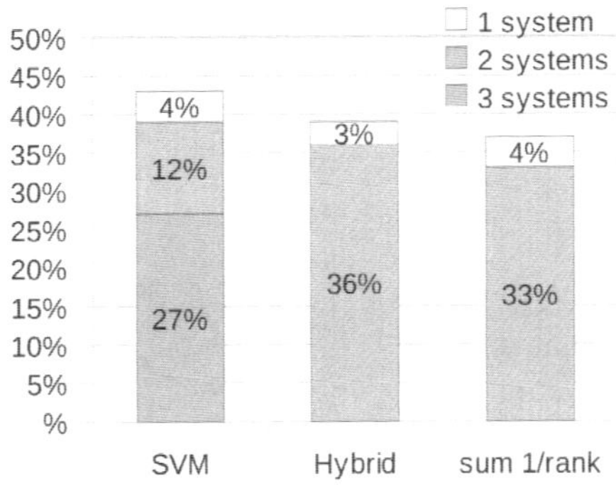

Figure 3: First rank

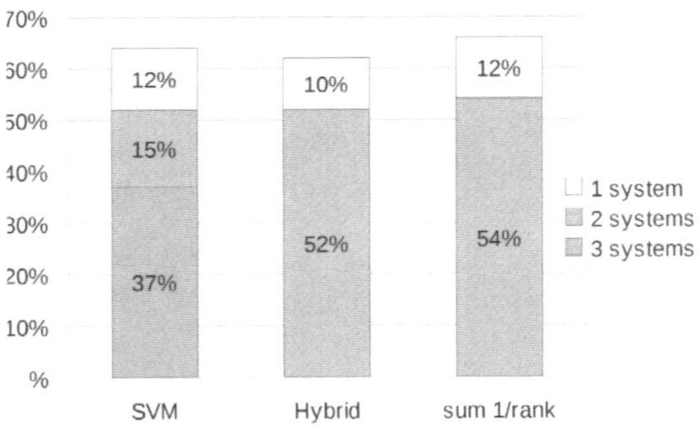

Figure 4: Top five ranks

see, in most of the cases, the three approaches often rank the correct answers found by all the systems. The best approach is the SVM-based one. It ranks 98 % of the correct answers given by the 3 systems in top 5 ranks. It also ranks better correct answers given by 2 systems (60% are ranked in the top 5 ranks versus about 48 % with the two other methods).

The rank-based method is globally reliable for selecting correct answers in the top 5 ranks. This behavior is consistent with the fact that our QA systems, when they found a correct answer, generally rank it in first positions.

Some correct answers given by only one system remain in the first position, and about 10% of them remain in the top 5 ranks and are not superseded by common wrong answers. However the major part of these correct single-system answers are discarded after the 5 first ranks (39% of them by the SVM method, 45% by the rank-based method and 53% by the hybrid method). In that case, a ML method is a better solution for deciding, however an improvement would be possible only if other features could be found for a better characterization of a correct answer, or maybe by enlarging the training base.

According to these results, we also can expect that with more QA systems, a fusion approach would be more effective.

8 Conclusion

Improving QA systems is a very difficult task, given the variability of the pairs (question / answering passages), the complexity of the processes and the variability of they performances. Thus, an improvement can be searched by the hybridization of different QA systems. We studied hybridization at different levels, internal combination of processes and merging of end-results. The first combination type did not proved to be useful, maybe because each system has its global coherence leading their modules to be more interdependent than expected. Thus it appears that combining different strategies is better realized with the combination of their end-results, specially when these strategies obtain good results. We proposed different combination methods, based on the confidence scores, the answer rank, that are adapted to the QA context, and a ML-method which considers more features for characterizing the answers. This last method obtains the better results, even if the simpler ones also show good results. The proposed methods can be applied to other QA systems, as the features used are generally provided by the systems.

References

R.M. Aceves-Pérez, M. Montes-y Gómez, L. Villaseñor-Pineda, and L.A. Ureña-López. 2008. Two approaches for multilingual question answering: Merging passages vs. merging answers. *International Journal of Computational Linguistics & Chinese Language Processing*, 13(1):27–40.

G. Bernard, S. Rosset, O. Galibert, E. Bilinski, and G. Adda. 2009. The LIMSI participation to the QAst 2009 track. In *Working Notes of CLEF 2009 Workshop*, Corfu, Greece, October.

G. De Chalendar, T. Dalmas, F. Elkateb-gara, O. Ferret, B. Grau, M. Hurault-plantet, G. Illouz, L. Monceaux, I. Robba, and A. Vilnat. The question answering system QALC at LIMSI: experiments in using Web and WordNet.

Arnaud Grappy and Brigitte Grau. 2010. Answer type validation in question answering systems. In *Adap-*

tivity, Personalization and Fusion of Heterogeneous Information, RIAO '10, pages 9–15.

Arnaud Grappy, Brigitte Grau, Mathieu-Henri Falco, Anne-Laure Ligozat, Isabelle Robba, and Anne Vilnat. 2011. Selecting answers to questions from web documents by a robust validation process. In *The 2011 IEEE/WIC/ACM International Conference on Web Intelligence*.

Arnaud Grappy. 2009. *Validation de rponses dans un systme de questions rponses*. Ph.D. thesis, Universit Paris Sud, Orsay.

Valentin Jijkoun and Maarten De Rijke. 2004. Answer Selection in a Multi-Stream Open Domain Question Answering System. In *Proceedings 26th European Conference on Information Retrieval (ECIR'04), volume 2997 of LNCS*, pages 99–111. Springer.

Thorsten Joachims. 2006. Training linear SVMs in linear time. In *Proceedings of the 12th ACM SIGKDD international conference on Knowledge discovery and data mining*, KDD '06, pages 217–226, New York, NY, USA. ACM.

Alessandro Moschitti, Silvia Quarteroni, Roberto Basili, and Suresh Manandhar. 2007. Exploiting Syntactic and Shallow Semantic Kernels for Question Answer Classification. In *Proceedings of the 45th Annual Meeting of the Association of Computational Linguistics*, pages 776–783, Prague, Czech Republic, June. Association for Computational Linguistics.

Ludovic Quintard, Olivier Galibert, Gilles Adda, Brigitte Grau, Dominique Laurent, Veronique Moriceau, Sophie Rosset, Xavier Tannier, and Anne Vilnat. 2010. Question Answering on Web Data: The QA Evaluation in Quaero. In *LREC'10*, Valletta, Malta, May.

Joseph A. Shaw and Edward A. Fox. 1994. Combination of multiple searches. In *TREC-2*. NIST SPECIAL PUBLICATION SP.

Alberto Tellez-Valero, Manuel Montes Gomez, Luis Villasenor Pineda, and Anselmo Penas. 2010. Towards multi-stream question answering using answer validation. *Informatica*, 34(1):45–54.

Dave Toney, Sophie Rosset, Aurlien Max, Olivier Galibert, and Eric Bilinski. 2008. An Evaluation of Spoken and Textual Interaction in the RITEL Interactive Question Answering System. In European Language Resources Association (ELRA), editor, *Proceedings of the Sixth International Language Resources and Evaluation (LREC'08)*, Marrakech, Morocco, May.

A Generalised Hybrid Architecture for NLP

Alistair Willis
Department of Computing
The Open University,
Milton Keynes, UK
a.g.willis@open.ac.uk

Hui Yang
Department of Computing
The Open University,
Milton Keynes, UK
h.yang@open.ac.uk

Anne De Roeck
Department of Computing
The Open University,
Milton Keynes, UK
a.deroeck@open.ac.uk

Abstract

Many tasks in natural language processing require that sentences be classified from a set of discrete interpretations. In these cases, there appear to be great benefits in using hybrid systems which apply multiple analyses to the test cases. In this paper, we examine a general principle for building hybrid systems, based on combining the results of several, high precision heuristics. By generalising the results of systems for sentiment analysis and ambiguity recognition, we argue that if correctly combined, multiple techniques classify better than single techniques. More importantly, the combined techniques can be used in tasks where no single classification is appropriate.

1 Introduction

The success of hybrid NLP systems has demonstrated that complex linguistic phenomena and tasks can be successfully addressed using a combination of techniques. At the same time, it is clear from the NLP literature, that the performance of any specific technique is highly dependent on the characteristics of the data. Thus, a specific technique which performs well on one dataset might perform very differently on another, even on similar tasks, and even if the two datasets are taken from the same domain. Also, it is possible that the properties affecting the effectiveness of a particular technique may vary within a single document (De Roeck, 2007).

As a result of this, for many important NLP applications there is no single technique which is clearly to be preferred. For example, recent approaches to the task of anaphora resolution include syntactic analyses (Haghighi and Klein, 2009), Maximum Entropy models (Charniak and Elsner, 2009) and Support Vector Machines (Yang et al., 2006; Versley et al., 2008). The performance of each of these techniques varies depending upon the particular choice of training and test data.

This state of affairs provides a particular opportunity for hybrid system development. The overall performance of an NLP system depends on complex interactions between the various phenomena exhibited by the text under analysis, and the success of a given technique can be sensitive to the different properties of that text. In particular, the text's or document's properties are not generally known until the document comes to be analysed. Therefore, there is a need for systems which are able to *adapt* to different text styles at the point of analysis, and select the most appropriate combination of techniques for the individual cases. This should lead to hybridising techniques which are robust or adaptive in the face of varying textual styles and properties.

We present a generalisation of two hybridisation techniques first described in Yang et al. (2012) and Chantree et al. (2006). Each uses hybrid techniques in a detection task: the first is emotion detection from suicide notes, the second is detecting nocuous ambiguity in requirements documents. The distinguishing characteristic of both tasks is that a successful solution needs to accommodate uncertainty in the outcome. The generalised methodology described here is particularly suited to such tasks, where as well as selecting between possible solutions, there is a need to identify a class of instances where no single solution is most appropriate.

Proceedings of the Workshop on Innovative Hybrid Approaches to the Processing of Textual Data (Hybrid2012), EACL 2012, pages 97–105,
Avignon, France, April 23 2012.

2 Hybridisation as a Solution to Classification Tasks

The methodology described in this paper proposes hybrid systems as a solution to NLP tasks which attempt to determine an appropriate interpretation from a set of discrete alternatives, in particular where no one outcome is clearly preferable. One such task is nocuous ambiguity detection. For example, in sentence (1), the pronoun *he* could refer to *Bill*, *John* or to *John's father*.

(1) When Bill met John's father, he was pleased.

Here, there are three possible antecedents for *he*, and it does not follow that all human readers would agree on a common interpretation of the anaphor. For example, readers might divide between interpreting *he* as *Bill* or as *John's father*. Or perhaps a majority of readers feel that the sentence is sufficiently ambiguous that they cannot decide on the intended interpretation. These are cases of *nocuous ambiguity* (Chantree et al., 2006), where a group of readers do not interpret a piece of text in the same way, and may be unaware that the misunderstanding has even arisen.

Similarly, as a classification task, sentiment analysis for sentences or fragments may need to accommodate instances where multiple sentiments can be identified, or possibly none at all. Example (2) contains evidence of both *guilt* and *love*:

(2) Darling wife, — I'm sorry for everything.

Hybrid solutions are particularly suited to such tasks, in contrast to approaches which use a single technique to select between possible alternatives. The hybrid methodology proposed in this paper approaches such tasks in two stages:

1. Define and apply a set of heuristics, where each heuristic captures an aspect of the phenomenon and estimates the likelihood of a particular interpretation.

2. Apply a combination function to either combine or select between the values contributed by the individual heuristics to obtain better overall system performance.

The model makes certain assumptions about the design of heuristics. They can draw on a multitude of techniques such as a set of selection features based on domain knowledge, linguistic analysis and statistical models. Each heuristic is a *partial descriptor* of an aspect of a particular phenomenon and is intended as an "expert", whose opinion competes against the opinion offered by other heuristics. Heuristics may or may not be independent. The crucial aspect is that each of the heuristics should seek to *maximise precision* or complement the performance of another heuristic.

The purpose of step 2 is to maximise the contribution of each heuristic for optimal performance of the overall system. Experimental results analysed below show that selecting an appropriate mode of combination helps accommodate differences between datasets and can introduce additional robustness to the overall system. The experimental results also show that appropriate combination of the contribution of high precision heuristics significantly increases recall.

For the tasks under investigation here, it proves possible to select combination functions that allow the system to identify behaviour beyond classifying the subject text into a single category. Because the individual heuristics are *partial* descriptions of the whole language model of the text, it is possible to reason about the interaction of these partial descriptions, and identify cases where either none, or many, of the potential interpretations of the text are possible. The systems use either a machine learning technique or a voting strategies to combine the individual heuristics.

In sections 3 and 4, we explore how the previously proposed solutions can be classed as instances of the proposed hybridisation model.

3 Case study: Sentiment Analysis

Following Pang et al. (2002) and the release of the polarity 2.0 dataset, it is common for sentiment analysis tasks to attempt to classify text segments as either of positive or negative sentiment. The task has been extended to allow sentences to be annotated as displaying both positive and negative sentiment (Wilson et al., 2009) or indicating the degree of intensity (Thelwall et al., 2010).

The data set used for the 2011 i2b2 shared challenge (Pestian et al., 2012) differs from this model by containing a total of 15 different sentiments to classify the sentences. Each text fragment was labelled with zero, one or more of the 15 sentiments. For example, sentence (2) was annotated with both *Love* and *Guilt*. The fragments varied between phrases and full sentences, and the task aims to identify all the sentiments displayed by each text fragment.

In fact, several of the proposed sentiments were identified using keyword recognition alone, so the hybrid framework was applied only to recognise the sentiments *Thankfulness*, *Love*, *Guilt*, *Hopelessness*, *Information* and *Instruction*; instances of the other sentiments were too sparse to be reliably classified with the hybrid system. A keyword cue list of 984 terms was manually constructed from the training data based on their frequency in the annotated set; no other public emotion lexicon was used. This cue list was used both to recognise the sparse sentiments, and as input to the CRF.

3.1 Architecture

An overview of the architecture is shown in figure 1. Heuristics are used which operate at the word level (Conditional Random Fields), and at the sentence level (Support Vector Machine, Naive Bayes and Maximum Entropy). These are combined using a voting strategy that selects the most appropriate combination of methods in each case.

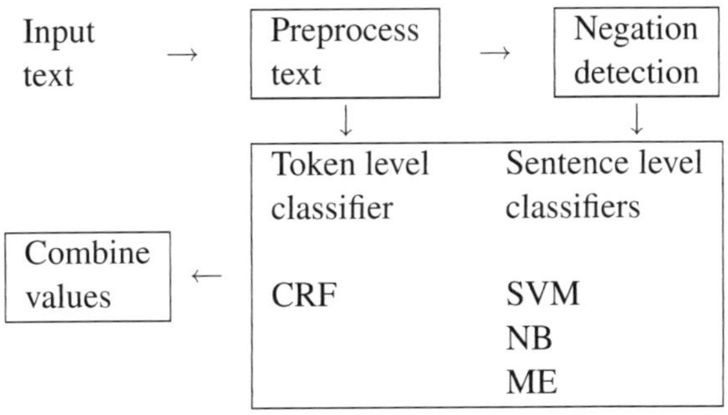

Figure 1: Architecture for sentiment classification task

The text is preprocessed using the tokeniser, POS tagger and chunker from the Genia tagger, and parsed using the Stanford dependency parser. This information, along with a negation recogniser, is used to generate training vectors for the heuristics. Negation is known to have a major effect on sentiment interpretation (Jia et al., 2009).

3.2 Sentiment recognition heuristics

The system uses a total of four classifiers for each of the emotions to be recognised. The only token-level classification was carried out using CRFs (Lafferty et al., 2001) which have been successfully used on Named Entity Recognition tasks. However, both token- and phrase-level recognition are necessary to capture cases where sentences convey more than one sentiment. The CRF-based classifiers were trained to recognise each of the main emotions based on the main keyword cues and the surrounding context. The CRF is trained on the set of features shown in figure 2, and implemented using CRF++[1].

Feature	Description
Words	word, lemma, POS tag, phrase chunk tag
Context	2 previous words and 2 following words with lemma, POS tags and chunk tags
Syntax	Dependency relation label and the lemma of the governer word in focus
Semantics	Is it negated?

Figure 2: Features used for CRF classifier

Three sentence-level classifiers were trained for each emotion, those being Naive Bayes and Maximum Entropy learners implemented by the MALLET toolkit[2], and a Support Vector Machine model implemented using SVM light[3] with the linear kernel. In each case, the learners were trained using a feature vector using the two feature vectors as shown in figure 3.

Feature vector	Description
Words	word lemmas
Semantics	negation terms identified by the negative term lexicon, and cue terms from the emotion term lexicon

Figure 3: Features used for sentence-level classifiers

A classifier was built for each of the main emotions under study. For each of the six emotions, four learners were trained to identify whether the text contains an instance of that emotion. That is, an instance of text receives 6 groups of results, and each group contains 4 results obtained from different classifiers estimating whether one particular emotion occurs. The combination function predicts the final sentiment(s) exhibited by the sentence.

[1]`http://crfpp.sourceforge.net/`
[2]`http://mallet.cs.umass.edu/`
[3]`http://svmlight.joachims.org/`

3.3 Combination function

To combine the outputs of the heuristics, Yang et al. (2012) use a voting model. Three different combination methods are investigated:

Any If a sentence is identified as an emotion instance by any one of the ML-based models, it is considered a true instance of that emotion.

Majority If a sentence is identified as an emotion instance by two or more of the ML-based models, it is considered a true instance of that emotion.

Combined If a sentence is identified as an emotion instance by two or more of the ML-based models *or* it is identified as an emotion instance by the ML-based model with the best precision for that emotion, it is considered a true instance of that emotion.

This combined measure reflects the intuition that where an individual heuristic is reliable for a particular phenomenon, then that heuristic's vote should be awarded a greater weight. The precision scores of the individual heuristics is shown in table 1, where the heuristic with the best precision for that emotion is highlighted.

Emotion	CRF	NB	ME	SVM
Thankfulness	**60.6**	58.8	57.6	52.6
Love	76.2	68.5	**77.6**	76.9
Guilt	58.1	46.8	35.3	**58.3**
Hopelessness	73.5	63.3	68.7	**74.5**
Information	53.1	41.0	48.1	**76.2**
Instruction	**76.3**	63.6	70.9	75.9

Table 1: Precision scores (%) for individual heuristics

3.4 Results

Table 2 reports the system performance on 6 emotions by both individual and combined heuristics.

In each case, the best performer among the four individual heuristics is highlighted. As can be seen from the table, the *Any* combinator and the *Combined* combinators both outperform each of the individual classifiers. This supports the hypothesis that hybrid systems work better overall.

3.5 Additional comments

The overall performance improvement obtained by combining the individual measures raises the question of how the individual elements interact. Table 3 shows the performance of the combined systems on the different emotion classes. For each emotion, the highest precision, recall and f-measure is highlighted.

As we would have expected, the *Any* strategy has the highest recall in all cases, while the *Majority* strategy, with the highest bar for acceptance, has the highest precision for most cases. The *Any* and *Combined* measures appear to be broadly comparable: for the measures we have used, it appears that the precision of the individual classifiers is sufficiently high that the combination process of improving recall does not impact excessively on the overall precision.

A further point of interest is that table 2 demonstrates that the Naive Bayes classifier often returns the highest f-score of the individual classifiers, even though it never has the best precision (table 1). This supports our thesis that a successful hybrid system can be built from multiple classifiers with high precision, rather than focussing on single classifiers which have the best individual performance (the *Combined* strategy favours the highest precision heuristic).

4 Nocuous ambiguity detection

It is a cornerstone of NLP that all text contains a high number of potentially ambiguous words or constructs. Only some of those will lead to misunderstandings, where two (or more) participants in a text-mediated interchange will interpret the text in different, and incompatible ways, without realising that this is the case. This is defined as nocuous ambiguity (Willis et al., 2008), in contrast to innocuous ambiguity, where the text is interpreted in the same way by different readers, even if that text supports different possible analyses.

The phenomenon of nocuous ambiguity is particularly problematic in high stake situations. For example, in software engineering, a failure to share a common interpretation of requirements stated in natural language may lead to incorrect system implementation and the attendant risk of system failure, or higher maintenance costs. The systems described by Chantree et al. (2006) and Yang et al. (2010a) aim not to *resolve* ambigu-

Emotion	Individual heuristics CRF	NB	ME	SVM	Hybrid models Any	Majority	Combined
Thankfulness	59.5	59.6	**61.9**	60.3	63.9	63.0	64.2
Love	63.7	**69.3**	66.5	61.5	72.0	70.3	71.0
Guilt	35.3	**40.5**	27.7	37.8	46.3	29.9	45.8
Hopelessness	63.2	**64.1**	59.9	57.0	67.3	65.4	67.3
Information	42.3	**47.7**	43.7	43.4	50.2	45.5	47.8
Instruction	**65.7**	65.7	63.4	58.8	72.1	65.4	72.0

Table 2: F-scores (%) for individual and combined heuristics (sentiment analysis)

	Any			Majority			Combined		
	P	R	F	P	R	F	P	R	F
Thankfulness	52.6	**81.6**	63.9	**60.6**	65.7	63.0	55.0	77.1	**64.2**
Love	68.7	**75.6**	**72.0**	**77.9**	64.0	70.3	74.6	67.7	71.0
Guilt	46.6	**46.2**	**46.3**	50.0	21.4	29.9	**50.5**	41.9	45.8
Hopelessness	64.1	**70.8**	67.3	**80.3**	55.2	65.4	66.3	68.4	**67.3**
Information	40.9	**64.9**	**50.2**	**49.9**	41.8	45.5	45.2	50.7	47.8
Instruction	68.5	**76.1**	**72.1**	**80.8**	54.9	65.4	70.3	73.7	72.0

Table 3: Precision, recall and F-scores (%) for the combined systems (sentiment analysis)

ous text in requirements, but to *identify* where instances of text might display nocuous ambiguity.

These systems demonstrate how, for hybrid systems, the correct choice of combination function is crucial to how the individual heuristics work together to optimise overall system performance.

4.1 Nocuous Ambiguity: Coordination

Chantree et al. (2006) focus on coordination attachment ambiguity, which occurs when a modifier can attach to one or more conjuncts of a coordinated phrase. For example, in sentence (3), readers may divide over whether the modifier *short* attaches to both *books* and *papers* (wide scope), or only to *books* (narrow scope).

(3) I read some short books and papers.

In each case, the coordination involves a near conjunct, (*books* in (3)), a far conjunct, (*papers*) and a modifier (*short*). The modifier might also be a PP, or an adverb in the case where a VP contains the conjunction. In disambiguation, the task would be to identify the correct scope of the modifier (i.e. which of two possible bracketings is the correct one). For nocuous ambiguity detection, the task is to identify to what extent people interpret the text in the same way, and to flag the instance as nocuous if they diverge relative to some threshold.

4.1.1 The dataset

17 human judgements were collected for each of 138 instances of sentences exhibiting coordination ambiguity drawn from a collection of software requirements documents. The majority of cases (118 instances) were noun compounds, with some adjective and some preposition modifiers (36 and 18 instances respectively). Participants were asked to choose between wide scope or narrow scope modifier attachment, or to indicate that they experienced the example as ambiguous. Each instance is assigned a *certainty* for wide and narrow scope modification reflecting the distribution of judgements. For instance, if 12 judges favoured wide scope for some instance, 3 judges favoured narrow scope and 1 judge thought the instance ambiguous, then the certainty for wide scope is 71% (12/17), and the certainty for narrow scope is 18% (3/17).

A key concept in nocuous ambiguity is that of an *ambiguity threshold*, τ. For some τ:

- if at least τ judges agree on the interpretation

of the text, then the ambiguity is *innocuous*,

- otherwise the ambiguity is *nocuous*.

So for $\tau = 70\%$, at least 70% of the judges must agree on an interpretation. Clearly, the higher τ is set, the more agreement is required, and the greater the number of examples which will be considered nocuous.

4.1.2 Selectional heuristics

A series of heuristics was developed, each capturing information that would lead to a preference for either wide or narrow scope modifier attachment. Examples from Chantree et al. (2006) propose seven heuristics, including the following:

Co-ordination Matching If the head words of the two conjuncts are frequently co-ordinated, this is taken to predict wide modifier scope.

Distributional Similarity If the head words of the two conjuncts have high distributional similarity (Lee, 1999), this is taken to predict wide modifier scope.

Collocation Frequency If the head word of the near conjunct has a higher collocation with the modifier than the far conjunct, this is taken to predict narrow modifier scope.

Morphology If the conjunct headwords have similar morphological markers, this is taken to predict wide modifier scope (Okumura and Muraki, 1994).

As with the sentiment recognition heuristics (section 3.2), each predicts one interpretation of the sentence with high precision, but potentially low recall. Recall of the *system* is improved by combining the heuristics, as described in the next section. Note that for the first three of these heuristics, Chantree et al. (2006) use the British National Corpus[4], accessed via the Sketch Engine (Kilgarriff et al., 2004), although a domain specific corpus could potentially be constructed.

4.1.3 Combining the heuristics

Chantree et al. (2006) combine the heuristics using the logistic regression algorithms contained in the WEKA machine learning package (Witten and Frank, 2005). The regression algorithm was trained against the training data so that the text was interpreted as nocuous *either* if there was evidence for both wide and narrow modifier scope *or* if there was no evidence for either.

This system performed reasonably for mid-range ambiguity thresholds (around $50\% < \tau < 80\%$; for high and low thresholds, naive baselines give very high accuracy). However, in subsequent work, Yang et al. (2010b) have demonstrated that by combining the results in a similar way, but using the LogitBoost algorithm, significant improvements can be gained over the logistic regression approach. Their paper suggests that LogitBoost provides an improvement in accuracy of up to 21% in the range of interest for τ over that of logistic regression.

We believe that this improvement reflects that LogitBoost handles interacting variables better than logistic regression, which assumes a linear relationship between individual variables. This supports our hybridisation method, which assumes that the individual heuristics can interact. In these cases, the heuristics bring into play different types of information (some structural, some distributional, some morphological) where each relies on partial information and favours one particular outcome over another. It would be unusual to find strong evidence of both wide and narrow scope modifier attachment from a single heuristic and the effect of one heuristic can modulate, or enhance the effect of another. This is supported by Chantree et al.'s (2006) observation that although some of the proposed heuristics (such as the morphology heuristic) perform poorly on their own, their inclusion in the regression model does improve the overall performance of the system

To conclude, comparing the results of Chantree et al. (2006) and Yang et al. (2010b) demonstrates that the technique of combining individual, high precision heuristics is a successful one. However, the combination function needs careful consideration, and can have as large an effect on the final results as the choice of the heuristics themselves.

4.2 Nocuous Ambiguity: Anaphora

As example (1) demonstrates, nocuous ambiguity can occur where there are multiple possible antecedents for an anaphor. Yang et al. (2010a) have addressed the task of nocuous ambiguity detection for anaphora in requirements documents, in sentences such as (4), where the pronoun *it* has

[4] `http://www.natcorp.ox.ac.uk/`

three potential antecedents (italicised).

(4) *The procedure* shall convert *the 24 bit image* to *an 8 bit image*, then display it in a dynamic window.

As with the coordination task, the aim is to identify nocuous ambiguity, rather than attempt to disambiguate the sentence.

4.2.1 The dataset

The data set used for the anaphora task consisted of 200 sentences collected from requirements documents which contained a third person pronoun and multiple possible antecedents. Each instance was judged by at least 13 people.

The concept of ambiguity threshold, τ, remains central to nocuous ambiguity for anaphora. The definition remains the same as in section 4.1.1, so that an anaphor displays innocuous ambiguity if there is an antecedent that at least τ judges agree on, and nocuous ambiguity otherwise. So if, say, 75% of the judges considered *an 8 bit image* to be the correct antecedent in (4), then the sentence would display nocuous ambiguity at $\tau = 80\%$, but innocuous ambiguity at $\tau = 70\%$.

For *innocuous* cases, the potential antecedent NP with certainty of at least τ is tagged as *Y*, and all other NPs are tagged as *N*. For *nocuous* cases, potential antecedents with τ greater than 0 are tagged as *Q* (questionable), or are tagged *N* otherwise ($\tau = 0$, ie. unselected).

4.2.2 Selectional Heuristics

The approach to this task uses only one selection function (Naive Bayes), but uses the output to support two different voting strategies. Twelve heuristics (described fully in Yang et al. (2010a)) fall broadly into three types which signal the likelihood that the NP is a possible antecedent:

linguistic such as whether the potential antecedent is a definite or indefinite NP

contextual such as the potential antecedent's recency, and

statistical such as collocation frequencies.

To treat a sentence, the classifier is applied to each of the potential antecedents and assigns a pair of values: the first is the predicted class of the antecedent (*Y*, *N* or *Q*), and the second is the associated probability of that classification.

Given a list of class assignments to potential antecedents with associated probabilities, a *weak positive threshold*, W_Y, and a *weak negative threshold*, W_N:

if the list of potential antecedents contains:
  one Y, no Q, one or more N
or
  no Y, one Q, one or more N but no *weak negatives*
or
  one *strong positive* Y , any number of Q or N
then
  the ambiguity is INNOCUOUS
else
  the ambiguity is NOCUOUS

where a classification Y is *strong positive* if its associated probability is greater than W_Y, and a classification N is *weak negative* if its associated probability is smaller than W_N.

Figure 4: Combination function for nocuous anaphora detection with weak thresholds

4.2.3 The combination function

As suggested previously, the choice of combination function can strongly affect the system performance, even on the same set of selectional heuristics. Yang et al. (2010a) demonstrate two different combination functions which exploit the selectional heuristics in different ways. Both combination functions use a voting strategy.

The first voting strategy states that a sentence exhibits innocuous ambiguity if either:

- there is a single antecedent labelled *Y*, and all others are labelled *N*, or
- there is a single antecedent labelled *Q*, and all others are labelled *N*.

The second strategy is more sophisticated, and depends on the use of *weak thresholds*: intuitively, the aim is to classify the text as innocuous if is (exactly) one *clearly* preferred antecedent among the alternatives. The combination function is shown in figure 4. The second clause states that a single potential antecedent labelled Q can be enough to suggest innocuous ambiguity if all the alternatives are N with a high probability.

	Model without weak thresholds			Model with weak thresholds		
τ	P	R	F	P	R	F
0.50	27.2	55.0	45.7	24.1	95.0	**59.7**
0.60	33.9	67.5	56.3	30.9	97.5	**68.1**
0.70	45.1	76.2	66.9	43.9	98.4	**78.8**
0.80	58.0	85.0	77.7	56.1	97.9	**85.5**
0.90	69.1	88.6	83.9	67.4	98.4	**90.1**
1.0	82.2	95.0	92.1	82.0	99.4	**95.3**

Table 4: Precision, Recall and f-measure (%) for the two combination functions (anaphora)

Task	Selectional heuristics	Combination functions
Sentiment analysis	CRF NB SVM ME	Voting - any - majority - combined
Nocuous ambiguity (coordination)	3 distributional metrics 4 others	logistic regression LogitBoost
Nocuous ambiguity (anaphora)	NB	Voting Voting (+ threshold)

Table 5: Hybridisation approaches used

The performance of the two voting strategies is shown in table 4. It is clear that the improved overall performance of the strategy with weak thresholds is due to the improved *recall* when the functions are combined; the precision is comparable in both cases. Again, this shows the desired combinatorial behaviour; a combination of high precision heuristics can yield good overall results.

5 Conclusion

The hybridised systems we have considered are summarised in table 5. This examination suggests that hybridisation can be a powerful technique for classifying linguistic phenomena. However, there is currently little guidance on principles regarding hybrid system design. The studies here show that there is room for more systematic study of the design principles underlying hybridisation, and for investigating systematic methodologies.

This small scale study suggests several principles. First, the sentiment analysis study has shown that a set of heuristics and a suitable combination function can outperform the best individually performing heuristic or technique. In particular, our results suggest that hybrid systems of the kind described here are most valuable when there is significant interaction between the various linguistic phenomena present in the text. This occurs both with nocuous ambiguity (where competition between the different interpretations creates disagreement overall), and with sentiment analysis (where a sentence can convey multiple emotions). As a result, hybridisation is particularly powerful where there are multiple competing factors, or where it is unclear whether there is sufficient evidence for a particular classification.

Second, successful hybrid systems can be built using multiple heuristics, even if each of the heuristics has low recall on its own. Our case studies show that with the correct choice of hybridisation functions, high precision heuristics can be combined to give good overall recall while maintaining acceptable overall precision.

Finally, the mode of combination matters. The voting system is successful in the sentiment analysis task, where different outcomes are not exclusive (the presence of *guilt* does not preclude the presence of *love*). On the other hand, the logitBoost combinator is appropriate when the different interpretations are exclusive (narrow modifier scope does preclude wide scope). Here, logitBoost can be interpreted as conveying the degree of uncertainty among the alternatives. The coordination ambiguity case demonstrates that the individual heuristics do not need to be independent, but if the method of combining them assumes independence, the benefits of hybridisation will be lost (logistic regression compared to LogitBoost).

This analysis has highlighted the interplay between task, heuristics and combinator. Currently, the nature of this interplay is not well understood, and we believe that there is scope for investigating the broader range of hybrid systems that might be applied to different tasks.

Acknowledgments

The authors would like to thank the UK Engineering and Physical Sciences Research Council who funded this work through the MaTREx project (EP/F068859/1), and the anonymous reviewers for helpful comments and suggestions.

References

Francis Chantree, Bashar Nuseibeh, Anne De Roeck, and Alistair Willis. 2006. Identifying nocuous ambiguities in natural language requirements. In *Proceedings of 14th IEEE International Requirements Engineering conference (RE'06)*, Minneapolis/St Paul, Minnesota, USA, September.

Eugene Charniak and Micha Elsner. 2009. EM works for pronoun anaphora resolution. In *Proceedings of the 12th Conference of the European Chapter of the Association for Computational Linguistics (EACL '09)*, pages 148–156.

Anne De Roeck. 2007. The role of data in NLP: The case for dataset profiling. In Nicolas Nicolov, Ruslan Mitkov, and Galia Angelova, editors, *Recent Advances in Natural Language Processing IV*, volume 292 of *Current Issues in Linguistic Theory*, pages 259–266. John Benjamin Publishing Company, Amsterdam.

Aria Haghighi and Dan Klein. 2009. Simple coreference resolution with rich syntactic and semantic features. In *Proceedings of the 2009 Conference on Empirical Methods in Natural Language Processing*, pages 1152–1161, Singapore, August.

Lifeng Jia, Clement Yu, and Weiyi Meng. 2009. The effect of negation on sentiment analysis and retrieval effectiveness. In *The 18th ACM Conference on Information and Knowledge Management (CIKM'09)*, Hong Kong, China, November.

Adam Kilgarriff, Pavel Rychly, Pavel Smrz, and David Tugwell. 2004. The sketch engine. Technical Report ITRI-04-08, University of Brighton.

John Lafferty, Andrew McCallum, and Fernando Pereira. 2001. Conditional random fields: Probabilistic models for segmenting and labeling sequence data. In *Proceedings of the International Conference on Machine Learning (ICML-2001)*, pages 282–289.

Lillian Lee. 1999. Measures of distributional similarity. In *Proceedings of the 37th Annual Meeting of the Association for Computational Linguistics*, pages 25–32, College Park, Maryland, USA, June. Association for Computational Linguistics.

Akitoshi Okumura and Kazunori Muraki. 1994. Symmetric pattern matching analysis for english coordinate structures. In *Proceedings of the 4th Conference on Applied Natural Language Processing*, pages 41–46.

Bo Pang, Lillian Lee, and Shivakumar Vaithyanathan. 2002. Thumbs up? Sentiment classification using machine learning techniques. In *Proceedings of the Conference on Empirical Methods in Natural Language Processing*, pages 79–86, Philadelphia, July.

John P. Pestian, Pawel Matykiewicz, Michelle Linn-Gust, Brett South, Ozlem Uzuner, Jan Wiebe, K. Bretonnel Cohen, John Hurdle, and Christopher Brew. 2012. Sentiment analysis of suicide notes: A shared task. *Biomedical Informatics Insights*, 5(Suppl 1):3–16.

Mike Thelwall, Kevan Buckley, Georgios Paltoglou, Di Cai, and Arvid Kappas. 2010. Sentiment in short strength detection informal text. *Journal of the American Society for Information Science & Technology*, 61(12):2544–2558, December.

Yannick Versley, Alessandro Moschitti, Massimo Poesio, and Xiaofeng Yang. 2008. Coreference systems based on kernels methods. In *Proceedings of the 22nd International Conference on Computational Linguistics (Coling 2008)*, pages 961–968, Manchester, August.

Alistair Willis, Francis Chantree, and Anne DeRoeck. 2008. Automatic identification of nocuous ambiguity. *Research on Language and Computation*, 6(3-4):355–374, December.

Theresa Wilson, Janyce Wiebe, and Paul Hoffmann. 2009. Recognizing contextual polarity: An exploration of features for phrase-level sentiment analysis. *Computational Linguistics*, 35(3):399–433.

Ian H. Witten and Eibe Frank. 2005. *Data mining: Practical machine learning tools and techniques*. Morgan Kaufmann, 2nd edition.

Xiaofeng Yang, Jian Su, and Chew Lim Tan. 2006. Kernel-based pronoun resolution with structured syntactic knowledge. In *Proceedings of the 21st International Conference on Computational Linguistics and 44th Annual Meeting of the ACL*, pages 41–48, Sydney, July.

Hui Yang, Anne De Roeck, Vincenzo Gervasi, Alistair Willis, and Bashar Nuseibeh. 2010a. Extending nocuous ambiguity analysis for anaphora in natural language requirements. In *18th International IEEE Requirements Engineering Conference (RE'10)*, Sydney, Australia, Oct.

Hui Yang, Anne De Roeck, Alistair Willis, and Bashar Nuseibeh. 2010b. A methodology for automatic identification of nocuous ambiguity. In *23rd International Conference on Computational Linguistics (COLING 2010)*, Beijing, China.

Hui Yang, Alistair Willis, Anne De Roeck, and Bashar Nuseibeh. 2012. A hybrid model for automatic emotion recognition in suicide notes. *Biomedical Informatics Insights*, 5(Suppl. 1):17–30, January.

Incorporating Linguistic Knowledge in Statistical Machine Translation: Translating Prepositions

Reshef Shilon
Dept. of Linguistics
Tel Aviv University
Israel

Hanna Fadida
Dept. of Computer Science
Technion
Israel

Shuly Wintner
Dept. of Computer Science
University of Haifa
Israel

Abstract

Prepositions are hard to translate, because their meaning is often vague, and the choice of the correct preposition is often arbitrary. At the same time, making the correct choice is often critical to the coherence of the output text. In the context of statistical machine translation, this difficulty is enhanced due to the possible long distance between the preposition and the head it modifies, as opposed to the local nature of standard language models. In this work we use monolingual language resources to determine the set of prepositions that are most likely to occur with each verb. We use this information in a transfer-based Arabic-to-Hebrew statistical machine translation system. We show that incorporating linguistic knowledge on the distribution of prepositions significantly improves the translation quality.

1 Introduction

Prepositions are hard to translate. Prepositional phrases modify both nouns and verbs (and, in some languages, other parts of speech); we only focus on verbs in this work. When a prepositional phrase modifies a verb, it can function as a complement or as an adjunct of the verb. In the former case, the verb typically determines the preposition, and the choice is rather arbitrary (or idiomatic). In fact, the choice of preposition can vary among synonymous verbs even in the same language. Thus, English *think* takes either *of* or *about*, whereas *ponder* takes no preposition at all (we view direct objects as prepositional phrases with a null preposition in this work.) Hebrew *hkh* "hit" takes the accusative preposition *at*, whereas the synonymous *hrbic* "hit" takes *l* "to". Arabic *tfAdY* "watch out" takes a direct object or *mn* "from", whereas *A$fq* "be careful of" takes *En* "on" and *tHrz* "watch out" takes *mn* "from".[1]

In the latter case, where the prepositional phrase is an adjunct, the choice of preposition does convey some meaning, but this meaning is vague, and the choice is often determined by the noun phrase that follows the preposition (the *object* of the preposition). Thus, temporals such as *last week*, *on Tuesday*, or *in November*, locatives such as *on the beach*, *at the concert*, or *in the classroom*, and instrumentals such as *with a spoon*, are all translated to prepositional phrases with *the same* preposition, *b* "in", in Hebrew (*b+šbw' š'br*, *b+ywm šliši*, *b+nwbmbr*, *b+ym*, *b+qwncrT*, *b+kth*, and *b+kp*, respectively).

Clearly, then, prepositions cannot be translated literally, and the head that they modify, as well as the object of the preposition, have to be taken into account when a preposition is chosen to be generated. Standard phrase-based statistical machine translation (MT) does not always succeed in addressing this challenge, since the coherence of the output text is determined to a large extent by an n-gram language model. While such language models can succeed to discriminate in favor of the correct preposition in local contexts, in long-distance dependencies they are likely to fail.

We propose a method for incorporating linguistic knowledge pertaining to the distribution of prepositions that are likely to occur with verbs in a transfer-based statistical machine translation system. First, we use monolingual language resources to rank the possible prepositions that various verbs subcategorize for. Then, we use this information in an Arabic-to-Hebrew MT system.

[1] To facilitate readability we use a transliteration of Hebrew using Roman characters; the letters used, in Hebrew lexicographic order, are abgdhwzxTiklmnspcqršt. For Arabic we use the transliteration scheme of Buckwalter (2004).

Proceedings of the Workshop on Innovative Hybrid Approaches to the Processing of Textual Data (Hybrid2012), EACL 2012, pages 106–114,
Avignon, France, April 23 2012.

The system is developed in the framework of Stat-XFER (Lavie, 2008), which facilitates the explicit expression of synchronous (extended) context-free transfer rules. We use this facility to implement rules that verify the correct selection of prepositions by the verbs that subcategorize them. We show that this results in significant improvement in the translation quality.

In the next section we briefly survey related work. Section 3 introduces the Stat-XFER framework in which our method is implemented. We present the problem of translating prepositions between Hebrew and Arabic in Section 4, and discuss possible solutions in Section 5. Our proposed method consists of two parts: acquisition of verb-preposition mappings from corpora (Section 6), and incorporation of this knowledge in an actual transfer-based MT system (Section 7). Section 8 provides an evaluation of the results. We conclude with suggestions for future research.

2 Related Work

An explicit solution to the challenges of translating prepositions was suggested by Trujillo (1995), who deals with the problem of translating spatial prepositions between Spanish and English in the context of a lexicalist transfer-based MT framework. Trujillo (1995) categorizes spatial prepositions according to a lexical-semantic hierarchy, and after parsing the source language sentence, uses the representation of prepositions in the transfer process, showing improvement in performance compared to other transfer-based systems. This requires resources much beyond those that are available for Arabic and Hebrew.

More recent works include Gustavii (2005), who uses transformation-based learning to infer rules that can correct the choice of preposition made by a rule-based MT system. Her reported results show high accuracy on the task of correctly generating a preposition, but the overall improvement in the quality of the translation is not reported. Li et al. (2005) focus on three English prepositions (*on*, *in* and *at*) and use WordNet to infer semantic properties of the immediate context of the preposition in order to correctly translate it to Chinese. Again, this requires language resources that are unavailable to us. WordNet (and a parser) are used also by Naskar and Bandyopadhyay (2006), who work on English-to-Bengali translation.

The closest work to ours is Agirre et al. (2009), who translate from Spanish to Basque in a rule-based framework. Like us, they focus on prepositional phrases that modify verbs, and include also the direct object (and the subject) in their approach. They propose three techniques for correctly translating prepositions, based on information that is automatically extracted from monolingual resources (including verb-preposition-head dependency triplets and verb subcategorization) as well as manually-crafted selection rules that rely on lexical, syntactic and semantic information. Our method is similar in principle, the main differences being: (i) we incorporate linguistic knowledge in a *statistical* decoder, facilitating scalability of the MT system, (ii) we use much more modest resources (in particular, we do not parse either of the two languages), and (iii) we report standard evaluation measures.

Much work has been done regarding the automatic acquisition of subcategorization frames in English (Brent, 1991; Manning, 1993; Briscoe and Carroll, 1997; Korhonen, 2002), Czech (Sarkar and Zeman, 2000), French (Chesley and Salmon-alt, 2006), and several other languages. The technique that we use here (Section 6) can now be considered standard.

3 Introduction to Stat-XFER

The method we propose is implemented in the framework of Stat-XFER (Lavie, 2008), a statistical machine translation engine that includes a declarative formalism for symbolic transfer grammars. A grammar consists of a collection of synchronous context-free rules, which can be augmented by unification-style feature constraints. These transfer rules specify how phrase structures in a source-language correspond and transfer to phrase structures in a target language, and the constraints under which these rules should apply. The framework also includes a transfer engine that applies the transfer grammar to a source-language input sentence at runtime, and produces collections of scored word- and phrase-level translations according to the grammar. Scores are based on a log-linear combination of several features, and a beam-search controls the underlying parsing and transfer process.

Crucially, Stat-XFER is a statistical MT framework, which uses statistical information to weigh word translations, phrase correspondences and target-language hypotheses; in contrast to other paradigms, however, it can utilize both automatically-created and manually-crafted language resources, including dictionaries, morphological processors and transfer rules. Stat-XFER has been used as a platform for developing MT systems for Hindi-to-English (Lavie et al., 2003), Hebrew-to-English (Lavie et al., 2004), Chinese-to-English, French-to-English (Hanneman et al., 2009) and many other low-resource language pairs, such as Inupiaq-to-English and Mapudungun-to-Spanish.

In this work, we use the Arabic-to-Hebrew MT system developed by Shilon et al. (2010), which uses over 40 manually-crafted rules. Other resources include Arabic morphological analyzer and disambiguator (Habash, 2004), Hebrew morphological generator (Itai and Wintner, 2008) and a Hebrew language model compiled from available corpora (Itai and Wintner, 2008).

While our proposal is cast within the framework of Stat-XFER, it can be in principle adapted to other syntax-based approaches to MT; specifically, Williams and Koehn (2011) show how to employ unification-based constraints to the target-side of a string-to-tree model, integrating constrain evaluation into the decoding process.

4 Translating prepositions between Hebrew and Arabic

Modern Hebrew and Modern Standard Arabic, both closely-related Semitic languages, share many orthographic, lexical, morphological, syntactic and semantic similarities, but they are still not mutually comprehensible. Machine translation between these two languages can indeed benefit from the similarities, but it remains a challenging task. Our current work is situated in the framework of the only direct MT system between these two languages that we are aware of, namely Shilon et al. (2010).

Hebrew and Arabic share several similar prepositions, including the frequent *b* "in, at, with" and *l* "to". However, many prepositions exist in only one of the languages, such as Arabic *En* "on, about" or Hebrew *šl* "of". Hebrew uses a preposition, *at*, to introduce definite direct objects (which motivates our choice of viewing direct objects as special kind of prepositional phrases, which may sometimes be introduced by a null preposition). The differences in how the two languages use prepositions are significant and common, as the following examples demonstrate.

(1)

AErb	*Al+wzyr*	*En*	*Aml+h*
expressed.3ms	the+minister	on	hope+his

'The minister expressed his hope' (Arabic)

h+šr	*hbi'*	*at*	*tqwt+w*
the+minister	expressed.3ms	acc	hope+his

'The minister expressed his hope' (Hebrew)

(2)

HDr	*Al+wzyr*	*Al+jlsp*
attended.3ms	the+minister	the+meeting

'The minister attended the meeting' (Arabic)

h+šr	*nkx*	*b+*	*h+išibh*
the+minister	attended.3ms	in	the+meeting

'The minister attended the meeting' (Hebrew)

In (1), the Arabic preposition *En* "on, about" is translated into the Hebrew accusative marker *at*. In contrast, (2) demonstrates the opposite case where the Arabic direct object (no preposition) is translated into a Hebrew prepositional phrase introduced by *b* "in". Clearly, despite the lexical and semantic similarity between many Hebrew and Arabic prepositions, their licensing by semantically-equivalent verbs is different in both languages.

An important issue is the selection of prepositions to model. We focus on a small list of the most common prepositions in both languages. The list was constructed by counting prepositions in monolingual corpora from the news domain in the two languages (500K tokens in Arabic, 120K tokens in Hebrew). In total, the Arabic data includes 70K prepositions, which comprise 14% of the corpus tokens, whereas the Hebrew data includes 19K prepositions, or 16% of the tokens. Not surprisingly, the most frequent prepositions were those that are commonly used to introduce complements. The data are listed in Table 1.

Based on these data, we decided to focus on the set of top nine Arabic prepositions (*fy, l, b, mn, ElY, AlY, En, mE* and the direct object), and the top six Hebrew prepositions (*b, l, m, 'l, 'm,* and the direct object), comprising over 80% of all preposition occurrences in our corpora.[2] These are also the most common complement-preceding prepositions, and therefore pose the main challenge for the task of machine translation.

[2]The preposition *k* "as" is omitted since it is translated directly to itself in most cases.

	Arabic				Hebrew			
Rank	Preposition	Count	%	$\sum\%$	Preposition	Count	%	$\sum\%$
1	*fy* "in"	13128	18.7	18.7	*b* "in"	6030	31.6	31.6
2	dir-obj	12626	17.9	36.7	*l* "to"	3386	17.7	49.3
3	*l* "to"	9429	13.4	50.1	dir-obj	3250	17.0	66.3
4	*b* "in, with"	7253	10.3	60.4	*m* "from"	1330	6.9	73.3
5	*mn* "from"	6859	9.7	70.2	*'l* "on"	1066	5.5	78.9
6	*ElY* "on"	5304	7.5	77.8	*k* "as"	354	1.8	80.7
7	*AlY* "to"	4458	6.3	84.1	*'m* "with"	338	1.7	82.5
8	*En* "on, about"	1871	2.6	86.8	*bin* "between"	191	1.0	84.6
9	*mE* "with"	1380	1.9	88.8	*'d* "until"	159	0.8	85.4
10	*byn* "between"	1045	1.4	90.3	*lpni* "before"	115	0.6	86.0

Table 1: Counts of Arabic and Hebrew most frequent prepositions. The columns list, for each preposition, its count in the corpus, the percentage out of all prepositions, and the accumulated percentage including all the higher-ranking prepositions.

5 Possible solutions

In order to improve the accuracy of translating prepositions in a transfer-based system, several approaches can be taken. We discuss some of them in this section.

First, accurate and comprehensive statistics can be acquired from large monolingual corpora of the target language regarding the distribution of verbs with their subcategorized prepositions and the head of the noun phrase that is the object of the preposition. As a backoff model, one could use a bigram model of only the preposition and the head of the following noun phrase, e.g., (*on, Wednesday*). This may help in the case of temporal and locative adjuncts that are less related to the preceding verb. Once such data are acquired, they may be used in the process of scoring hypotheses, if a parser is incorporated in the process.

One major shortcoming of this approach is the difficulty of acquiring the necessary data, and in particular the effect of data sparsity on the accuracy of this approach. In addition, a high quality parser for the target language must be available, and it must be incorporated during the decoding step, which is a heavy burden on performance.

Alternatively, one could acquire lexical and semantic mappings between verbs, the type of their arguments, the selectional restrictions they impose, and the possible prepositions used to express such relations. This can be done using a mapping from surface forms to lexical ontologies, like WordNet (Fellbaum, 1998), and to a syntactic-semantic mapping like VerbNet (Schuler, 2005) which lists the relevant preceding preposition. Similar work has been done by Shi and Mihalcea (2005) for the purpose of semantic parsing. These lexical-semantic resources can help map between the verb and its possible arguments with their thematic roles, including selectional restrictions on them (expressed lexically, using a WordNet synset, like *human* or *concrete*).

The main shortcoming of this solution is that such explicit lexical and semantic resources exist mainly for English. In addition, even when translating into English, this information can only assist in limiting the number of possible prepositions but not in determining them. For example, one can talk *about* the event, *after* the event, or *at* the event. The information that can determine the correct preposition is in the source sentence.

Finally, a potential solution is to allow translation of source-language prepositions to a limited set of possible target-language prepositions, and then use both target-language constraints on possible verb-preposition matches and an n-gram language model to choose the most adequate solution. Despite the fact that this solution does not model the probability of the target preposition given its verb and the original sentence, it limits the number of possible translations by taking into account the target-language verb and the possible constraints on the prepositions it licenses. This method is also the most adequate for a scenario that employs a statistical decoder, such as the one used in Stat-XFER. This is the solution we advocate in this paper. We describe the acquisition of Hebrew verb–preposition statistics in the following section, and the incorporation of this knowledge in a machine translation system in Section 7.

6 Acquisition of verb–preposition data

To obtain statistics on the relations between verbs and prepositions in Hebrew we use the *TheMarker, Knesset* and *Arutz 7* corpora (Itai and Wintner, 2008), comprising 31M tokens. The corpora include 1.18M (potentially inflected) verb tokens, reflecting 4091 verb (lemma) types.

The entire corpus was morphologically analyzed and disambiguated (Itai and Wintner, 2008). We then collected all instances of prepositions that immediately follow a verb; this reflects the assumption that such prepositions are likely to be a part of the verb's subcategorization frame. A special treatment of the direct object case was required, because a Hebrew direct object is introduced by the accusative marker *at* when it is definite, but not otherwise. Since constituent order in Hebrew is relatively free, the noun phrase that immediately follows the verb can also be its subject. Therefore, we only consider such noun phrases if they do not agree with the verb in gender and number (and are therefore not subjects).

We then use maximum likelihood estimation to obtain the conditional probability of each preposition following a verb. The result is a database of verb-preposition pairs, with an estimate of their probabilities. Examples include *nkll* "be included", for which *b* "in" has 0.91 probability; *hstpq* "be satisfied" *b* "in" (0.99); *xikh* "wait" *l* "to" (0.73); *ht'lm* "ignore" *m* "from" (0.83); and *htbss* "base" *'l* "on" (0.93). Of course, some other verbs are less clear-cut.

From this database, we filter out verb-preposition pairs whose score is lower than a certain threshold. We are left with a total of 1402 verbs and 2325 verb-preposition pairs which we use for Arabic-to-Hebrew machine translation, as explained in the next section. Note that we currently ignore the probabilities of the prepositions associated with each verb; we only use the probabilities to limit the set of prepositions that are licensed by the verb. Ranking of these prepositions is deferred to the language model.

7 Incorporating linguistic knowledge

We implemented the last method suggested in Section 5 to improve the quality of the Arabic-to-Hebrew machine translation system of Shilon et al. (2010) as follows.

First, we modified the output of the Hebrew morphological generator to reflect also, for each verb, the list of prepositions licensed by the verb (Section 6). Stat-XFER uses the generator to generate inflected forms of lemmas obtained from a bilingual dictionary. Each such form is associated with a feature structure that describes some properties of the form (e.g., its gender, number and person). To the feature structures of verbs we add an additional feature, ALLOWED_PREPS, whose value is the list of prepositions licensed by the verb. For example, the feature structure of the Hebrew verb *sipr* "tell" is specified as:

```
(allowed_preps = (*OR* at l))
```

Thus, whenever the Hebrew generator returns an inflected form of the verb *sipr*, the feature ALLOWED_PREPS lists the possible prepositions *at* and *l* "to", that are licensed by this verb.

Then, we modified the transfer grammar to enforce constraints between the verb and its objects. This was done by adding a new non-terminal node to the grammar, OBJ, accounting for both direct and indirect objects. The idea is to encode the actual preposition (in fact, its surface form) as a feature of the OBJ node (Figure 1), and then, when a sentence is formed by combining a verb with its subject and object(s), to check the value of this

```
{OBJ_ACC_AT,0}
OBJ::OBJ [NP] -> ["AT" NP]
(X1::Y2)
((X1 def) = +)
((Y2 prep) = AT) #mark preposition
(X0 = X1)
(Y0 = Y2

{OBJ_PP,0}
OBJ::OBJ [PREP NP] -> [PREP NP]
(X1::Y1)
(X2::Y2)
((Y0 prep) = (Y1 lex)) #mark prep.
(X0 = X1)
(Y0 = Y1)

{OBJ_NP_PP_B, 0}
OBJ::OBJ [NP] -> ["B" NP]
(X1::Y2)
((Y0 prep) = B) #mark preposition
(X0 = X1)
(Y0 = Y2)
```

Figure 1: Propagating the surface form of the preposition as a feature of the OBJ node.

```
{S_VB_NP_OBJ_swap, 1}
S::S [VB NP OBJ] -> [NP VB OBJ]
(X1::Y2)
(X2::Y1)
(X3::Y3)
((X1 num) = singular) # Arabic agr.
((X1 per) = (X2 per))
((Y1 num) = (Y2 num)) # Hebrew agr.
((Y1 gen) = (Y2 gen))
((Y1 per) = (Y2 per))
((Y2 allowed_preps) = (Y3 prep))
```

Figure 2: Enforcing agreement between a verb VB and its object OBJ on the Hebrew side.

feature against the ALLOWED_PREPS feature of the verb (Figure 2).

Consider Figure 1. The first rule maps an Arabic direct object noun phrase to a Hebrew direct object, and marks the preposition *at* on the Hebrew OBJ node as the value of the feature PREP. The second rule maps an Arabic prepositional phrase to Hebrew prepositional phrase, marking the Hebrew OBJ (referred to here as Y1 lex) with the value of the feature PREP. The third rule maps an Arabic noun phrase to a Hebrew prepositional phrase introduced by the preposition *b* "in".

The rule in Figure 2 enforces sentence-level agreement between the feature ALLOWED_PREPS of the Hebrew verb (here, Y2 allowed_preps) and the actual preposition of the Hebrew object (here, Y3 prep).

To better illustrate the effect of these rules, consider the following examples, taken from the system's actual output (the top line is the Arabic input, the bottom is the Hebrew output). There can be four types of syntactic mappings between Arabic and Hebrew arguments: (NP, NP), (NP, PP), (PP, NP) and (PP, PP). Examples (3) and (4) demonstrate correct translation of the Arabic direct object into the Hebrew direct object (with and without the Hebrew definite accusative marker *at*, respectively). Example (5) demonstrates the correct translation of the Arabic direct object to a Hebrew PP with the preposition *l* "to". Example (6) demonstrates the correct translation of an Arabic PP introduced by *En* "on, about" to a Hebrew direct object, and Example (7) demonstrates the translation of Arabic PP introduced by *b* "in, with" into a Hebrew PP introduced by *'m* "with".

(3) *rAyt* *Al+wld*
see.past.1s the+boy

raiti *at* *h+ild*
see.past.1s acc.def the+boy
'I saw the boy'

(4) *rAyt* *wldA*
see.past.1s boy.acc.indef

raiti *ild*
see.past.1s boy
'I saw a boy'

(5) *Drb* *Al+Ab* *Al+wld*
hit.past.3ms the+father the+boy

h+ab *hrbic* *l+* *h+ild*
the+father hit.past.3ms to the+boy
'The father hit the boy'

(6) *AErb* *Al+wzyr* *En* *Aml+h*
express.past.3ms the+minister on hope+his

h+šr *hbi'* *at* *tqwt+w*
the+minister express.past.3ms acc.def. hope+his
'The minister expressed his hope'

(7) *AjtmE* *Al+wzyr* *b+* *Al+wld*
meet.past.3ms the+minister in the+boy

h+šr *npgš* *'m* *h+ild*
the+minister meet.past.3ms with the+boy
'The minister met the boy'

In (3), the input Arabic NP is definite and is marked by accusative case. A designated rule adds the string *at* before the corresponding Hebrew output, to mark the definite direct object. We create a node of type OBJ for both (direct) objects, with the feature PREP storing the lexical content of the preposition in the target language. Finally, in the sentence level rule, we validate that the Hebrew verb licenses a direct object, by unifying the feature PREP of OBJ with the feature ALLOWED_PREPS of the verb VB.

In (4), a similar process occurs, but this time no additional *at* token is added to the Hebrew output (since the direct object is indefinite). The same preposition, *at*, is marked as the PREP feature of OBJ (we use *at* to mark the direct object, whether the object is definite or not), and again, the feature PREP of OBJ is validated against the feature ALLOWED_PREPS of VB.

Example (5) is created using a rule that maps an Arabic direct object to a Hebrew prepositional phrase introduced by a different preposition, here *l* "to". Such rules exist for every Hebrew preposition from the set of common prepositions we focus on, since we have no prior knowledge of which preposition should be generated. We mark the lexical preposition *l* on the feature PREP of the Hebrew OBJ node, and again, this is validated in the sentence level against the prepositions allowed by the verb.

In example (6) we use rules that map an Arabic prepositional phrase to a Hebrew noun phrase. Here, the Arabic preposition is not translated at all, and the Hebrew definite accusative marker *at* is added, depending on the definiteness of the Hebrew noun phrase. The only difference in example (7) compared to previous examples is the translation of the Arabic preposition into a different Hebrew preposition. This is implemented in the bilingual lexicon, in a lexical entry that maps the Arabic preposition *b* "in, with" to the Hebrew preposition *'m* "with".

These rules help to expand the lexical variety of the prepositions on one hand (as in Example (7)), while at the same time disqualifying some hypotheses that employ prepositions that are not licensed by the relevant verb, using unification-style constraints. After this process, the lattice may still include several different hypotheses, from which the decoder statistically chooses the best one.

8 Evaluation

To evaluate the contribution of the proposed method, we created a test set of 300 sentences from newspaper texts, which were manually translated by three human translators. Of those, we selected short sentences (up to 10 words), for which the bilingual lexicon used by the system had full lexical coverage. This resulted in a set of 28 sentences (still with three reference translations each), which allowed us to focus on the actual contribution of the preposition-mapping solution rather than on other limitations of the MT system. Unfortunately, evaluation on the entire test set without accounting for full lexical coverage yields such low BLEU scores that the comparison between different configurations of the system is meaningless.

As a baseline system, we use exactly the same setup, but withhold any monolingual linguistic knowledge regarding verb-prepositions relations:

1. We omit the restrictions (stated in the grammar) on which prepositions Hebrew verbs license, such that each verb can be followed by each preposition.

2. We limit the lexical variance between prepositions in the lexicon, to only allow translation-pairs that occur in the bilingual dictionary. For example, we use the mapping of Arabic *ElY* "on" to Hebrew *'l* "on" (which occurs in the bilingual dictionary), but remove the mapping of Arabic *ElY* "on" to Hebrew *b* "in", which does not carry the same meaning.

Table 2 lists the BLEU (Papineni et al., 2002) and METEOR (Denkowski and Lavie, 2011) scores of both systems.

	BLEU	METEOR
Baseline	0.325	0.526
With prepositions	0.370	0.560

Table 2: Automatic evaluation scores.

The system that incorporates linguistic knowledge on prepositions significantly ($p < 0.05$) outperforms the baseline system. A detailed analysis of the obtained translations reveals that the baseline system generates prepositions that are not licensed by their head verb, and the language model fails to choose the hypothesis with the correct preposition, if such a hypothesis is generated at all.

As an example of the difference between the outputs of both systems, consider Figure 3. The Arabic input is given in (8). The output of the system that incorporates our treatment of prepositions is given in (9). Here, the Hebrew verb *hdgiš* "emphasize" is followed by the correct definite accusative marker *at*. The output of the baseline system is given in (10). Here, the Hebrew verb *aišr* "approve" is followed by the wrong preposition, *'l* "on", which is not licensed in this location. Consequently, the lexical selections for the following words of the translation differ and are not as fluent as in (9), and the output is only partially coherent.

(8)

Akd	*AlHryry*	*ElY*	*AltzAm+h*	*b+*	*Al+byAn*	*Al+wzAry*
emphasize.past.3ms	AlHaryry	on	obligation+his	in	the+announcement	the+ministerial

l+	*Hkwmp*	*Al+whdp*	*Al+wTnyp*
to	government	the+unity	the+national

'Alharyry emphasized his obligation in the ministerial announcement to the national government'

(9)

alxriri	*hdgiš*	*at*	*xwbt+w*	*b+*	*h+hwd'h*
Alharyry	emphasize.past.3ms	def.acc	obligation+his	in	the+announcement

h+mmšltit	*l+*	*mmšlt*	*h+axdwt*	*h+lawmit*
the+governmental	to	government	the+unity	the+national

'Alharyry emphasized his obligation in the governmental announcement to the national government'

(10)

alxriri	*aišr*	*'l*	*zkiwn*	*šl+w*	*b+*	*h+hwd'h*	*h+mmšltit*
Alharyry	confirm.past.3ms	on	permit	of+his	in	the+announcement	the+governmental

l+	*mmšlt*	*h+axdwt*	*h+lawmit*
to	government	the+unity	the+national

'Alharyry confirmed on his permit in the governmental announcement to the national government'

Figure 3: Example translation output, with and without handling of prepositions.

9 Conclusion

Having emphasized the challenge of (machine) translation of prepositions, specifically between Hebrew and Arabic, we discussed several solutions and proposed a preferred method. We extract linguistic information regarding the correspondences between Hebrew verbs and their licensed prepositions, and use this knowledge for improving the quality of Arabic-to-Hebrew machine translation in the context of the Stat-XFER framework. We presented encouraging evaluation results showing that the use of linguistic knowledge regarding prepositions indeed significantly improves the quality of the translation.

This work can be extended along various dimensions. First, we only focused on verb arguments that are prepositional phrases here. However, our Hebrew verb-subcategorization data include also information on other types of complements, such as subordinate clauses (introduced by the complementizer *š* "that") and infinitival verb phrases. We intend to extend our transfer grammar in a way that will benefit from this information in the future. Second, we currently do not use the weights associated with specific prepositions in our subcategorization database; we are looking into ways to incorporate this statistical information in the decoding phase of the translation.

Furthermore, our database contains also statistics on the distribution of nouns following each preposition (which are likely to function as the heads of the object of the preposition); such information can also improve the accuracy of translation, and can be incorporated into the system. Another direction is to acquire and incorporate similar information on deverbal nouns, which license the same prepositions as the verbs they are derived from. For example, *xtimh 'l hskm* "signing.noun an agreement", where the Hebrew preposition *'l* "on" must be used, as in the corresponding verbal from *xtm 'l hskm* "signed.verb an agreement". We will address such extensions in future research.

Acknowledgements

We are grateful to Alon Itai, Alon Lavie, and Gennadi Lembersky for their help. This research was supported by THE ISRAEL SCIENCE FOUNDATION (grant No. 137/06).

References

Eneko Agirre, Aitziber Atutxa, Gorka Labaka, Mikel Lersundi, Aingeru Mayor, and Kepa Sarasola. 2009. Use of rich linguistic information to translate prepositions and grammar cases to Basque. In *Proceedings of the XIII Conference of the European*

Association for Machine Translation, EAMT-2009, pages 58–65, May.

Michael R. Brent. 1991. Automatic acquisition of subcategorization frames from untagged text. In *Proceedings of the 29th annual meeting on Association for Computational Linguistics*, pages 209–214.

Ted Briscoe and John Carroll. 1997. Automatic extraction of subcategorization from corpora. In *Proceedings of the 5th ACL Conference on Applied Natural Language Processing*, pages 356–363.

Tim Buckwalter. 2004. *Buckwalter Arabic Morphological Analyzer Version 2.0*. Linguistic Data Consortium, Philadelphia.

Paula Chesley and Susanne Salmon-alt. 2006. Automatic extraction of subcategorization frames for French. In *Proceedings of the Language Resources and Evaluation Conference, LREC-2006*.

Michael Denkowski and Alon Lavie. 2011. Meteor 1.3: Automatic metric for reliable optimization and evaluation of machine translation systems. In *Proceedings of the Sixth Workshop on Statistical Machine Translation*, pages 85–91.

Christiane Fellbaum, editor. 1998. *WordNet: An Electronic Lexical Database*. Language, Speech and Communication. MIT Press.

Ebba Gustavii. 2005. Target language preposition selection – an experiment with transformation-based learning and aligned bilingual data. In *Proceedings of EAMT-2005*, May.

Nizar Habash. 2004. Large scale lexeme based arabic morphological generation. In *Proceedings of Traitement Automatique du Langage Naturel (TALN-04)*, Fez, Morocco.

Greg Hanneman, Vamshi Ambati, Jonathan H. Clark, Alok Parlikar, and Alon Lavie. 2009. An improved statistical transfer system for French–English machine translation. In *StatMT '09: Proceedings of the Fourth Workshop on Statistical Machine Translation*, pages 140–144.

Alon Itai and Shuly Wintner. 2008. Language resources for Hebrew. *Language Resources and Evaluation*, 42(1):75–98, March.

Anna Korhonen. 2002. *Subcategorisation acquisition*. Ph.D. thesis, Computer Laboratory, University of Cambridge. Techical Report UCAM-CL-TR-530.

Alon Lavie, Stephan Vogel, Lori Levin, Erik Peterson, Katharina Probst, Ariadna Font Llitjós, Rachel Reynolds, Jaime Carbonell, and Richard Cohen. 2003. Experiments with a Hindi-to-English transfer-based MT system under a miserly data scenario. *ACM Transactions on Asian Language Information Processing (TALIP)*, 2(2):143–163.

Alon Lavie, Shuly Wintner, Yaniv Eytani, Erik Peterson, and Katharina Probst. 2004. Rapid prototyping of a transfer-based Hebrew-to-English machine translation system. In *Proceedings of TMI-2004: The 10th International Conference on Theoretical and Methodological Issues in Machine Translation*, Baltimore, MD, October.

Alon Lavie. 2008. Stat-XFER: A general search-based syntax-driven framework for machine translation. In Alexander F. Gelbukh, editor, *CICLing*, volume 4919 of *Lecture Notes in Computer Science*, pages 362–375. Springer.

Hui Li, Nathalie Japkowicz, and Caroline Barrière. 2005. English to Chinese translation of prepositions. In Balázs Kégl and Guy Lapalme, editors, *Advances in Artificial Intelligence, 18th Conference of the Canadian Society for Computational Studies of Intelligence*, volume 3501 of *Lecture Notes in Computer Science*, pages 412–416. Springer, May.

Christopher D. Manning. 1993. Automatic acquisition of a large subcategorization dictionary from corpora. In *Proceedings of the 31st annual meeting on Association for Computational Linguistics*, pages 235–242.

Sudip Kumar Naskar and Sivaji Bandyopadhyay. 2006. Handling of prepositions in English to Bengali machine translation. In *Proceedings of the Third ACL-SIGSEM Workshop on Prepositions*, pages 89–94.

Kishore Papineni, Salim Roukos, Todd Ward, and Wei-Jing Zhu. 2002. BLEU: a method for automatic evaluation of machine translation. In *ACL '02: Proceedings of the 40th Annual Meeting on Association for Computational Linguistics*, pages 311–318.

Anoop Sarkar and Daniel Zeman. 2000. Automatic extraction of subcategorization frames for Czech. In *Proceedings of the 18th conference on Computational linguistics*, pages 691–697.

Karin Kipper Schuler. 2005. *Verbnet: a broad-coverage, comprehensive verb lexicon*. Ph.D. thesis, University of Pennsylvania, Philadelphia, PA.

Lei Shi and Rada Mihalcea. 2005. Putting pieces together: Combining framenet, verbnet and wordnet for robust semantic parsing. In Alexander F. Gelbukh, editor, *CICLing*, volume 3406 of *Lecture Notes in Computer Science*, pages 100–111. Springer.

Reshef Shilon, Nizar Habash, Alon Lavie, and Shuly Wintner. 2010. Machine translation between Hebrew and Arabic: Needs, challenges and preliminary solutions. In *Proceedings of AMTA 2010: The Ninth Conference of the Association for Machine Translation in the Americas*, November.

Indalecio Arturo Trujillo. 1995. *Lexicalist machine translation of spatial prepositions*. Ph.D. thesis, University of Cambridge, April.

Philip Williams and Philipp Koehn. 2011. Agreement constraints for statistical machine translation into German. In *Proceedings of the Sixth Workshop on Statistical Machine Translation*, pages 217–226, Edinburgh, Scotland, July.

Combining Different Summarization Techniques for Legal Text

Filippo Galgani **Paul Compton** **Achim Hoffmann**
School of Computer Science and Engineering
The University of New South Wales
Sydney, Australia
{galganif,compton,achim}@cse.unsw.edu.au

Abstract

Summarization, like other natural language processing tasks, is tackled with a range of different techniques - particularly machine learning approaches, where human intuition goes into attribute selection and the choice and tuning of the learning algorithm. Such techniques tend to apply differently in different contexts, so in this paper we describe a hybrid approach in which a number of different summarization techniques are combined in a rule-based system using manual knowledge acquisition, where human intuition, supported by data, specifies not only attributes and algorithms, but the contexts where these are best used. We apply this approach to automatic summarization of legal case reports. We show how a preliminary knowledge base, composed of only 23 rules, already outperforms competitive baselines.

1 Introduction

Automatic summarization tasks are often addressed with statistical methods: a first type of approach, introduced by Kupiec et al.(1995), involves using a set of features of different types to describe sentences, and supervised learning algorithms to learn an empirical model of how those features interact to identify important sentences. This kind of approach has been very popular in summarization; however the difficulty of this task often requires more complex representations, and different kinds of models to learn relevance in text have been proposed, such as discourse-based (Marcu, 1997) or network-based (Salton et al., 1997) models and many others. Domain knowledge usually is present in the choice of features and algorithms, but it is still an open issue how best to capture the domain knowledge required to identify what is relevant in the text; manual approaches to build knowledge bases tend to be tedious, while automatic approaches require large amounts of training data and the result may still be inferior.

In this paper we present our approach to summarize legal documents, using knowledge acquisition to combine different summarization techniques. In summarization, different kinds of information can be taken in account to locate important content, at the sentence level (e.g. particular terms or patterns), at the document level (e.g. frequency information, discourse information) and at the collection level (e.g. document frequencies or citation analysis); however, the way such attributes interact is likely to depend on the context of specific cases. For this reason we have developed a set of methods for identifying important content, and we propose the creation of a Knowledge Base (KB) that specifies which content should be used in different contexts, and how this should be combined. We propose to use the Ripple Down Rules (RDR) (Compton and Jansen, 1990) methodology to build this knowledge base: RDR has already proven to be a very effective way of building KBs, had has been used successfully in several NLP task (see Section 2). This kind of approach differs from the dominant supervised learning approach, in which we first annotate text to identify relevant fragments, and then we use supervised learning algorithms to learn a model; one example in the legal domain being the work of Hachey and Grover (2006). Our approach eliminates the need for separate manual annotation of text, as the rules are built by a human who judges the relevance of text and directly creates the set of rules as the one process, rather than annotating the text and then separately tuning the learning model.

We apply this approach to the summarization of legal case reports, a domain which has an increasing need for automatic text processing, to cope with the large body of documents that is case law.

Proceedings of the Workshop on Innovative Hybrid Approaches to the Processing of Textual Data (Hybrid2012), EACL 2012, pages 115–123,
Avignon, France, April 23 2012. ©2012 Association for Computational Linguistics

Table 1: Examples of catchphrases list for two cases.

COSTS - proper approach to admiralty and commercial litigation - goods transported under bill of lading incorporating Himalaya clause - shipper and consignee sued ship owner and stevedore for damage to cargo - stevedore successful in obtaining consent orders on motion dismissing proceedings against it based on Himalaya clause - stevedore not furnishing critical evidence or information until after motion filed - whether stevedore should have its costs - importance of parties cooperating to identify the real issues in dispute - duty to resolve uncontentious issues at an early stage of litigation - stevedore awarded 75% of its costs of the proceedings
MIGRATION - partner visa - appellant sought to prove domestic violence by the provision of statutory declarations made under State legislation - "statutory declaration" defined by the Migration Regulations 1994 (Cth) to mean a declaration "under" the Statutory Declarations Act 1959 (Cth) in Div 1.5 - contrary intention in reg 1.21 as to the inclusion of State declarations under s 27 of the Acts Interpretation Act - statutory declaration made under State legislation is not a statutory declaration "under" the Commonwealth Act - appeal dismissed

Countries with "common law" traditions, such as Australia, the UK and the USA, rely heavily on the concept of precedence: on how the courts have interpreted the law in individual cases, in a process that is known as *stare decisis* (Moens, 2007), so legal professionals: lawyers, judges and scholars, have to deal with large volumes of past court decisions.

Automatic summarization can greatly enhance access to legal repositories; however, legal cases, rather than summaries, often contain lists of catchphrases: phrases that present the important legal points of a case. The presence of catchphrases can aid research of case law, as they give a quick impression of what the case is about: "*the function of catchwords is to give a summary classification of the matters dealt with in a case. [...] Their purpose is to tell the researcher whether there is likely to be anything in the case relevant to the research topic*" (Olsson, 1999). For this reason, rather than constructing summaries, we aim at extracting catchphrases from the full text of a case report. Examples of catchphrases from two case reports are shown in Table 1.

In this paper we present our approach towards automatic catchphrase extraction from legal case reports, using a knowledge acquisition approach according to which rules are manually created to combine a range of diverse methods to locate catchphrase candidates in the text.

2 Related Work

Different kinds of language processing have been applied to the legal domain, for example, automatic summarization, retrieval (Moens, 2001), machine translation (Farzindar and Lapalme, 2009), and citation analysis (Zhang and Koppaka, 2007; Galgani and Hoffmann, 2010). Among these tasks, the most relevant to catchphrase extraction is the work on automatic summarization, with the difference that catchphrases usually cover many dimensions of one case, giving a broader representation than summaries. Examples of automatic summarization systems developed for the legal domain are the work of Hachey and Grover (Hachey and Grover, 2006) to summarize the UK House of Lords judgements, and PRODSUM (Yousfi-Monod et al., 2010), a summarizer of case reports for the CanLII database (Canadian Legal Information Institute) (see also (Moens, 2007) for an overview). Both systems rely on supervised learning algorithms, using sentences tagged as important to learn how to recognize important sentences in the text: in this case the domain knowledge is incorporated mainly in the choice of features. This contrasts with our approach where the human intuition goes also in the weights given to different attributes in different contexts.

Ripple Down Rules

As we propose to use rules manually created for specifying how to identify relevant text, our approach is based on incremental Knowledge Acquisition (KA). A KA methodology which has already been applied to language processing tasks is Ripple Down Rules (RDR) (Compton and Jansen, 1990). In RDR, rules are created by domain experts without a knowledge engineer, the knowledge base is built with incremental refinements from scratch, while the system is in use; the domain expert monitors the system and whenever it performs incorrectly he or she flags the error and provides a rule based on the case which generated the error, which is added to the knowledge base and corrects the error. RDR is essentially an error-driven KA approach, the incremental refinement of the KB is achieved by patching the errors it makes, in the form of exception rule structure.

The strength of RDR is easy maintenance: the point of failure is automatically identified, the expert patches the knowledge only locally, considering the case at hand, and new rules are placed by the system in the correct position and checked for consistency with all cases previously correctly classified, so that unwanted indirect effects of rule interactions are avoided (Compton and Jansen, 1990). The manual creation of rules, in contrast with machine learning, requires a smaller quantity of annotated data, as the human in the loop can identify the important features in a single case, whereas learning techniques require multiple instances to identify important features.

RDR have been used to tackle natural language processing tasks with the system KAFTIE (Pham and Hoffmann, 2004) (for summarization in (Hoffmann and Pham, 2003)). Knowledge bases built with RDR were shown to outperforms machine learning in legal citation analysis (2010) and in open information extraction (Kim et al., 2011); while Xu and Hoffmann (2010) showed how a knowledge base automatically built from data can be improved using manual knowledge acquisition from a domain expert with RDR.

3 Dataset

We use as the source of our data the legal database AustLII[1], the Australasian Legal Information Institute (Greenleaf et al., 1995), one of the largest sources of legal material on the net, which provides free access to reports on court decisions in all major courts in Australia.

We created an initial corpus of 2816 cases accessing case reports from the Federal Court of Australia, for the years 2007 to 2009, for which author-made catchphrases are given and extracted the full text and the catchphrases of every document. Each document contains on average 221 sentences and 8.3 catchphrases. In total we collected 23230 catchphrases, of which 15359 (92.7%) were unique, appearing only in one document in the corpus. These catchphrases are used to evaluate our extracts using Rouge, as described in Section 4.

To have a more complete representation of these cases, we also included citation information. Citation analysis has proven to be very useful in automatic summarization (Mei and Zhai, 2008; Qazvinian and Radev, 2008). We downloaded citation data from LawCite[2]. It is a service provided by AustLII which, for a given case, lists cited cases and more recent cases that cite the case. We downloaded the full texts and the catchphrases (where available) from AustLII, of both cited (previous) cases and more recent cases that cite the current one (citing cases). Of the 2816 cases, 1904 are cited at least by one other case (on average by 4.82 other cases). We collected the catchphrases of these citing cases, searched the full texts to extract the location where a citation is explicitly made, and extracted the containing paragraph(s). For each of the 1904 cases we collected on average 21.17 citing sentences, and we extracted an average of 35.36 catchphrases (from one or more other documents). From previous cases referenced by the judge, we extracted on average 67.41 catchphrases for each case.

We also extracted, using LawCite, references to any type of legislation made in the report. We located in the full text the sentences where each section or Act is mentioned; then we accessed the full texts of the legislation on AustLII, and extracted the title of the sections (for example, if section 477 is mentioned in the text, we extract the corresponding title: *CORPORATIONS ACT 2001 - SECT 477 Powers of liquidator*).

Our dataset thus contains the initial 2816 cases with given catchphrases, and all cases related to them by incoming or outgoing citations, with catchphrases and citing sentences explicitly identified, and the references to Acts and sections of the law.

4 Evaluation method

As it was not reasonable to involve legal experts in this sort of exploratory study, we looked for a simple way to evaluate candidate catchphrases automatically by comparing them with the author-made catchphrases from our AustLII corpus (considered as our "gold standard"), to quickly assess the performances of various methods on a large number of documents. As our system extracts sentences from text as candidate catchphrases, we propose an evaluation method which is based on Rouge (Lin, 2004) scores between extracted sentences and given catchphrases. This method was used also in (Galgani et al., 2012). Rouge includes several measures to quantitatively compare system-generated summaries to human-generated summaries, counting the number of overlapping n-grams of various lengths, word pairs and word sequences between two or more summaries.

Somewhat different from the standard use of Rouge (which would involve comparing the whole block of catchphrases to the whole block of extracted sentences), we evaluated extracted sentences individually so that the utility of any one catchphrase is minimally affected by the others, or by their particular order. On the other hand we want to extract sentences that contain an entire individual catchphrase, while a sentence that

[1] http://www.austlii.edu.au/

[2] http://www.lawcite.org

contains small pieces of different catchphrases is not as useful.

We therefore compare each extracted sentence with each catchphrase individually, using Rouge. If the recall (on the catchphrase) is higher than a threshold, the catchphrase-sentence pair is considered a match. For example if we have a 10-word catchphrase, and a 15 words candidate sentence, if they have 6 words in common we consider this as a match using Rouge-1 with a threshold of 0.5, but not a match with a threshold of 0.7 (requiring at least 7/10 words from the catchphrase to appear in the sentence). Using other Rouge scores (Rouge-SU or Rouge-W), the order and sequence of tokens are also considered in defining a match. In this way, once a matching criterion is defined, we can divide all the sentences in "**relevant**" sentences (those that match at least one catchphrase) and "**not relevant**" sentences (those that do not match any catchphrase).

Once the matches between single sentences and catchphrases are defined for a single document and a set of extracted (candidate) sentences, we can compute precision and recall as:

$$Recall = \frac{MatchedCatchphrases}{TotalCatchphrases}$$

$$Precision = \frac{RelevantSentences}{ExtractedSentences}$$

The recall is the number of catchphrases matched by at least one extracted sentence, divided by the total number of catchphrases; the precision is the number of sentences extracted which match at least one catchphrase, divided by the number of extracted sentences. This evaluation method gives us a way to compare the performance of different extraction systems automatically, by giving a simple but reasonable measure of how many of the desired catchphrases are generated by the systems, and how many of the sentences extracted are useful. This is different from the use of standard Rouge overall scores, where precision and recall do not relate to the number of catchphrases or sentences, but to the number of smaller units such as n-grams, skip-bigrams or sequences, which makes it more difficult to interpret the results.

5 Relevance Identification

Different techniques can be used to extract important fragments from text. Approaches such as (Hoffmann and Pham, 2003; Galgani and Hoffmann, 2010) used regular expressions to recognize patterns in the text, based on cue phrases or particular terms/constructs. However, when manually examining legal texts, we realised that to recognize important content, several aspects of the text need to be considered. Looking at one sentence by itself is clearly not enough to decide its importance: we must consider also document-scale information to know what the present case is about, and at the same time we need to look at corpus-wide information to decide what is peculiar to the present case. For this reason we developed several ways of locating potential catchphrases in legal text, based on different kinds of attributes, which form the building blocks for our rule system.

Using the NLTK library[3] (Bird et al., 2009), we collected all the words in the corpus, and obtained a list of stemmed terms (we used the Porter stemmer). Then for each term (stem) of each document, we computed the following numerical attributes:

1. Term frequency (**Tf**): the number of occurrences of the term in this document.
2. **AvgOcc**: the average number of occurrences of the term in the corpus.
3. Document frequency (**Df**): computed as the number of document in which the term appear at least once divided by the total number of documents.
4. **TFIDF**: computed as the rank of the term in the document (i.e. TFIDF(term)=10 means that the term has the 10 highest TFIDF value for this document).
5. **CpOcc**: how many times the term occurs in the set of all the known catchphrases present in the corpus.
6. The **FcFound** score: from (Galgani 2012), this uses the known catchphrases to compute the ratio between how many times (that is in how many documents) the term appears both in the catchphrases and in the text of the case, and how many times in the text [4] :

$$FcFound(t) = \frac{NDocs_{text\&catchp.}(t)}{NDocs_{text}(t)}$$

[3]http://www.nltk.org/

[4]Attributes 5 and 6 use information from the set of existing catchphrases. We consider this set as a general resource and believe that the corpus of catchphrases comprises most of the relevant words and phrases, and as such can be deemed a general resource and can be applied to new data without loss of performances, as it was shown in (Galgani et al., 2012).

7. **CitSen**: how many times the term occurs in all the sentences (from other documents) that cite the target case.

8. **CitCp**: how many times the term occurs in all the catcphrases of other documents that cite or are cited by the target case.

9. **CitLeg**: how many times the term occurs in the section titles of the legislation cited by the target case.

Three more non-numeric attributes were also used for each term:

10. The Part Of Speech (**POS**) tag of the term (obtained using the NLTK default part of speech tagger, a classifier-based tagger trained on the PENN Treebank corpus).

11. We extracted a set of legal terms from (Olsson, 1999), which lists a set of possible titles and subtitles for judgements. The existence of a term in this set is used as an attribute (**Legal**).

12. If the term is a proper noun (**PrpNoun**), as indicated by the POS tagger.

Furthermore, we also use four sentence-level attributes:

13. Specific words or phrases that must be present in the sentence, i.e. "court" or "whether".

14. If the sentence contains a citation to another case (**HasCitCase**).

15. If the sentence contains a citation to an act or a section of the law (**HasCitLaw**).

16. A constraint on the length of the sentence (**Length**).

When constructing our set of features, we included different kinds of information that can be used to recognize important content. Each of the different features can be used to locate potential catchphrases in a case. In (Galgani et al., 2011) automatic extraction methods based on these attributes were compared to each other, and it was shown that citation-based methods in general outperform text-only methods. However, we believe that different methods best apply to different contexts (for different documents and sentences), and we propose to combine them using manually created rules.

6 Building a Knowledge Base

Our catchphrase extraction system is based on creating a knowledge base of rules that specify which sentences should be extracted from the full text, as candidate catchphrases. These rules are acquired and organized in a knowledge base according to the RDR methodology.

As the rules are created looking at examples, we built a tool to facilitate the inspection of legal cases. The user, for each document, can explore the relevant sentences and see which ones are most similar to the (given) catchphrases of the case. The interface also shows citation information, the catchphrases, relevant sentences of cited/citing cases, and which parts of the relevant legislation are cited. For a document the user can see the "best" sentences: those that are more similar to the catchphrases, or those similar to one particular catchphrase. For each sentence, frequency information is also shown, according to the attributes described in Section 5.

In order to make a rule, the user looks at one example of a relevant sentence, together with all the frequency and citation information, the catchphrases and other information about the document. The user can then set different constraints for the attributes: attributes 1 to 12 refer to a single term, with attributes 1-9 being numeric (for these the user can specify a maximum and/or minimum value) while attributes 10-12 require an exact value (a POS tag or a True/False value). The user specifies how many terms which satisfy that constraint, must be present in a single sentence for it to be extracted (for example, there must be at least 3 terms with $FcFound > 0.1$). It is also possible to insert proximity constraints, such as: the 3 terms must be no more than 5 tokens apart (they must be within a window of 5 tokens). We call this set of constraints on terms, a condition. A rule is composed of a conjunction of conditions (for example: there must be 3 terms with $FcFound > 0.1$ and $AvgOcc < 1$ AND 2 terms with $CpOcc > 20$ and $CitCp > 1$). There is no limit on the number of conditions that form a rule. The conclusion of a rule is always "the sentence is relevant".

To acquire rules from the user, we follow the RDR approach, according to which the user looks at an instance that is currently misclassified and formulates a rule to correct the error. In our case, the user is presented with a sentence that matches at least one catchphrase (a relevant sentence), but is not currently selected by the knowledge base.

Looking at the sentence at hand, and at the attributes values for the different terms, the user specifies a possible rule condition, and can then test it on the entire dataset. This gives an immediate idea on how useful the condition is, as the user can see how many sentences would be selected by that condition and how many of these sentences are relevant (similar enough to at least one catchphrase, as defined in Section 4). At the same time the user can inspect manually other sentences matched by the condition, and refine the condition accordingly. When he/she is satisfied with one condition, they can add and test more conditions for the rule, and see other examples, to narrow down the number of cases matched by the rule and improve the precision while at the same time trying to include as many cases as possible.

When looking at the number of sentences matched by adding a condition, we can also compute the probability that the improvement given by the rule/condition is random. As initially described in (Gaines and Compton, 1995), for a two class problem (sentence is relevant/not relevant), we can use a binomial test to calculate the probability that such results could occur randomly. That is, when a condition is added to an existing rule, or added to an empty rule we compute the probability that the improvement is random. The probability of selecting randomly n sentences and getting x or more relevant sentences is:

$$r = \sum_{k=x}^{n} \binom{n}{k} p^k (1-p)^{n-k} = \frac{n! p^x (1-p)^{n-x}}{x!(n-x)!}$$

where p is the random probability, i.e. the proportion of relevant sentences among all sentences selected by the current rule. If we know how many relevant sentences the new condition select (x), we can calculate this probability which can guide the user in creating a condition that minimize the value of r.

As an example, the user may be presented with the following sentence:

> As might have been expected, the bill of lading contains a "Himalaya" clause in the widest terms which is usual in such transactions.

which we know to be relevant, being similar to a given catchphrase:

> *goods transported under bill of lading incorporating Himalaya clause*

Looking at the attributes the user proposes a condition, for example based on the term *lading* and *Himalaya* (that are peculiar of this document), a possible condition is:

> SENTENCE contains at least 2 terms with $CpOcc > 1$ and $FcFound > 0.1$ and $CitCp > 1$ and $TFIDF < 4$ and $AvgOcc < 1$

Testing the condition on the dataset we can see that it matches 1392 sentences, of which 849 are relevant (precision = 0.61), those sentences cover a total of 536 catchphrases (there are cases in which a number of sentences match the same catchphrase). The probability that a random condition would have this precision is also computed (10e-136). To improve the precision we can look at the two other terms that occurs in the catchphrase (*bill* and *clause*) and add another condition, for example:

> SENTENCE also contains at least 2 terms with $CpOcc > 20$ and $FcFound > 0.02$ and $CitCp > 1$ and $isLegal$ and $TFIDF < 16$

The rule with two conditions now matches 429 sentences of which 347 are relevant (precision=0.81), covering 331 catchphrases. The probability that a random condition added to the first one would bring this improvement is 10e-19. The user can look at other matches of the rule, for example:

> That is to say, the Tribunal had to determine whether the applicant was, by reason of his war-caused incapacity alone, prevented from continuing to undertake remunerative work that he had been undertaking.

remunerative and *war-caused* are matched by the first condition, and *Tribunal* and *work* by the second. If the user is satisfied the rule is committed to the knowledge base. In this way the creation, testing and integration of the rule in the system is done at the same time.

During knowledge acquisition this same interaction is repeated: the user looks at examples, creates conditions, tests them on the dataset until he/she is satisfied, and then commits the rule to the knowledge base, following the RDR approach. When creating a rule the user is guided both by particular examples shown by the system, and by statistics computed on the large dataset. Some rules of our KB are presented in Table 2.

Table 2: Examples of rules inserted in the Knowledge Base

SENTENCE contains at least 2 terms with $Tf > 30$ and $CpOcc > 200$ and $AvgOcc < 2.5$ and $TFIDF < 10$ within a window of 2
SENTENCE contains at least 2 terms with $Tf > 5$ and $CpOcc > 20$ and $FcFound > 0.02$ and $CitCp > 1$ and $TFIDF < 15$ and contains at least 2 terms with $Tf > 5$ and $CpOcc > 2$ and $FcFound > 0.11$ and $AvgOcc < 0.2$ and $TFIDF < 5$
SENTENCE contains at least 10 terms with $CitCp > 10$ and contains at least 6 terms with $CitCp > 20$
SENTENCE contains the term $corporations$ with $Tf > 15$ and $CitCp > 5$

7 Preliminary Results and Future Development

After building the knowledge acquisition interface, we conducted a preliminary KA session to verify the feasibility of the approach, and the appropriateness of the rule language. We conducted a KA session creating a total of 23 rules (which took on average 6.5 minutes for each to be specified, tested and commited). These 23 rules extracted a total of 12082 sentences, of which 10565 were actually relevant, i.e. matched a least one catchphrase, where we used Rouge-1 with a similarity threshold of 0.5 to define a match. These sentences are distributed among 1455 different documents. The overall precision of the KB is thus is 87.44% and the total number of catchphrases covered is 6765 (29.12% of the total).

Table 3 shows the comparison of this Knowledge Base with four other methods: Random is a random selection of sentences, Citations is a methods that use only citation information to select sentences (described in (Galgani et al., 2011)); in particular it selects those sentences that are most similar to the catchphrases of cited and citing documents. As a state-of-the-art general purpose summarizer, we used LexRank (Erkan and Radev, 2004), an automatic tool that first builds a network in which nodes are sentences and a weighted edge between two nodes shows the lexical cosine similarity, and then performs a random walk to find the most central nodes in the graphs and takes them as the summary. We downloaded the Mead toolkit[5] and applied LexRank to all the documents to rank the sentences. For every method we extracted the 5 top ranked sentences. Finally, because our rules have matches in only 1455 documents (out of a total of 2816), we used a mixed approach in which for each document, if there is any sentence(s) selected by the KB we select those, otherwise we take the best 5 sentences as given by the Citation method. This method is called KB+Citations. We can see from the Table that the Knowledge Base outperforms all other methods in precision, followed by KB+Citations, while KB+Citations obtains higher recall.

Table 3: Performances measured using Rouge-1 with threshold 0.5. SpD is the average number of extracted sentences per document.

Method	SpD	Precision	Recall	F-measure
KB	4.29	0.874	0.291	0.437
Citations	4.56	0.789	0.527	0.632
KB+CIT	7.29	0.828	0.553	0.663
LexRank	4.87	0.563	0.402	0.469
Random	5.00	0.315	0.233	0.268

Table 4: Performances measured using Rouge-1 with threshold 0.7. SpD is the average number of extracted sentences per document.

Method	SpD	Precision	Recall	F-measure
KB	4.29	0.690	0.161	0.261
Citations	4.56	0.494	0.233	0.317
KB+CIT	7.28	0.575	0.265	0.363
LexRank	4.87	0.351	0.216	0.267
Random	5.00	0.156	0.098	0.120

Note that we can vary the matching criterion (as described in Section 4) and only consider more strict matches, in this case only sentences more similar to catchphrases are considered relevant. We can see the results of setting a higher similarity threshold (0.7) in Table 4. All the approaches give lower precision and recall, but the margin of the knowledge base over the other methods increases, with a relative improvement of precision of 40% over the citation method.

While the precision level of the KB alone is higher than any other method, the recall is low when compared to other approaches. We only conducted a preliminary KA session, which took slightly more than 2 hours. Figure 1 shows precision and recall of the KB as new rules are in-

[5] www.summarization.com/mead/

serted into the system. We can assume that a more comprehensive set of rules, capturing more sentences and addressing different types of contexts, should cover a greater number of catchphrases, while keeping the precision at a high value; however, the rules constructe so far only fire for some cases, and many cases are not covered at all.

Even with this limited KB, we can use the citation method as fall-back to select sentences for those cases that are not matched by the rules. Using this approach, as we can see from Tables 3 and 4 (method KB+CIT), that obtain the highest recall while keeping the precision very close to the precision of the KB alone.

For future work we plan not only to expand the KB in general with more rules, in order to improve recall, but also to construct rules specifically for those cases that are not already covered, applying those rules in a selective way, only for these of documents (and not for those which already have a sufficient number of catchphrases candidates). In doing this we will seek to generalize our experience of applying the citation approach to documents where the KB did not produce catchphrases. We also hypothesize that the recall level of the rules is low because they select several sentences that are similar among them, and thus match the same catchphrases, so that for some documents we have a set of relevant sentences which cover only some aspects of the case. Using a similarity-based re-ranker would allow us to discard sentences to similar to those already selected.

In future developments we also plan to develop further the structure of the knowledge base into an RDR tree, writing exception rules (rule with conclusion "not relevant") that can patch the existing rules whenever an error is found. The current knowledge base only consists of a list of rules while the RDR methodology will let us organize the rules so they are used in different situations depending on which previous rule has fired.

8 Conclusion

This paper presents our hybrid approach to text summarization, based on creating rules to combine different types of statistical information about text. In contrast to supervised learning, where human intuition applies only to attribute and algorithm selection, here human intuition also applies to the organization of features in rules, but still guided by the available dataset.

We have applied our approach to a particular summarization problem: creating catchphrases for legal case reports. Catchphrases are considered to be a significant help to lawyers searching through cases to identify relevant precedents and are routinely used when browsing documents. We created a large dataset of case reports, corresponding catchphrases and both incoming and outgoing citations to cases and legislation. We created a Knowledge Acquisition framework based on Ripple Down Rules, and defined a rich rule language that includes different aspects of the case under consideration. We developed a tool that facilitates the inspection of the dataset and the creation of rules by selecting and specifying features depending on the context of the present case and using different information for different situations. A preliminary KA session shows the effectiveness of the rule approach: with only 23 rules we can obtain a significantly higher precision (87.4%) than any automatic method tried. We are confident that a more extensive knowledge base would further improve the performances and cover a larger portion of the cases, improving the recall.

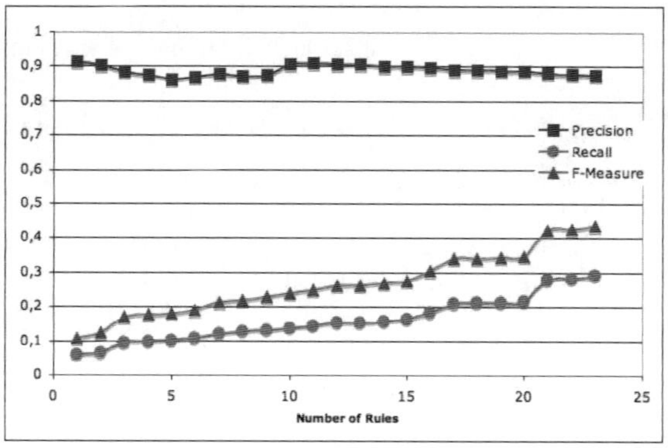

Figure 1: Precision, Recall and F-measure as the size of the KB increases

References

Steven Bird, Ewan Klein, and Edward Loper. 2009. *Natural Language Processing with Python.* O'Reilly Media.

P. Compton and R. Jansen. 1990. Knowledge in context: a strategy for expert system maintenance. In *AI '88: Proceedings of the second Australian Joint Conference on Artificial Intelligence*, pages 292–306, New York, NY, USA. Springer-Verlag New York, Inc.

G. Erkan and D.R. Radev. 2004. LexRank: Graph-based lexical centrality as salience in text summarization. *Journal of Artificial Intelligence Research*, 22(2004):457–479.

Atefeh Farzindar and Guy Lapalme. 2009. Machine translation of legal information and its evaluation. *Advances in Artificial Intelligence*, pages 64–73.

B. R. Gaines and P. Compton. 1995. Induction of ripple-down rules applied to modeling large databases. *J. Intell. Inf. Syst.*, 5:211–228, November.

Filippo Galgani and Achim Hoffmann. 2010. Lexa: Towards automatic legal citation classification. In Jiuyong Li, editor, *AI 2010: Advances in Artificial Intelligence*, volume 6464 of *Lecture Notes in Computer Science*, pages 445 –454. Springer Berlin Heidelberg.

Filippo Galgani, Paul Compton, and Achim Hoffmann. 2011. Citation based summarization of legal texts. Technical Report 201202, School of Computer Science and Engineering, UNSW, Australia.

Filippo Galgani, Paul Compton, and Achim Hoffmann. 2012. Towards automatic generation of catchphrases for legal case reports. In Alexander Gelbukh, editor, *the 13th International Conference on Intelligent Text Processing and Computational Linguistics*, volume 7182 of *Lecture Notes in Computer Science*, pages 415–426, New Delhi, India. Springer Berlin / Heidelberg.

G. Greenleaf, A. Mowbray, G. King, and P. Van Dijk. 1995. Public Access to Law via Internet: The Australian Legal Information Institute. *Journal of Law and Information Science*, 6:49.

Ben Hachey and Claire Grover. 2006. Extractive summarisation of legal texts. *Artif. Intell. Law*, 14(4):305–345.

Achim Hoffmann and Son Bao Pham. 2003. Towards topic-based summarization for interactive document viewing. In *K-CAP '03: Proceedings of the 2nd international conference on Knowledge capture*, pages 28–35, New York, NY, USA. ACM.

Myung Hee Kim, Paul Compton, and Yang Sok Kim. 2011. Rdr-based open ie for the web document. In *Proceedings of the sixth international conference on Knowledge capture*, K-CAP '11, pages 105–112, New York, NY, USA. ACM.

Julian Kupiec, Jan Pedersen, and Francine Chen. 1995. A trainable document summarizer. In *SIGIR '95: Proceedings of the 18th annual international ACM SIGIR conference on Research and development in information retrieval*, pages 68–73, New York, NY, USA. ACM.

Chin-Yew Lin. 2004. Rouge: A package for automatic evaluation of summaries. In Stan Szpakowicz Marie-Francine Moens, editor, *Text Summarization Branches Out: Proceedings of the ACL-04 Workshop*, pages 74–81, Barcelona, Spain, July. Association for Computational Linguistics.

Daniel Marcu. 1997. From discourse structures to text summaries. In *In Proceedings of the ACL Workshop on Intelligent Scalable Text Summarization*, pages 82–88.

Q. Mei and C.X. Zhai. 2008. Generating impact-based summaries for scientific literature. *Proceedings of ACL-08: HLT*, pages 816–824.

Marie-Francine Moens. 2001. Innovative techniques for legal text retrieval. *Artificial Intelligence and Law*, 9(1):29–57, 03.

Marie-Francine Moens. 2007. Summarizing court decisions. *Inf. Process. Manage.*, 43(6):1748–1764.

Justice Leslie Trevor Olsson. 1999. *Guide To Uniform Production of Judgments*. Australian Institute of Judicial Administration, Carlton South, Vic, 2nd edition.

Son Bao Pham and Achim Hoffmann. 2004. Incremental knowledge acquisition for building sophisticated information extraction systems with kaftie. In *in 5th International Conference on Practical Aspects of Knowledge Management*, pages 292–306. Springer-Verlag.

Vahed Qazvinian and Dragomir R. Radev. 2008. Scientific Paper Summarization Using Citation Summary Networks. *Proceedings of the 22nd International Conference on Computational Linguistics (Coling 2008)*, pages 689–696.

Gerard Salton, Amit Singhal, Mandar Mitra, and Chris Buckley. 1997. Automatic text structuring and summarization. *Inf. Process. Manage.*, 33(2):193–207.

Han Xu and Achim Hoffmann. 2010. Rdrce: Combining machine learning and knowledge acquisition. In Byeong-Ho Kang and Debbie Richards, editors, *Knowledge Management and Acquisition for Smart Systems and Services*, volume 6232 of *Lecture Notes in Computer Science*, pages 165–179. Springer Berlin / Heidelberg.

Mehdi Yousfi-Monod, Atefeh Farzindar, and Guy Lapalme. 2010. Supervised machine learning for summarizing legal documents. In *Canadian Conference on Artificial Intelligence 2010*, volume 6085 of *Lecture Notes in Artificial Intelligence*, pages 51–62, Ottawa, Canada, may. Springer.

Paul Zhang and Lavanya Koppaka. 2007. Semantics-based legal citation network. In *ICAIL '07: Proceedings of the 11th international conference on Artificial intelligence and law*, pages 123–130, New York, NY, USA. ACM.

Author Index

Association for Computational Linguistics
209 N. Eighth Street
Stroudsburg, Pennsylvania 18360

CURRAN ASSOCIATES INC
proceedings
.com

TALAF 2012: African Language Processing

Held at JEP-TALN-RECITAL 2012

Grenoble, France
4 – 7 June 2012

ISBN: 978-1-62276-496-9